RUN *with* POWER

RUN *with* POWER

The Complete Guide to Power Meters *for* Running

JIM VANCE

VELO press

Boulder, Colorado

Acute Training Load™, Chronic Training Load™, Intensity Factor™, Normalized Graded Pace™, Normalized Power™, Performance Management Chart™, Training Stress Score™, and Variability Index™ are trademarks of Peaksware, LLC.

Ironman® is a registered trademark of World Triathlon Corporation.

Figures 2.2, 2.3, and 2.4 were adapted for this book with permission of Stryd.
Figures 2.1, 7.1, and 7.3 were adapted for this book with permission of Joe Friel.

▼velopress®

3002 Sterling Circle, Suite 100
Boulder, Colorado 80301-2338 USA
(303) 440-0601 · Fax (303) 444-6788 · E-mail velopress@competitorgroup.com

Distributed in the United States and Canada by Ingram Publisher Services

A Cataloging-in-Publication record for this book is available from the Library of Congress.
ISBN 978-1-937715-43-4

For information on purchasing VeloPress books, please call (800) 811-4210, ext. 2138, or visit www.velopress.com.

This paper meets the requirements of ANSI/NISO Z39.48-1992 (Permanence of Paper).

Cover design by Pete Garceau
Interior design by Brenda Gallagher
Figures 2.2, 2.3, 2.4, 4.1a, 4.2a, 4.3a, 4.6a, 5.3a, 5.4a, 5.5a, 5.6a, 8.2, 8.3, 8.4, 8.5, 8.6, 8.7, and 9.1a illustrated by Charles Chamberlin

Text set in Andada

16 17 18 / 10 9 8 7 6 5 4 3 2 1

CONTENTS

Introduction:
The Future Is Here

We are on the cusp of a performance revolution in the sport of running. The science of training and the art of coaching are entering a new relationship, one much stronger than we've ever seen. With the advent of the power meter for running, we now have a tool to measure athletic performance directly, objectively, and with precise repeatability. We can measure the athlete's power output not only throughout the days and weeks of training, but also during competition. This lets us plan for each event's specific demands and capitalize on the athlete's specific strengths. The power meter is easily the most powerful tool we've ever had to analyze running form, fitness, and potential. When used correctly, it will make you a better, faster runner.

You may think you've heard this story before, and in a way, you have. When heart rate monitors first came on the market, there was a period of time when many people didn't bother learning how to use the technology. Today, however, if you are using *only* a heart rate monitor—or simply a stopwatch—you're considered out of touch with technology, since you're not using GPS. The advent of GPS was a significant step, and it can still be a useful training tool. But once you learn of the full range of the power meter's capabilities, you will see that GPS was just scratching the surface, especially for athletes who have high goals.

What Will Happen?

The sub-2-hour marathon is today's most prominent running barrier, equivalent to the mythical 4-minute-mile barrier broken by Roger Bannister in 1954. Today, we see similar doubt about the 2-hour marathon, with many scoffing at the idea that humans are capable of running that fast. Countless articles, publications, and forums have discussed and debated the feat. Many top runners and experts disagree on whether it is possible, when it might happen (if ever), what it would take from an athlete to accomplish it, and what the course requirements would be for such a spectacular performance.

For years, many thought the sub-1-hour half-marathon was not likely or possible. Yet the sub-1-hour half-marathon was first recorded in 1993, and by 2011 that so-called barrier had been broken more than 150 times.

Look back to the mid-1990s, when a group of young East African men came onto the distance-running scene and rewrote the record books for 5000 and 10,000 meters, month after month, year after year. We went from wondering if anyone other than Saïd Aouita could run sub-13 minutes for the 5000 meters, as he did in 1987, to seeing it done more than 250 times by 2011. As I write this, the record stands at nearly a 4-minute-mile pace: 12:37. Heck, the men's mile is now down to 3:43. That's over 4 seconds faster per lap than Bannister ran! The women's world record for the mile still stands at 4:12. Could a woman break the 4-minute-mile barrier? I believe we are closer than we realize.

Call me overly optimistic, but I believe we'll see a sub-2-hour marathon very soon, probably by the Olympic year 2028 at the latest. And that's just the beginning. Yes, 2028 sounds like the distant future, but many of us remember the blitz of those 1990s performances like they were yesterday.

The problem with a belief that a particular performance is impossible, or that the prospect is too far away for any of us to see in our lifetime, is that this viewpoint looks at the result, not at the process of getting there. As a professional coach, however, I believe that the results come when the process of training improves.

I am a coach who is big on data and technological training tools. In cycling, we have power meters, which have done wonders for training and performance. In swimming, we've profited from important studies with force plates, swim flumes, and video technology for stroke analysis as well as the insights from bold and knowledgeable coaches creating new periodization models and training plans. In many endurance sports, the processes of training and performance have improved as much as the technology, but in the running world, we've been very limited in our use and advancement of technological tools throughout history. That has now changed.

What Can We See?

What we've been missing with running is a way to measure output consistently, throughout an entire season, in races, across different terrains, course profiles, weather conditions, and more. This tool is here now, and it's so simple that it's hard to believe it didn't arrive long ago, but I believe surpassing the sub-2-hour marathon mark will be just the beginning. Every world record will fall, from the marathon to the 100 meters. In fact, as the power meter becomes available for other sports, the records for every field event—from the horizontal jumps to the high jump and pole vault, and all throwing disciplines—will be broken as well.

This will be because of a simple tool, the power meter, and that tool for running is now available to you. With the power meter, we can measure your output directly, in the actual process of performance, not just indirectly through recorded times or other postperformance marks. Using this tool, we will know much more than we have ever known, with metrics and measurements we've never even considered or knew could exist, and this information will open the floodgates to a new level of high performance.

New technology can be intimidating, and there will be some who will reject the very idea of using a power meter. They'll say that they are happy with the way they're doing things. But I guarantee that if you embrace this opportunity to learn how to train with a power meter, you will find yourself a smarter and faster athlete, thanks to a training schedule improved by power data. The initial onslaught of data and feedback for coaches and athletes will be overwhelming, but those who study it and learn to use the information to their competitive advantage will be the ones who set themselves apart. Once the best athletes come into contact with the best coaches, who know and understand how to use this technology and data to design training programs and improve an athlete's weaknesses, the next revolution will begin, with performances that will leave us dropping our jaws. If you don't believe me, take a look at the history of running and training, and you will see that the writing is already on the wall. History tends to repeat itself. The future is here.

1 Why Use a Power Meter for Running?

Do you have high goals? Are you trying to qualify for an event or place high at a certain race? Perhaps you simply want to run a faster time than you've run before. The higher you set your goals and the better you become, the more commitment you'll need to reach your next level, however you define it. And as your goals become more challenging, the margin for error in your training and performance will become ever smaller. Many of your competitors are just as good as you are, and some of them are better. It's crucial that you get your training right.

Training is stressful on the body. It has to be, because fitness is really just the ability of your body to tolerate a level of stress. The faster you go, the more stress you put on your body for a given level of fitness. But for as long as runners have been training, our ability to measure the amount of stress we put into our bodies has been quite limited.

We can track volume easily—we don't need anything more sophisticated than a training diary to record how long and how far we train each day. But volume is not a very accurate way to measure stress.

Workout intensity is the real key to fitness, but the usual ways we measure intensity, such as a scale of perceived exertion, are subjective. Heart rate (HR) is a tool we've used to infer intensity in the past, but it's flawed, too. In addition to the fact that heart rate does not measure intensity directly, it can also be affected by factors unrelated to training, such as diet, temperature, and stress.

With a power meter, you can take control of your training and racing to improve every aspect of your running career.

Pace may seem as straightforward as training volume at first, but in fact it is hard to quantify; varying terrain and elevation can markedly affect pace. Windy, hot, or cold conditions can also affect pace negatively or positively, adding to the challenge of quantifying the intensity.

All of these tools are helpful in creating a snapshot to measure fitness, and yet none of them give us an impartial way to monitor training intensity with repeatable precision. But when we measure stress incorrectly, our training suffers. We become more vulnerable to injury. We may suffer from a lack of recovery. We may get intensity wrong. Any one of those setbacks can derail a training plan.

What we need, clearly, is a better way to measure the stress we are inflicting in our daily training routines. And that's exactly what the power meter provides, and it is why the power meter has the potential to revolutionize your run training.

With a power meter, you can measure your performance and training stress more precisely than ever before, and take control of your training and racing to improve every aspect of your running career. No longer will you wonder whether you are meeting the intensity, recovery, pace, and volume goals of your training plan. Instead, you will erase any doubts about your training, and you will be able to monitor changes and improvements in every aspect of your running fitness.

Why Power?

If you're a triathlete, a bicycle racer, or a fan of either pro sport, you are probably already familiar with the use of power meters in cycling. The power meter transformed training and racing in the cycling world. It has surpassed every other training tool because it delivers an objective and repeatable assessment of overall fitness without any of the drawbacks of previous measurement methods, such as heart rate, speed, and perceived exertion. In fact, the advantages of the cycling power meter are so great—and the margin of error so small in the world of competitive cycling and triathlon—that to ignore the information and the advantage from a power meter would be to concede victory before the race had started.

In the running world, we have recently seen a surge in the popularity of GPS units, and we've seen these units get smaller and smaller as usage has grown. The increased adoption of GPS shows that the running world, like the cycling world, is open to embracing technology and its benefits.

While the GPS unit is a useful tool, its contribution to training pales in comparison with the advantages the power meter can provide. The leap in technology is something like the difference between using a typewriter and a computer. In the history of running technology, a stopwatch is probably equivalent to using a typewriter—pretty good at its job, but severely limited in scope. Running's step up to heart rate monitors was a revelation, but in retrospect, it was like moving from the typewriter to what we would now regard as an old, heavy, slow desktop computer. Today's GPS wrist units are like the first cellphones, much like a flip-phone. The portable power meter for running is the next step, equivalent to the laptop, tablet, and smartphone coming into existence all at once. And while you can still accomplish a lot with a desktop computer, you likely will be much more effective in many ways if you add the laptop, tablet, and smartphone to your arsenal. This is what the power meter brings to the world of training and racing for competitive running.

I am sure you are wondering what makes this technology so great. Here are just some of the ways a power meter for running can positively affect training and performance:

SPECIFICITY

One of the core principles in sports training is the principle of specificity. Simply stated, in order to become better at a specific task, you must practice or train that task. For example, doing cross-country skiing in the off-season can certainly help your running, but you could never expect to become a great runner by doing only cross-country skiing. The reverse is also true, of course: You can't expect to be a great cross-country skier by simply doing run training all the time.

Power meters help us see how well our specific training is improving our fitness. More to the point, the power meter can help you prepare for the specific demands of the target race you're preparing for. If you want to prepare for a hilly course, or a race that requires a lot of spikes in pacing (and thus in your power outputs), you can use your power meter to prepare for that, measuring with great precision the improvement in your surges or hill climbs.

Once you know what you're preparing for, your power meter can help you to better plan and strategize for the event to maximize your performance potential on the day.

TECHNICAL IMPROVEMENTS

Imagine making a small change in your run form and seeing a major change in power (whether good or bad). The power meter can help you understand which aspects of your running technique you need to focus on and which you can improve or even abandon. This understanding becomes especially helpful when learning or trying a new technical change. It also is a huge asset late in a race, when you may be tired and need help to stay focused on going as fast as you can. The power meter can help with that simply by monitoring your pace and power and telling you accurately what you have left in reserve.

OBJECTIVE FITNESS MEASUREMENTS

Fitness may seem pretty simple to measure: Just look at how fast you ran. But not all courses are the same, and conditions vary constantly. What if you ran entirely into a headwind? Or had a constant tailwind? Yes, pace is a good tool for analyzing your training, but power and pace together are an even more powerful way to measure training and fitness. Add in heart rate (HR) and you've got some very objective data to work with.

What these variables can tell you about your fitness includes when you're about to hit a performance plateau and need to consider a change in your training. If you can avoid a plateau in your fitness while continuing to get better and better, your confidence will grow. Of course, your performances are likely to get better too, putting you in a better position to achieve your running goals.

If you get injured, you can use these measurements to understand exactly how much fitness you've lost, or better yet, bolster your confidence by showing you how *little* fitness you have actually lost. In some cases, the data from your power meter can even tell you if you are still suffering from an injury that you thought you had put behind you (or, more likely, that you are pretending to

SPEED PER WATT

Possibly the most important concept in this book, and arguably the biggest advantage of a power meter, is a better understanding of how the watts you produce are converted into speed. This insight into your running is something you could never measure until now.

OBJECTIVE FEEDBACK ON PERIODIZATION

At the end of your season, the data you've accumulated from your power meter can be invaluable in assessing how well your training plan worked and how to move forward with your run training. How did your training go for the year? Was there a particular type of training you responded to especially well? Training you didn't respond well to? Was there a point where things started to go backward and your performance declined? Being able to see this lets you learn a lot about yourself as an athlete, and your power meter data gives you an unparalleled view of your season's ups and downs.

PACING

A strong fitness base gives you a margin of error to race with, even when it comes to your pacing. If you make a mistake in pacing, you can minimize the damage—if you're fit enough. But add in tough competition, challenging courses, and rough conditions, and you might not be able to overcome that pacing mistake. This makes pacing a critical skill for success, especially as you set your goals higher.

A power meter can help you establish and maintain the correct pace, even on courses where establishing the right rhythm is difficult. For example, if you're preparing for a hilly course that requires perfect pacing, your power meter can help you dial in the exact output pace you need to hold throughout the varying terrain.

Here's another way a power meter can help with pacing: Many runners look at pace as a governor; it's their tool for holding back during a race to make sure they don't overdo it in the early going, or get carried away midrace as the field sorts out. But sometimes with a taper, an athlete might be rested enough to run even faster than he or she expected; in this case, holding back to a predetermined pace might prevent the runner from doing as well as he or she could. A power meter gives you an objective assessment of your running condition and can help you determine—even in the middle of a race—when you have the form to open the throttle.

Training with Heart Rate *and* Power

If you already use a heart rate monitor in your training and racing, you might be wondering why you need a power meter. The main reason is that heart rate always lags behind effort. While power is a precise view of your immediate condition and always represents the work you are doing at the moment you are doing it, heart rate is like looking in the rear-view mirror: It tells you what has already happened. If you suddenly up your pace and move into a sprint, for example, your heart will need a few moments to respond to your muscles' request for more oxygen (in the form of increased blood flow). While your power output has increased, and the amount of work you are doing is greater, your heart rate is still ticking along at its previous beat. The same holds true when you back off from a rapid pace: Your speed and power output decrease, but your heart keeps thumping along until your body rebalances its systems.

But that doesn't mean there isn't a lot of value in HR data from a workout or race. It's just that to make heart rate a truly valuable tool for analysis, it needs to be compared with other performance metrics. When we take HR data and compare it with an actual performance output, like pace and power, that changes the game. Now we can begin to measure economy and efficiency, two essential training concepts that will greatly improve your training. Briefly, economy is a measure of oxygen usage—how many meters of distance you are getting from each milliliter of oxygen. Efficiency is a measure of how much speed you are getting for the watts you are producing. All of this will be covered in later chapters; for now, the message is that if you already use heart rate, a power meter will greatly enhance what you get out of it.

Training with Power Versus Training by Feel

There is a misconception I have found among many cyclists and triathletes (and I am sure it will be true of some runners, too) that using a power meter and analyzing its data somehow means they can't train according to feel, or that they must train and race only by the numbers on the power meter. I am not sure where this misconception comes from; it might arise from people assuming that the power meter does all the thinking and does not allow any deviation. But the power meter doesn't think, and it isn't designed to stifle innovation in training. Quite the contrary; the power meter is designed to help stimulate innovation in training.

The best coaches and athletes are the ones who innovate, who devise training sessions and periodization plans that meet the individual needs, strengths, and weaknesses of the athlete on a regular, daily basis. Sometimes athletes feel good and are able to push the pace, and sometimes not, even if they're doing the same thing they did the day before.

The ability to read the signs of fatigue, to listen to the body to squeeze out every possible ounce of training, is something that requires careful observation by both the coach and runner in order to maximize performance potential. A power meter supports this because it's not about pace (time, distance, cadence); it's about power and the work actually accomplished.

If you coach yourself, one of the biggest challenges you face is not having an objective expert at your side who can remove all emotion from the decision making. The power meter can help fill that role, giving you factual data so that you can evaluate your training and make smart decisions for your future training sessions.

To be sure, nothing in the world is perfect, and that includes the running power meter. Some power meters can account for wind, while some can't. Some can account for the type of shoes you use or the terrain you run on, but others can't.

A power meter also cannot tell you how your legs feel, or where your mind is at. It can't tell you when to make a move in a race. But a power meter can help you learn your own strengths and weaknesses, and it can supplement your gut feelings and ability to read your body. It can tell you when you can increase your efforts and when you need to hold back, and it can help tell you how hard to push, both in training and during a race. As much as anything, the power meter can make you faster and fitter than ever before.

This book will give you a great understanding of the current state of power meter technology and how we can use it. It's the first book of its kind, and I will be the first to admit that there is plenty more to learn about power meters in the years ahead. But I am confident that the power meter can help you improve your training and fitness right now, starting today. I am also convinced that this book has the right information to get you started so that you can use your power meter effectively. In the following chapters, we'll define the concept of power, then explore the many ways to use power measurements in your daily training and racing. So let's get going on the path to better running.

moves us away from the ground. We don't feel the return force, of course, but it's there; the action (force in) and reaction (acceleration forward) of movement is expressed in Newton's Third Law of Motion, which says that every action has an equal and opposite reaction. It is this force and its return force that allows us to move a distance. The greater the force and the greater the distance traveled, the more work you've accomplished.

We can express the definition of *work* in a simple equation where work is W, force is F, and distance is D:

$$W = F \times D$$

That is, work equals force times distance.

As mentioned earlier, power is a work rate. Therefore, without much fiddling, we can express the definition of power in another equation, where power is P and time is T:

$$P = W/T$$

Power equals work divided by time. This is the basic definition of power. The tidy equation tells us that the work you expend while running divided by the time it takes you to do it equals the amount of power you are generating.

Problem is, it is not a very useful equation as an aid in our run training. After all, when we think about running, one of the key metrics we're after is velocity—we want to know how fast we're going. While we are running, we commonly associate velocity with cadence—how rapidly we're putting one foot in front of the other. And after a run, we analyze our velocity in terms of elapsed time: How long did that run take?

Velocity is simply a measurement of distance divided by time, and distance and time are the two most fundamental measurements we use every day in our training. So how do we get velocity into the picture? Fortunately, it's not very difficult. First, we can break down our basic expression of power by inserting our earlier definition of work as follows:

$$P = (F \times D)/T$$

That is, power equals force times distance, divided by time. Bringing distance back into the picture means that we now have one of the components we need to define velocity. You probably remember from your days in school doing story problems that distance is equal to velocity multiplied by the time you travel at that velocity, or:

$$D = V \times T$$

Now, using basic algebra, we will substitute this equation for distance into the power equation. The earlier equation for power, $P = (F \times D)/T$, thus becomes:

$$P = [F \times (V \times T)]/T$$

Since time is present on the top and bottom of the fraction, those two cancel each other out. This leaves us with:

$$P = [F \times (V)]$$

some type of sensor that measures either force or speed (or both), or estimates those metrics. Beyond that, the designs differ.

If you're familiar with cycling power meters, you know that some measure from the pedal, some from the crankarm, and others from the rear wheel's hub. In the past, we even had some that measured from the chain and its tension and speed, while another estimated based on Newton's Third Law of action-reaction, measuring movement in one direction to estimate another.

The diversity of the types of power meters in the cycling world is likely to be duplicated for running; as more running power meters come on the market, the way they estimate, measure, or calculate power will change, creating a variety of types of products.

The current power meters for running use sensors at the chest or core of the body, or through sensors at the shoe, such as an insole. I believe we will soon see foot pods as a way to measure power, and perhaps in the years to come we will see other types of sensors we can't even imagine yet, as cadence is quite simple to measure through the foot, leg, hand, or even through the rotation of the body. All a product has to do is find a way to measure the force or estimate it based on other forces.

Types of Power

There are three types of power in running. They are defined by the planes in which we move through space, and the work rate we accomplish in each of those planes. These planes are horizontal power, vertical power, and lateral power.

Power meters differ not only in how they measure or estimate power, but also in how they present the data to athletes. Some may give total power (a number that is the sum of all three planes), while some may provide power data for only one or two of these planes. The methods of reporting power will continue to evolve; down the road we might find some power meters that can give us the ratio of power produced in each plane, or even the most effective power being produced, a vector of how well the power we produce is helping us go in the direction we want. But knowledge of each plane and what it represents is important for using these power meters effectively.

At the time of this writing, power meters can be divided into two groups: those that measure two planes and those that measure all three. I've taken the liberty of classifying them as two-dimensional (2D) and three-dimensional (3D) power meters, and we will use the 2D and 3D designations throughout this book. Both types of power meters can deliver accurate results and at the moment there is no reason to assume that a 2D meter is inferior to a 3D unit.

There are some distinct differences I should clarify, as the advantages and disadvantages of each power meter can differ. A power meter that can measure power at the ground contact point can take wind into account if the runner is facing a headwind or tailwind, as the force applied to the ground to run forward will be relative to the wind force the runner faces or has at his or her back. Any power meter based as a sensor on the body cannot do that at this time, but in the future it may be able to do so.

A power meter sensor in a shoe will likely have a shorter life span than a sensor on the body simply due to the force repeatedly placed upon it, causing wear and tear. It can, however, measure force production directly, rather than estimating it.

There will always be a challenge with both of these types of power meters in terms of terrain affecting the data, because soft surfaces can dissipate the force you put into the ground. Even if you're directly measuring power from the shoe, the cushioning within the shoe can affect the values it calculates.

Are these differences extremely important? Not unless you run with a lot of tail- or headwinds, or you run frequently on soft sand. As long as the

air. There's a limit to how much vertical power is useful, however; after all, if horizontal power is zero and vertical power is 100 percent, the individual isn't actually running—he or she is simply jumping up and down in place. So while there must be some amount of vertical power expended to get the feet off the ground, there comes a point at which that vertical movement is using energy that you can better employ in a horizontal plane, in order to be faster.

You may have seen runners who oscillate their heads greatly up and down as they run, perhaps in concert with a long, loping stride. These runners have high vertical power. They likely have lower horizontal power than they would like. These runners tend to have a noticeably upright posture when they run, making for a highly vertical body position. When they apply force directly underneath them, the return force comes back directly up their body; this translates to more upward movement than forward motion.

If you watch elite runners, you'll likely notice very little head oscillation. Most of their movements are forward and back, in the horizontal plane. These runners tend to have some amount of forward lean, allowing them to apply forces effectively in a rearward direction. The return force being applied through their body and that forward lean leads directly to horizontal power.

LATERAL POWER

Not every movement we do in running is forward, back, up or down. We have some lateral movements as well. Lateral movements in running include some of the rotation of the hips and shoulders, and the hands, elbows, knees, and feet. Some of us have more lateral movement than others, and since horizontal power is the main component in generating forward movement, lateral motion can diminish our forward speed.

When we run, the alternating motion of transferring our weight from one foot and leg to the other means there have to be some lateral motions and movements in order for us to propel ourselves forward. However, as with vertical power, there is a limit to the amount of power and work we want to burn up in lateral planes.

How much lateral movement (lateral power) will you see in your power graphs? It depends on where you measure the power and movement. In the upper body, there is a lot of lateral motion of the shoulders, and some at the hips as well. At the feet, where ground forces are applied and reactive forces are returned, there is very little lateral movement to measure; only about 2 percent of total power generated shows up here as lateral power. If your power meter measures high on the body, you will see a higher value than from a power meter measuring inside the shoe. In all cases, the value will be quite small compared to horizontal and vertical power.

Runners with high lateral power tend to

- Have hands and part of their arms cross the centerline of their body;
- Have elbows that move left and right, rather than forward and back;
- Have feet that kick out to the side after toeing off the ground; and
- Have knees that move outward on the drive phase of the force into the ground.

These are just a small sample of the lateral movements you might see among a field of runners. Obviously, if you have many or all of these movements at work, you can understand how the generation of these lateral forces is reducing your horizontal power, most likely leading to a slower pace.

The sum of horizontal, vertical, and lateral power is the total power output of the athlete. There is inevitably some overlap of movements among these planes; after all, we operate in a three-dimensional world, where we move through three planes at one time. No runner could possibly solely generate horizontal power, to the total exclusion of the other two. How much overlap we see depends on our movements and running style, and the direction of each force produced. And while the power meter cannot control our output movements, it can be the most effective tool yet for monitoring and improving our running form, helping us to find the best way to turn movement into forward motion.

Seeing Fitness with Power

Probably the most exciting aspect of any technological training tool is actually seeing the benefits of your hard work pay off as you become faster and fitter. After all, what good is a tool to help you train if you can't tell that you're getting fitter?

When it comes to power meters, many runners probably think the goal is to push the watts as high as possible. After all, more watts means more power, right? So watts must be what we want. In fact, however, watts are only part of the story. Let me explain.

Running is as much about efficiency as it is about maximum power and speed. Yes, the higher the work rate you can hold, the more work you can do over a period of time. But is that alone accomplishing what you want? No matter the distance you run, from sprinting to the marathon, the biomechanical efficiency at which you run will be as great a determinant of your speed as sheer power. Biomechanical efficiency is what controls your expenditure of power in the horizontal, lateral, and vertical planes, and the transfer of your power from one plane to another.

As a runner fatigues during an effort or race, he or she will likely see a breakdown in technique. Typically, this means we will probably see more vertical and lateral power generated as the runner's movements become less disciplined, and less power will be generated in the horizontal plane.

Figure 2.2 shows an effort of an elite runner running a step test on a treadmill, where the speed increases in steps and the athlete's horizontal, vertical, and lateral power are displayed graphically during each interval.

You'll notice that as the speed increases, the total power of the athlete increases. However, there is no increase in vertical power: As the athlete increased the speed during the session, there was actually a decrease in the vertical oscillations. This is a good result; the athlete is fairly efficient in his vertical movements and is seeing a good increase in horizontal power. You can also see that the lateral power values are small and consistent. The faster and longer any athlete goes, however, the more inefficient he or she will become. There comes a point where increases in pace and intensity are exponential in their energy costs, and that is because the body produces forces at such a high speed that it can't control the movements as well as it could before.

Figure 2.3 shows the same test with a runner who is not elite. As with the previous example, you can see that the total power increases with each interval. In this case, however, the only consistent power increase is in the horizontal measurement, while the vertical power trace is much more ragged. Within each interval, vertical power starts off high, then decreases as horizontal power increases. It is likely that this athlete starts each interval with high force production upward and slower cadence (due to high vertical oscillation), instead of concentrating on horizontal power production. Then, with a decrease in vertical power and vertical force production comes an opportunity to increase cadence, leading to increases in horizontal power, as shown.

Figure 2.4 tracks the cadence from this novice runner, showing the increase of steps per minute (spm). When we put the two figures together, it is easy to see the relationship of force and cadence, as well as to see that as vertical power decreases, cadence and horizontal power increase. By examining

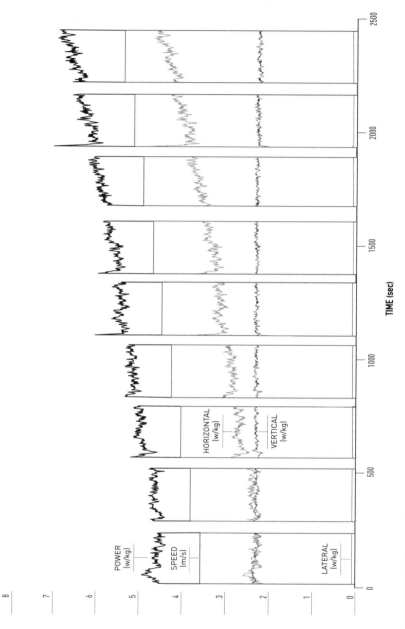

FIGURE 2.2 Changes in power via step test for elite runner

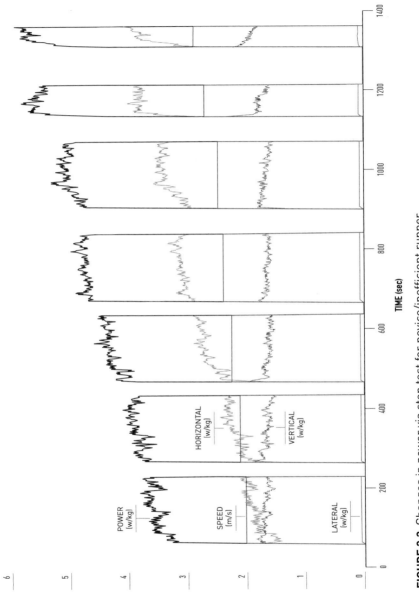

FIGURE 2.3 Changes in power via step test for novice/inefficient runner

the power data, this athlete can see the need to increase cadence in order to improve horizontal power and fitness.

Let's return to the vertical power trace. We already know that high force production in a vertical direction has little benefit for forward speed. From the traces in these figures, we can see that a higher cadence helps this runner limit vertical power loss and keep horizontal power high.

This is just one example of how an athlete can improve power output via changes in running technique, and a very good example of why it is important not to think of the power meter simply in terms of the gross generation of

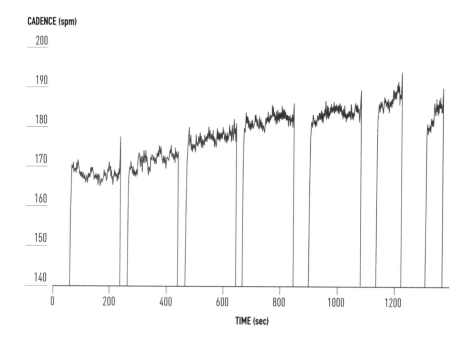

FIGURE 2.4 Cadence of a novice runner

watts. Don't get me wrong: Watts are absolutely important, but they are only one part of a complete picture that includes running technique and efficiency.

Here are some other ways that runners can see fitness and efficiency improvements with a power meter:

- An increase in watts held over a duration, specifically watts generated from horizontal power
- An increase in pace or speed while maintaining the same wattage
- A decrease in total power output for a given pace
- Lower heart rate for a given power and pace.

A power meter can also help pinpoint technical improvements in running, especially in the following ways:

- Decrease in vertical power for a given pace
- Decrease in lateral power for a given pace
- Decrease in total power for a given pace
- Increase in pace relative to any consistent power output, be it total, horizontal, vertical, or lateral.

You'll notice that some of these technical improvements have the same foundation as the fitness improvements. Technical improvements allow you to work easier for a given pace. Do not neglect the importance of power as a tool to measure your efficiency.

There are additional ways you can see technical and fitness improvements, even strategic improvements, such as the power output for a hill relative to the pace achieved, and more. We'll cover all that in the chapters to come.

Summary

Power is a work rate, measured in watts. Work is force times distance, while power is simply force times the speed at which the force is applied. Although as a runner you might think this is strictly moving your body forward, there is work being accomplished in different directions and planes. It's important to understand what those directions are, as well as what your cadence is, and what the sum of all forces mean to your running.

With a power meter, you can see a number of improvements in your fitness, as well as how technical changes in your run form affect your power. When you make changes to your run form, if you can see an increase in your horizontal power while at the same time you see decreases in vertical and lateral power, then you know you've made some very effective technical changes that should make you faster.

3 Getting Started

Now that you have your power meter, it is time to start learning how to use it. While I would love to begin this chapter by telling you how to use it to set a PR on your very first run, the fact is that you're going to have to start a little slower. While you should indeed strap it on and start recording data right away, the first order of business is to establish a performance baseline that will help you understand what your numbers mean for you.

The First Steps

In order for your power meter to record your movements correctly, you need to calibrate it. Calibrate incorrectly, or skip calibration altogether, and the numbers and data you collect will most likely be incorrect and not representative of what you're doing, and not lead to improvement in your training and running.

The calibration process for your power meter will likely involve using a smartphone app, or will involve adjusting settings on a GPS unit to let the power meter get to know you better. Some of these settings might include your weight or mass, or specifics such as your height or the placement of the meter, depending on the type of meter you're using. For example, if your power meter is insole-based, you might need to do some standing or walking calibrations, or other setups that define you as the user.

You'll likely be using either a GPS watch or a smartphone to connect wirelessly via ANT+ or Bluetooth to your power meter. We commonly call any separate readout device a head unit. Its job is to display the data collected from the power meter in real time and store that data for further analysis, post-race or post-workout, through analysis software.

Once you've calibrated the meter correctly, you should begin the process of using the power meter on all of your runs, so you can collect some basic data. My advice is to collect every bit of data on every run, even if you think the data may be unimportant. You can always delete or ignore a run later, but during the familiarization period, you should grab everything you can. Data to collect specifically includes the following:

- Easy runs, moderate runs, hard runs, and runs with hard intervals.
- Your whole run. Start recording at the start of your warm-up, and don't stop recording until the end of your cooldown.
- Recovery intervals. The rest periods in a hard workout are just as important to record as the intervals themselves. I'll have more information on this later in the book; for now, get in the habit of recording your recovery periods.
- No analysis! This is very important—for the first two weeks, don't even try to interpret the numbers.

Among this short list of guidelines, I know the last one will be the hardest to follow. That's understandable: You've just bought this cool new gadget, and here I am telling you to ignore it! Obviously, you are going to look at the numbers constantly to see what they say. How could you not? You wouldn't be a competitive athlete if you didn't, and there's nothing wrong with that. What I am trying to get at is something more subtle: I want you to train for two weeks as you normally would, as if you were not only training without the meter but as if you had never even heard of a power meter. In other words, wear your meter but run without any consideration for what it is saying. The idea here is to collect the data from your current training routine so that you establish a baseline of your own tendencies, strengths, and weaknesses.

Since we both know there is no way you are not going to look at your head unit, let me tell you about some of the trends you will notice when you run. You may begin to see a certain wattage range for each of the different intensities at which you run, from easy to hard. At easier paces, you'll likely see lower wattage than harder efforts. You may also begin to see an association between your power levels and the terrain and your effort: uphill, downhill, on the flat, with surges, and more. As best you can, just observe these tendencies for the first two weeks; don't do anything to influence them. That is, don't let the readout and the various power-level reports change the way you approach your running. Resist the temptation to see how many watts you can record on a hill. Just collect the data for now. In the following chapters, you'll see how these two weeks of baseline data will help you create a training program that will make you faster and fitter.

Key Data Metrics, Terms, and Concepts

Your new power meter is capable of collecting a sizable number of metrics, each fascinating in its own way. You are probably familiar with some, while others will likely be new to you unless you have used a power meter elsewhere, such as on your bike. Which metrics are visible on your head unit while you're running may vary, depending on whether you use a smartphone app or a GPS watch for your head unit, as well as which power meter you use. In addition, you can generally choose which metrics you want on your display.

What follows is an overview of the metrics that run power meters generally offer. Most or all of these can probably be displayed on your head unit; if not, they will likely be viewable on your computer through the software that comes with your meter or can be found in most training analysis software suites.

Down the road, after you have become familiar with your power meter and have developed your own approach on how to use it in your training, you may decide to focus on only a few metrics while ignoring the others. For now, though, here's an overview of the key data metrics and what they mean.

POWER

Power is expressed in watts, of course, but there are different ways to measure and display it. We can read it instantaneously on our head unit or view it as average power for durations of our choosing. We can record average power for one lap of whatever course we determine, or for the entire run session.

Some athletes enjoy seeing instantaneous power, while others find it very difficult to use due to the constant fluctuation in the wattage reading. This fluctuation is normal even while you are maintaining the same pace or effort level. Don't let it frustrate you. In general, the more experience you have as a runner, the less fluctuation you will see. As you learn to train with your power meter, it is likely that you will want either average or instantaneous power prominently displayed on your head unit. We will discuss more specifics on power later in this chapter.

HEART RATE

If you are an endurance athlete, you are likely familiar with training according to heart rate (HR), and might want to continue to use HR and HR zones for your training, even after you get a better understanding of how to use your power meter. Even if your power meter doesn't come with an HR monitor, you can likely still connect it to a head unit, especially if you are using a GPS watch.

Heart rate and power together yield an important ratio you will want to track over time to assess your training. More on that later, when we begin to discuss how to analyze power data.

PACE

Pace is probably the most popular metric in all of running. It is usually measured in minutes per mile (min/mi) or minutes per kilometer (min/km). Most athletes care about how fast they run, and judge their improvement and satisfaction with a session or race based on the pace they were able to run. The fact that you're reading this book shows you want to get faster, so pace is important to you. As we will see, the relationship between pace and power is vital for your success. Keeping pace as a prominent display on the head unit to compare with your power output will be a great way to begin to learn the relationship between the two as you are running.

DURATION/DISTANCE

Power, pace, and HR help us define intensity of a session. Two other important factors for every session are duration and distance. You can display either or both on your head unit. Before the popularity of GPS watches, most runners trained simply on duration over a known distance, using the measure of how long it took to do a run to better understand how fast or how hard they ran. Now with GPS watches, you can see not only duration, but also the distance traveled (so you don't have to run a predetermined course to judge speed and effort). Many GPS units can also record lap splits based on distance or time and save it for later analysis.

Runners commonly do workouts based on time. You may decide to do a fixed time, such as a 1-hour run, for example. Or you may decide to run intervals by time, such as 5 × 3 minutes with 3 minutes recovery between intervals. Some athletes might instead choose intervals or runs by distance, such as a 10 km run, or 5 × 1-km or 5 × 1-mile intervals. In any case, duration by lap or distance by lap might be helpful to include as a prominent data field on your head unit.

CADENCE

As you recall from Chapter 2, power is simply force times speed (the force applied by your body to the ground times the speed of your foot as you get it off the ground). This movement of the feet off the ground is called cadence, and it is usually represented in steps per minute (spm) for both feet total, or as revolutions per minute (rpm) if talking about one foot. So if one foot runs at 90 rpm, the spm is 180.

You've probably wondered what makes a good cadence for running. In fact, that is an excellent question. Though there is a lot of individual variance, it is indisputable that the slower the cadence, the slower the runner. A foot planted on the ground is not moving. The faster the foot gets off the ground, the higher the speed of the movement, which is critical for power. In general, a cadence of 90-plus rpm is ideal for most runners to achieve. If you are far from this number, or feel the need to work on your cadence—or are simply unsure of your cadence—adding this number to the display on your head unit can help you concentrate on keeping your cadence up.

OTHER

There are a number of other metrics we will examine in depth in upcoming chapters. As you become familiar with them, you may want to display some of them on your head unit. These metrics include Normalized Power (NP), Intensity Factor (IF), Training Stress Score (TSS), Efficiency Index (EI), kilojoules per kilometer (kJ/km), and various efficiency factors (EF).

To complicate things even more, there may be additional metrics developed over the next few years as we see the head unit firmware catch up with the needs and demands of the athletes using them and as we create new metrics to improve the process of analyzing run training. Many of these will depend on how the power meter collects, measures, or estimates power, as well as on the capabilities of the head unit. Some of these additional metrics might include balance of power between legs (left-right balance), or ratios of the various planes of power to help athletes see if they have extraneous movements in planes that don't help them.

KILOJOULES, AVERAGE POWER, NORMALIZED POWER, AND NORMALIZED GRADED PACE

There are important metrics you might not specifically use in the data fields of a head unit, but ones you need to know and understand to help your training with power. All of the following are key to measuring performance and training stress.

Kilojoules

In Chapter 2, I discussed how power is simply a work rate (the rate at which work is being accomplished). Work requires energy, and watts are simply a rate at which you are expending energy to run. The more work you do, the more energy you must expend to do it.

The energy we use to apply these forces comes from Calories. A Calorie (with a capital C) is 1,000 calories, and to more easily distinguish "Calories" from "calories," the term we use for Calories is kiloCalories. (The calorie, with a lowercase "c," is generally useful only in chemistry; the everyday food calorie is actually a Calorie.)

A kilojoule, or kJ, is the mechanical energy used to move your body in running, and it is represented by the kJ symbol on your head unit. Broadly speaking, the energy usually required to run 1 mile is approximately 100 Calories, but the mechanical efficiency of the runner will determine how well that energy is translated to speed or pace.

Cyclists and triathletes know that the ratio of kJ to kiloCalories is approximately 1:1, which makes nutritional calculations relatively straightforward, whether you are planning pre-race fueling or simply figuring out how much energy you just spent on your bike. The situation is not quite as clear-cut in our sport, however, because some power meters for running

Collect the data from your current training routine to establish a baseline of your own tendencies, strengths, and weaknesses.

measure work in two dimensions, whereas others measure in three dimensions. This makes the ratio of kJ to kiloCalories more complicated, because we have either an incomplete picture with a 2D power meter or possibly an overstated kJ total with a 3D meter. The differences for this calculation are not significant, however, and after working with both meter types, my research shows that the 100-Calories-per-mile ratio is a reasonable metric to use. By tying kiloCalories to mileage, you should be able to get a good sense of what your ratio is for kJ and kiloCalories with the particular power meter you use.

Aside from its potential role in determining caloric expenditure and meal planning, tracking kJ is a great way to determine your running efficiency. The simplest way to approach this is to record the kJ required for similar performances, and divide the kJ by the kilometers of the distance. The product of this calculation, kilojoules per kilometer (kJ/km), will give you an idea of the amount of work required to complete the distance. When you are able to reduce the mechanical energy required for running a certain pace, you have made a major improvement as a runner!

If you do tempo runs on a track or on a course on which you repeat the same workout regularly, you can compare your kJ/km figure to your pace to monitor improvements in efficiency. For example, if you complete a tempo run of 30 minutes and see an increase in kJ/km of 2 percent while at the same time you see an increase in pace of at least 3 to 5 percent, you have made a significant improvement in your efficiency. Your kJ/km figure represents the actual energy required to run at a high pace, while your pace figure tells you how well that work is translated to speed.

Average Power

If you've been using pace and HR data during your running, you're familiar with average HR and average pace for runs. Average power is similar: It is the total of all the watts generated during a run divided by the time the data was collected. As mentioned earlier in this chapter, your power meter collects data and displays the power measurement in a time range you can set in the head unit, in 1-, 5-, 10-, or 30-second averages. You can even set the data field of the head unit to display the average power for the entire run, and it will collect and display a rolling average during that time.

In fact, the power meter doesn't take a single sample in 1 second. It has taken numerous samples in a second and displayed the average for that second.

Average power is a basic value, which is simple to understand and use. However, it isn't always the best value for assessing how well a session or race went. That is where Normalized Power comes in as a more valuable metric.

Normalized Power: Why Not Just Average Power?

While average power is a simple and basic metric in widespread use, it isn't always the best metric for assessing the metabolic demand of a training session. Normalized Power (NP) is an adjusted expression of average power that better reflects the metabolic cost of a run than average power, and I find it to be a better metric for taking into account what you truly experienced on the run. Normalizing data allows us to scale the information and eliminate the effect of some gross influences and anomalies; in doing so, it yields a clearer picture of true effort.

You're probably saying, "OK, but what does normalizing mean?" Normalizing is the process of comparing the range of variability of power during a run with the average power of the run; the number it spits out gives you a more accurate picture of the true metabolic cost of the run.

Let me give you an example of how normalizing works, and then we can look at how it comes into play during a run. Let's say we have two runners of different weights and we want to compare their power outputs. Runner A has an average power on a run of 210 watts. Runner B has an average power of 150 watts. So in a hilly cross-country race, runner A is going to cream runner B, right? Not necessarily; average power alone does not tell the whole story. If we normalize the figures, however, we get a useful comparison that reflects the real world. In this case, we can normalize by dividing power by body weight. For example, if runner A weighs 180 pounds, his power (210) normalized for weight is 1.17 watts per pound (210 ÷ 180 = 1.17). If runner B weighs 120 pounds, her power (150) normalized for weight is 1.25 (150 ÷ 120 = 1.25). So even though A puts out far more power than B, B is actually more powerful pound for pound. That's a subtlety you might not see in reviewing average power, but you probably would see it when A and B race each other up a hill. All we've done here is normalize the data from these two runners according to their weight to get a better sense of what the data truly means. Without that normalizing, we wouldn't know that B is more powerful.

So how does NP work on a run? On flat terrain, runners must apply a force to get their feet off the ground (up against gravity), but some of the force is applied in a vector horizontally, to move forward. On the flat, gravity is a constant and very small variable.

As soon as the path goes uphill, runners must produce more watts to climb it. This is because they must now apply a force that can overcome the increased influence of gravity on them to maintain the pace in a more vertical direction (a more vertical vector than the flat) in addition to the force applied to go forward. The amount of influence of gravity and this change in the force required is relative to the steepness of the hill and the time spent climbing.

Over the top and down the other side, the watts produced to go downhill are far fewer than the amount needed to maintain the same pace on the flat, as now gravity assists the runners, and the force required to get their feet off the ground and move forward is much smaller. The movement downhill accelerates the athletes, because little force is required to produce forward motion.

Apart from track events, most racecourses are not perfectly flat. There are hills, which affect the output and also the demands placed on the runner. Add in surges in a race, such as at a start or in other key deciding moments in a race, and you can begin to see how the variance in power output needs to be accounted for to normalize the data.

Also, as athletes fatigue, they will likely produce more watts in the vertical and lateral planes, reducing efficiency. This means for a given pace, it is likely that runners will fatigue and not produce watts at the same efficiency as they did when fresher. For example, kJ burned per kilometer might be higher in the last kilometer of a 10-km run on the track, even if the athlete is running the same pace as before. So even though an athlete is running the same pace, the power is different, and the stress on the body to produce power can be higher just through time.

Normalized Power might be built into the software that comes with your power meter. You probably won't find it useful to display on your head unit, but when you review NP after a run you will probably see that it gives you a much better sense of what the run felt like than the average power figure. That is, it will give you a much better idea about the true energy cost of every run you do.

One last note about Normalized Power before we move on: If you are familiar with NP through your use of a power meter in cycling or triathlon, you're probably familiar with the extreme range of power outputs during a ride. In cycling, big surges and jumps are common, as is coasting along in the draft generating zero watts whenever possible.

In running, however, it is rare to see a number of high sprinting outputs in a race, especially in races of 5K and longer. Runners can never coast down a hill or sit in a pack, so the range of power outputs is generally small. And because of this small range, there usually is not a large difference between average power and Normalized Power values from a run workout, unless the workout includes a lot of intervals. Normalized Power is especially helpful, therefore, in analyzing interval workouts, but as you will see, NP is also important for other metrics that we'll introduce in later chapters.

Normalized Graded Pace

Just as Normalized Power is a scaling of power data and its variance to better understand the metabolic cost of each run, Normalized Graded Pace

(NGP) brings the same idea to pace data, given the variance of terrain and speed of the runner.

Consider this scenario to help explain it. A runner warms up for 20 minutes on a flat course by running 8-minute miles, a nice and easy pace for this runner. He then does 20 minutes of running at a 6-minute-per-mile pace on a very hilly course. Then, after being tired from the effort, he does a 20-minute cooldown jog at 10 minutes per mile on a flat course again. The average pace for this run is an 8-minute-per-mile pace, an easy warm-up pace for this athlete. But the average pace for this entire run doesn't come close to representing what the run was really like in terms of stress on the body. The 6-minute-pace portion on a tough, hilly course means the pace was probably much harder in that section alone. The athlete had easy parts of this run, but also much harder parts.

With GPS data, or data from an accelerometer on the body that can pick up changes in the slope of the terrain, we can normalize the gradient and changes in pace according to that gradient. We can account for the steepness of the slope of the inclines and declines, and how that affects the output of the athlete.

It is important to mention that the algorithm for NGP does not account for, nor include, any power data. This metric has been around longer than power meters in running, and in the past has been part of how we trained runners and compared performances on varying courses.

You're likely asking, "Why do I care about Normalized Graded Pace if I have Normalized Power?" Great question! Though we have power data, pace is far from obsolete as a data metric. After all, we all want to run a faster pace. Pace as a metric is enhanced with power data. NGP and NP will become key metrics in some of our other metric calculations, especially when we want comparisons with HR. More on that in the chapters ahead.

Putting It All Together

With a power meter, you now have the opportunity to take your training to a new level. You have data that can help you fine-tune your training and better understand your tendencies and needs, and assess your current fitness and technique through analysis of the data. Analysis can be a commitment in itself if you really want to learn and are serious about performance, and you'll continue to learn through the process of examining your run data. If you have no interest in doing analysis, you should reconsider whether a power meter is right for you, as the numbers will not really do you much good if you can't see the bigger picture of your training and trends in your fitness.

Do You Need Power-Analysis Software?

If you're serious about your training and your goals and have bought a power meter, then yes, you need power-analysis software. In order to maximize the return on your investment, you will want access to analytic tools. You don't have to spend an hour analyzing each run workout you do. Quite often, the details of the workout aren't the most important information; reviewing a few key metrics post-workout is fine. Or you can do a weekly or semi-regular summary to make sure things are on track, help plan future training, and give yourself confidence that you are training well and are on track to achieve your goals.

In the chapters ahead I will show you some basic, important metrics that your power software should help you to track and see. Some of the analysis I show might not be available to you in your software suite, but as this tool grows in popularity, I think many of these new metrics will begin to become standard across all analysis programs.

One of the challenges you face might lie in deciding which software to use. I have some analysis software programs listed in Appendix B, which you can review to determine which ones best meet your needs, budget, and goals.

Should I Get a Coach?

A number of runners want nothing to do with data. They simply want to run consistently, monitor their pace on a run, race well, peak at their local annual race, and have some bragging rights over training partners and friends. Other athletes have high goals, and the stakes get higher as the goals get higher. If you want to do well, you can't miss training days or mis-time your recovery. You've got to maximize what you can do for what is likely to be the constrained time you have available. If this describes you, then I would strongly encourage you to hire a coach. You may not need a full-time coach; I have worked with some athletes on a consulting basis, checking in from time to time to review their data and tell them what I see and answer their questions, so they can learn and go forward on their own, coaching themselves. This might be a good first step for you, if you're interested in learning but hesitant to commit to a coaching relationship.

Summary

Once you've calibrated your new power meter, you can begin using it with a head unit of your choice and start collecting data. At first you should not let the power numbers control your workouts; instead, just learn the basics from observing them during your workouts.

The head unit you choose should be able to display the metrics you are most interested in tracking. The head unit itself could be a smartphone or a GPS watch.

Normalized Power and Normalized Graded Pace help us account for the variance in a run to better assess the metabolic cost of the effort and intensity.

4 Running Intensity

In the first three chapters, I covered the basics of power and how they apply to running. Now I can begin to show you how the power meter can be an effective tool for your own training. The key to using the power meter effectively is to fully understand the power data it collects in terms of what the numbers mean specifically for you.

More than any other training variable, intensity is the key to fitness. Volume has long been a badge of honor for runners, who may share the total miles or kilometers from their training logs to show how hard they are working. But training effectively and efficiently is not about how far you run, nor about how long or how often. It's about how hard you run those miles, especially as your goals get higher. You have to know what your intensity is and what it should be, relative to your goals and needs.

One of the biggest advantages of a running power meter lies in its ability to define intensity, because pace alone can't really give us a complete picture. So let's discuss how the power meter presents intensity, beginning with the most important metric: functional threshold power.

Functional Threshold Power (rFTPw): The Most Important Number

In the world of power meters, the most important metric for an athlete is functional threshold power. You're probably familiar with the term "threshold" in endurance training; it is usually used to refer to the physiological change in the athlete's blood that can limit performance over the course of an hour or so. Some call this point the lactate threshold or the anaerobic threshold. There is also the aerobic threshold, where the anaerobic energy pathways begin to be used more significantly in energy production than the aerobic pathways. In my coaching world, however, we don't measure the

One big advantage of a running power meter is its ability to define intensity.

performance of an athlete by lactate levels or energy pathways. We measure performance by something that we can see: What is the best performance the runner can functionally hold for an hour? This level of performance is the functional threshold. When we use it in conjunction with power, we call it functional threshold power.

If you are a triathlete or cyclist, then you may already be familiar with the abbreviation FTP in connection with the power meter that you use on your bicycle. To avoid creating confusion with cycling's definition of FTP (as well as with functional threshold pace, a different metric that we will discuss later in this chapter), we will use the abbreviation rFTPw for running functional threshold power. The "r" at the beginning signifies running, to avoid confusion with cycling, and the "Pw" refers to power. This measure, rFTPw, represents the best power output that an athlete can hold while running for 60 minutes.

The measurement of rFTPw is important because it embraces the performance measures of work rate, intensity, and efficiency. In addition, rFTPw will help you establish your power zones. Specifically:

- Because it's a key representation of the work rate you are capable of holding for one hour, rFTPw is the strongest indicator of your potential. The greater the work rate you can sustain, the fitter and better you are.

- It is the base value for which intensity is defined specifically for you. Power outputs above your rFTPw are going to be harder efforts than those wattages that are below it. Of course you already know that doing high work rates is not easy. But what constitutes a high work rate? That depends on your rFTPw, so it is specific to you. For example, 200 watts will seem like a lot to a runner with an rFTPw of 180 watts, while a runner with an rFTPw of 300 watts will find 200 watts easy to sustain.

- It is a value at which your efficiency as a distance runner can be calculated and measured. Chapter 5 will discuss efficiency and how to monitor it during your training.

- It is the basis for establishing power zones, should you choose to use them. We will discuss power zones in Chapter 6, but if you have experience with HR zones, you'll find that power zones are very similar as a guide to intensities, with the zones defined by percentage ranges of rFTPw.

Okay, so the importance of rFTPw is clear; next we need to lay out how to determine your own rFTPw value.

How Can I Find My rFTPw?

There are a few different ways to determine rFTPw. You can do it in a lab by running a series of protocols on a treadmill while wearing a gas-exchange mask to measure the physiological markers for threshold and the watts you produce at that pace. However, I believe the best way to find your rFTPw is to do a field test. I haven't found any evidence that a lab test is any more accurate than a field test, but the field test is a lot less expensive and much easier to schedule. In addition, a field test is usually easily repeatable and generally very reliable when done properly and consistently under the same conditions. Ideally, you'll do your field test on a track or a flat road that you can return to regularly for follow-up tests, and where the effect of wind can be minimized or eliminated.

You can also calculate your rFTPw in other ways, including deriving it from your race results or your training logs. These methods can give you a reasonable estimate. We'll look at those methods later on, after we cover the field tests.

One important note before we get to the tests: Your rFTPw value will vary somewhat depending on whether you use a 2D power meter or a 3D meter. A 3D power meter will collect power data from three planes, while a 2D will collect it from only two planes. (Review this in Chapter 2.) As a result, there will likely be a small difference in the numbers you get for the same workout, test or effort. Among experienced runners, lateral power contributes only a small amount to total power; for novice or inefficient runners, the contribution is a bit greater. In any case, you should not derive an rFTPw value from a 2D power meter and expect it to be accurate for a 3D (and vice versa). This does not mean that one type of meter is more accurate than the other. It only means that for your power meter training to be useful, you need to stick with the same type of power meter for all your data collection. If you do change power meter types at some point, you will need to recalculate your rFTPw by conducting a new field test before using the new meter in your training.

By the way, neither of the two tests below are an all-out hour-long effort. As you can imagine, a full hour at maximum output can require some serious recovery time, and it can obviously be affected by motivation as well. In fact, it is very difficult to perform a full-hour effort that is representative of what you can reach in a race, and runners who attempt it usually struggle to get an FTP number that is an accurate measure of their potential. For all these reasons, it is better to undertake shorter tests that are designed to derive an accurate measure of rFTPw than to kill yourself in an hour-long effort and then find your training derailed for two weeks.

TEST 1: THE 3/9 TEST

This test comprises a 3-minute all-out segment and a 9-minute all-out segment with rest periods in between. It was originally designed by the Stryd running power meter company as a way to measure changes in threshold power without putting the athlete through a full hour-long test. Stryd also initially compared the results obtained from this test with blood lactate levels to try to find a correlation with rFTPw, but the 10 percent margin of error was too great to be used effectively. I liked the premise of this test, however, and did some basic trials with some of my athletes. I then made some changes to it, and compared it to the results we obtained with Test 2 (covered below). With a little tinkering, I was able to create this variation of the 3/9 Test that yields a reliable estimate of rFTPw, as long as the conditions and terrain are repeatable and consistent each time you conduct the test.

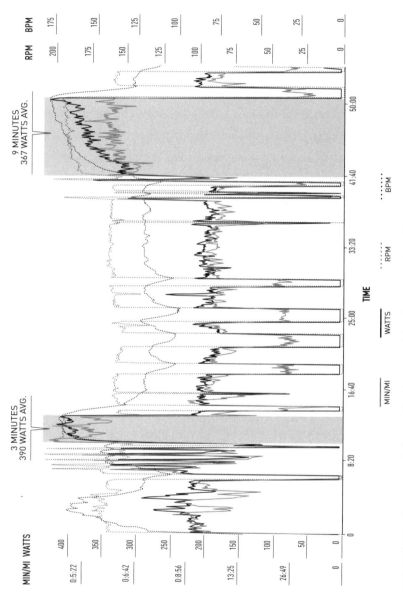

FIGURE 4.1a Power graph from a 3-minute and 9-minute test for rFTPw

For this test:

- Warm up 15 minutes, preparing for a hard effort at the end of it.
- Conduct a 3-minute interval at maximal effort.
- Recover with a 5-minute walk, 10-minute very easy jog, 5-minute walk, 5-minute easy jog, and 5-minute walk again (30 minutes total).
- Conduct a 9-minute interval at maximal effort.
- Cool down 10 to 15 minutes.
- Add the 3-minute average power value to the 9-minute average power value.
- Divide that total by 2.
- Take 90 percent of the quotient; that is your estimated rFTPw value.

Figure 4.1 shows the power file from an athlete doing the test in which I have highlighted the 3-minute and 9-minute intervals. This shows the

Duration	Distance	TSS
03:08.80	0.59 mi	6.8

Work	**73** kJ	IF	**1.24**
NP	**396** W	VI	**1.02**
Pa:Hr	**9.13** %	El. Gain	--
Grade	--	El. Loss	--
VAM	--	w/kg	**5.40**

	MIN	AVG	MAX	
Power	0	390	421	w
Heart Rate	0	165	172	bpm
Cadence	0	198	207	rpm
Speed	0.00	11.2	14.5	mph
Pace	00:00	05:21	04:09	min/mi

FIGURE 4.1b 3-minute data

Duration	Distance	TSS
09:02.09	1.46 mi	19.1

Work	**199** kJ	IF	**1.16**
NP	**370** W	VI	**1.01**
Pa:Hr	**4.98** %	El. Gain	--
Grade	--	El. Loss	--
VAM	--	w/kg	**5.10**

	MIN	AVG	MAX	
Power	0	367	434	w
Heart Rate	0	165	178	bpm
Cadence	0	194	202	rpm
Speed	0.00	9.72	14.0	mph
Pace	00:00	06:10	04:18	min/mi

FIGURE 4.1c 9-minute data

average values as 390 watts for the 3-minute interval and 367 watts for the 9-minute interval.

Using this test as the example, the sum of those two average powers is 757 watts. Divide 757 by 2, and the quotient is 378.5 watts. Ninety percent of 378.5 is 340.65, or 341 watts for rFTPw, as we only deal in whole numbers for FTP values. Ninety percent is a good starting point, but since there is a margin of error, and each athlete has unique traits and abilities, I will share with you how Test 2 can be used to help dial in a specific conversion to better estimate your rFTPw.

TEST 2: 30-MINUTE TIME TRIAL

This test was devised by Joe Friel, and it is one that I've used successfully for years to estimate an athlete's threshold pace. I've also used it to estimate threshold HR when training with HR zones. The test is simple but requires decent pacing skills. It is also a longer effort than the 3/9 Test, so injury risk is higher and the recovery time needed will be greater, but I find this 30-minute test is more accurate in predicting an athlete's rFTPw than the 3/9 Test. If you're worried about the recovery required for this effort, or if you're not very good at pacing yet, you might want to stick with the 3/9 Test. However, if you do this test along with the 3/9 Test at least two to three times in the early days of using your power meter, you'll be able to see how the tests correlate, so in the future you can use the less-stressful 3/9 Test to estimate rFTPw. More on that shortly.

It's important that you do this test on your own, as doing it alone just about guarantees that you cannot go as fast as you would in a race of 30 minutes. Remember, the goal here is to estimate what you could hold for 60 minutes, which is not the same effort as you'd expend in a 30-minute race with others. Running solo is an important factor in getting an accurate result.

For this test:

- Warm up 15 minutes, preparing for a hard effort afterward.
- Start a 30-minute time trial (best effort) on a flat road or track, collecting power data (collect pace and HR data as well, if possible).
- Cool down 10 to 15 minutes.
- Take the average power for the last 20 minutes of the time trial; this is your rFTPw value.

In Figure 4.2, I've zoomed in on the test portion of the file and isolated the data from the last 20 minutes of the test to make it easier to see. The athlete conducting this test is the same one who did the 3/9 Test above (Figure 4.1). In this 30-minute test, his estimated rFTPw value is 353, or approximately 3.5 percent higher than the 3/9 Test estimate—not bad in terms of consistency. If you do the 3/9 Test first, then the 30-minute test, and follow up with a few trials after that, you might find that 90 percent of the 3/9 Test needs to be adjusted slightly. However, I wouldn't expect it to change much; most athletes fall close to the 90 percent range, usually within ± 3.5 percent.

If you do both tests for the first three times you schedule a testing period, about every four to six weeks, and find you are consistently within a small percentage range difference, you can then do the 3/9 Test and adjust by the average percentage that is specific to you. Table 4.1 shows an athlete who did three separate tests, conducting both the 3/9 Test and the 30-minute TT test. The table shows the average watts from the different 3/9 Tests in the first column, the three 30-minute TT tests in the second column (with the final 20 minutes value listed), and the percentage difference in the third column.

Based upon this consistent difference in the values of the average of the 3/9 Test with the last 20 minutes of the TT, you can see the value of the 3/9 Test is about 8 percent higher than the harder 30-minute test. With these data in hand, an athlete can do the 3/9 Test and take 92 percent of the value to get an accurate rFTPw value.

My advice is to do both tests from time to time, especially when starting a new block of training or a new season, so you can make sure the conversion hasn't changed drastically based on fitness changes. One thing you may notice during the 30-minute Time Trial test is that your watts may rise as you get deeper into the test, despite the fact that your pace might not have gotten faster, or perhaps has even slowed a little. If so, you're not alone; I've seen this frequently,

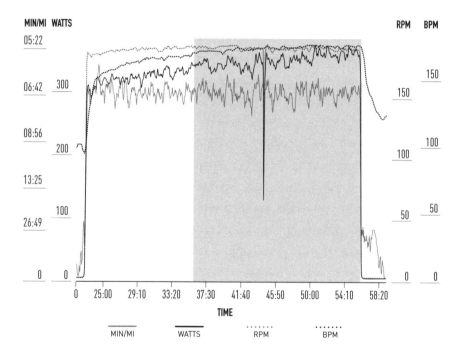

FIGURE 4.2a Power graph from a 30-minute time trial test, with power rising as pace stays relatively even and steady

and I attribute it to athletes producing watts more laterally and vertically as they become fatigued, due to extraneous movement patterns. These movements can include more head bobbing, some arm carriage changes, and other lateral swings. It actually happened to the runner in Figure 4.2. Look closely and you'll see that while he maintains his pace, his watts are clearly rising as the test goes on.

If you're wondering why we look at the last 20 minutes specifically, the reason has to do precisely with this increase in watts over time. If we look at the whole 30 minutes, the lower early wattages will reduce your average rFTPw value. If you're using a 3D power meter that gives you total power in three planes, you want to look at the total work rate. The highest amount of power you can produce for an hour, whether effective in helping you go faster or not, is the key value to know. This signifies the highest potential work rate you can sustain. If you can improve your efficiency (by converting extraneous movements to forward motion), you will be able to hold the same work rate while producing more speed.

If you're a triathlete or cyclist, you'll recognize that this is where cycling power and cycling FTP differ from running and rFTPw. Cyclists want to get their wattage numbers up, as the power meter on the bike

Duration	Distance	TSS
20:00	3.05 mi	32.4

Work	424 kJ	IF	1.00
NP	354 W	VI	1.00
Pa:Hr	1.75 %	El. Gain	--
Grade	--	El. Loss	--
VAM	--	w/kg	4.90

	MIN	AVG	MAX	
Power	0	353	387	w
Heart Rate	170	175	177	bpm
Cadence	172	193	198	rpm
Speed	6.03	9.15	11.4	mph
Pace	09:57	06:33	05:15	min/mi

Peak Power

☐ Entire Workout	236 w	
☐ Peak 10:00 min	362 w	
☐ Peak 12:00 min	358 w	
✔ **Peak 20:00 min**	**353 w**	
☐ Peak 30:00 min	346 w	
☐ Peak 01:00 h	257 w	

FIGURE 4.2b 30-minute time trial test data

measures the watts directly applied to moving the bike forward. When cyclists fatigue, their watts decrease because they can no longer produce power to move the bike forward as effectively as before. If a cyclist saw her watts increase even as she fatigued, she would be pretty excited!

Running power meters are different because they give the work rate that is being done by the body in two or three planes, depending on the power meter, not specifically what is being used effectively and applied to running forward. In Chapter 5, we will discuss how to use the power meter to gauge how efficient you are at producing speed per the watts you're generating.

I know you may be thinking that if the runner's watts will just keep going up and up, why stop at 30 minutes? Wouldn't the watts increase linearly until the end of the test? The answer is no, they won't. There is a maximal work rate the body can produce, and it likely won't continue to increase at the same rate until one hour has expired and suddenly stop there. The other reason to stop at 30 minutes, of course, is that a one-hour maximal work rate would exhaust an athlete for quite a while, possibly impinging on training for some time afterward.

Should you absolutely expect to see watts increase during your test? No, not necessarily. Your wattage reading might go down if you don't pace yourself well and can't produce a force or cadence that keeps your watt production up. In addition, any changes you do see could be small or large, depending on a

TABLE 4.1 3/9 and 30-Minute Time Trial Tests Percentage Differences

	Avg 3/9 Test	20 Min in TT Test	% Difference
Test 1	379	354	93.40
Test 2	418	383	91.63
Test 3	429	397	92.54

number of factors about you. That's another great thing about training with this tool: You're going to learn a lot about yourself as a runner.

OTHER CALCULATIONS FOR ESTIMATING RFTPW

There are other ways to estimate rFTPw if you don't have the time to test, or have a lot of data already collected. Are these methods as good as the two tests above? Yes, but there is a caveat: While they can be effective, that effectiveness depends on recent data. Your fitness changes over the course of a season (at least we hope so), so if you are in better shape now than you were a month ago, last month's data is not going to give you an accurate assessment. In fact, for all the tests that follow, the freshness of your data is usually more important than the way you estimate.

Races

If you have recently done a race that is close to an hour long and you collected power data from it, you can likely use the value from the race. The race might be a half-marathon for some, a 15K or 10K for others. When using this process to determine your rFTPw, you want to look for your peak 60-minute power value in the race file (the best 60-minute average power), then take the Normalized Power (NP) for that 60 minutes. If your race was well paced, these two numbers will be close to the same. If you ran a tough, hilly course, the NP figure will probably be somewhat higher.

If the race was between 50 and 60 minutes long, you can use the NP value for the entire race. If your race file is more than an hour long—up to 70 minutes—the NP value is probably pretty close. If the race was more than 70 minutes but not more than 90 minutes, you can increase the value by 0.5 percent for every minute over 70 (up to 90 minutes). Remember, rFTPw is the best value you can hold for an hour, not 70 to 90 minutes. You should be able to hold a higher intensity for 60 minutes than you can for time ranges greater than 60 minutes. If the race file is greater than 90 minutes, I do not suggest you use it to estimate rFTPw.

The number that you obtain will be useful as a reasonable estimate of your rFTPw, not a means to specifically benchmark it. Also, as mentioned earlier, if this race file is more than a month old, it is not likely to be a good indicator of your current rFTPw.

20-Minute Value

If you have some recent power files where you've trained or raced hard *on a rolling or flat course* for 20 minutes, you can use 95 percent of the average power for that peak 20 minutes as an approximate calculation of your rFTPw. The qualification of a rolling to flat course is important; an uphill race will inflate the value, and a downhill race will deflate it. It can be hard to find courses that are entirely flat, of course, so some rolling terrain is acceptable, as the descents will likely offset the climbs.

Self-Assessment

As a competitive runner for many years, I could usually predict my time before a race within a few seconds, even for longer distances such as 10K and half-marathon. I just knew my body—and my fitness. I had the same ability for estimating my FTP for cycling in my days as a triathlete. You might have a similar ability, and I would encourage you to estimate what your rFTPw is before your tests, just to get a sense of your perception of yourself and how close you are to the actual number you obtain. This applies even to the first time you conduct the tests, after just generally observing your watts on your runs for the first two weeks or so. You will learn a lot about yourself. After a while, a test may not even be necessary, as you'll know what you can do.

Software Modeling

Software programs are available that can predict your rFTPw based on your power outputs at different intensities. These models can be fairly reliable as long as the sample size is large and the collected data is accurate.

Once you have your rFTPw value, you should record it, make sure it is posted in your athlete settings in the analysis software you use, and mark it in your training log. It is an important number to track, not only for the reasons listed earlier, but also for the added metrics we will discuss in the coming chapters.

Functional Threshold Pace (rFTPa): The Other Important Number

In addition to functional threshold power, the other important metric to collect is running functional threshold pace, which we abbreviate as rFTPa, with "r" signifying running, and "Pa" signifying pace. This calculation is similar in principle to rFTPw, but instead of recording the best power you can hold for 1 hour, it is the best *pace* you can hold for that hour. The measurement predicts a flat course, with no wind, and with the athlete relatively fresh and able to maximize his or her fitness level.

Pace is critically important. In some ways, it is a more important measurement than sheer power, because the race is always won by who goes fastest, not who has the most watts. The emergence of power meters in the world of distance running hasn't made pace obsolete as a metric but has actually enhanced it! In Chapter 5, we will discuss how the relationship of pace and power can help you get more insight into your training and racing. Indeed, tracking pace within the context of power is likely the biggest benefit power meters provide as a training tool, in terms of making athletes faster and understanding the process of how to run faster.

How Can I Find rFTPa?

I am sure you're already thinking there are too many tests to do with this power meter—but I have good news! You can calculate your rFTPa from the same tests I listed for finding rFTPw, as long as you collect pace data in the tests as well.

TEST 1: THE 3/9 TEST

During the 3/9 Test, take the average pace from the two interval efforts and add 10 percent. The result is your estimated rFTPa. For example, our athlete from Figures 4.1 and 4.2 ran a 5:21 pace for the 3-minute interval and a 6:10 pace for the 9-minute interval. The average of these two is 5:45. Add 10 percent to this value, and he is at 6:20 minutes per mile for his rFTPa.

TEST 2: 30-MINUTE TIME TRIAL

In the 30-minute test, the pace for the final 20 minutes is usually an accurate indication of your rFTPa value. For example, the athlete from Figures 4.1 and 4.2 estimates 6:33 for his rFTPa in this 30-minute test, a difference of 13 seconds from Test 1. That's a 3.3 percent difference, which is very close to the small 3.5 percent difference we found in comparing the results of the 3/9 and 30-minute power tests.

Coincidentally, the rFTPa you collect from the final 20 minutes of this test is also a good indicator of your anaerobic threshold HR value (or lactate threshold HR if you prefer). If you are training with HR zones, you can use this number as your guide.

OTHER TESTS

Similarly to the rFTPw estimates, you can use a race file close to 60 minutes long, from a flat to rolling course, and take the pace of that 60 minutes. You can also use your own self-assessment. I find experienced runners can estimate their rFTPa quite accurately.

Keeping rFTPw and rFTPa Current

Fitness is a moving target, constantly changing for better or worse. It is important to stay aware of your current rFTPw and rFTPa. Unless you are certain your fitness hasn't changed much, files that are a month or more older are almost certainly not a good indicator of your current fitness level.

You should use your training log to help keep track of how hard efforts feel when training at similar intensities. Doing so will help you to home in on your self-awareness and ability to self-assess.

As you lay out your annual training plan, schedule your tests no more than six weeks apart. Preferably, you'll do them a little more often than that, as you learn more about yourself and your power as a runner. In addition, make sure that your testing is repeatable and reliable. This means resting a couple days before the test each time, so fatigue doesn't negatively affect the value. For example, you might want to treat your test like a B-priority race, where it is not a peak event but it is one that still matters to you.

If you can test on the same course or the same track each time, so much the better. Conduct the same warm-up routine each time, and if possible, try to replicate the conditions, such as heat, rain, cold, wind, and so on.

These thresholds are the most important metrics in training with power as a distance runner, so treat them as such. Give them your attention. If your numbers are improving, you are improving.

Defining Intensity

Now that we've established your threshold power and threshold pace, you have a benchmark from which to judge your intensity. Efforts that are above your threshold are obviously higher intensity for you than efforts below your threshold. This holds true for power (higher watts versus lower watts) and for pace (faster pace versus slower pace).

The higher your goals, the more intensity you must include in your training. This doesn't mean that your volume of training doesn't matter; volume does have benefits. But to gain high levels of fitness, athletes must push their

If you improve your efficiency, you will produce more speed at the same work rate.

limits, and the best way to push them is to train with intensity. If volume were the key to fitness, whoever put in the most miles would be the winner of all races. Ultra-marathoners would be the fastest and best runners around, in every type of race from 100 meters to 100 miles. But we know that isn't the case.

Volume has long been popular not only for describing training level (as well as for bragging rights), but also because there is a lot of benefit to long runs and loads of miles—to a point. In a race, however, it is speed that matters. Unfortunately, speed and intensity are harder to define or quantify than mileage. Until now, that is. With the arrival of the power meter, we can better define and describe intensity. Your functional threshold power is your baseline intensity, but there are other ways we can measure intensity with power.

Let's look at three metrics that help define intensity better for runners using power: Intensity Factor, peak power, and Variability Index.

Intensity Factor (IF)

If I tell you I did a run at 300 watts Normalized Power, or at 4 min/km, or at a 6:30 mile pace, do any of those numbers truly give you an idea of what they mean in terms of intensity for me as a runner? Probably not. What's missing is context. Was that fast for me? Was it slow? Was it a recovery run, a tempo run, a race effort? Without some sort of baseline to define how hard that run was, the numbers don't have any useful meaning.

With Intensity Factor, however, we can look at the watts from the effort and compare that to the baseline measurement, the rFTPw. The number we get is the context that allows you to better define and understand the intensity of your workouts, compare your workouts against each other, and even compare them with other runners. Intensity Factor tells you how hard you are actually running.

To find Intensity Factor, you simply take the value of the Normalized Power of your run and divide it by your rFTPw value. The equation is:

$$IF = NP/rFTPw$$

For example, if my rFTPw is 400w, the 300-watt run example from above was below my threshold. Doing the arithmetic yields an IF of 0.75, or about 75 percent of my rFTPw value. That defines it as a relatively easy run.

If my rFTPw was 300w, however, this run would come in at 100 percent of my rFTPw—that is, 1.00 IF. If the run was an hour long, that 1.00 effort would mean it was an all-out effort for the hour, because that is the definition of rFTPw, the best wattage you can hold for an hour.

And of course, if the IF of a run comes in greater than 1.00, it is a run above my threshold and of still higher intensity. Obviously, there is a limit to this. If you have an IF value higher than 1.00 for one hour or longer, you need to adjust your rFTPw value because by definition your rFTPw is equal to a one-hour best effort. If you're regularly exceeding it, you are doing better than your maximum for one hour, which means that your rFTPw value is inaccurate, and you need to retest or re-estimate based on your current data.

You can also use IF to plan your workouts for a specific goal event. If you understand the IF you want to maintain for a certain race or distance, you can prescribe workouts at the watts that represent that IF. This becomes especially helpful when training on courses that are extremely hilly, or when running in extremely windy conditions, where goal pace can be harder to simulate.

To determine in advance the correct IF for select races and distances, the first consideration has to be an estimation of how long you will be on the course. Clearly, the shorter the distance or time of a race, the faster you can go (you can't run a 10K at a pace faster than you can for 5K, for example). An athlete's speed has as much to do with the IF value as distance.

The efficiency discussion in Chapter 5 will further clarify how to use Intensity Factor. For now, get in the habit of calculating your IF values for the workouts you are using to simulate the intensity of your goal events. As you track these values over the seasons, you'll learn a great deal about how IF can help you train specifically for your goal events, and how to compare race efforts on different courses, and in different conditions.

Peak Power

Another way to look at how you're responding to your training is by tracking your peak power outputs. As stated earlier, the longer the duration of a run, the lower your power output, since time and power are inversely related. You can't sprint at super-high watts for more than a few seconds, so it is inevitable that as the duration of the run or race increases, power will decrease.

If we use power data to compare two track and field athletes, such as an Olympic sprinter and an Olympic 10K runner, we would find the sprinter is capable of very high watts for a few seconds, while a distance runner might only reach half that wattage figure for the same amount of time. But over the course of an hour, the 10K runner might be able to hold hundreds more watts than the sprinter.

The more power you can generate over a period of time, the greater your fitness and performance potential. All things being equal, the runner who can produce the most watts over a given duration is fitter and should win.

The challenge, of course, is that in running, all things are never equal. Efficiency of movement, measured in speed per watt, is a critical component in performance. The sprinter can't hold the watts a distance runner can, due to the mechanics the sprinter uses to produce his or her high power outputs. And the mechanics the distance runner uses won't allow her or him to produce the high power outputs needed for a blazing sprint. The biomechanical efficiency of the athlete makes a big difference, even within the same population of athletes competing in the same events. The key to determining efficiency is how much speed per watt the athlete produces. If the athlete is relatively efficient, we can look at peak power outputs and profiles to determine the potential of the athlete to perform relative to his or her goals.

The best power an athlete can produce for a given amount of time is defined as his or her peak power. Peak power values are expressed as P, followed by the number of minutes for the duration we are expressing. So the peak power output for 60 minutes would be expressed as P60. Some of the peak power outputs we will commonly look at in distance running are 2 hours, or 120 minutes (P120), 60 minutes (P60), 30 minutes (P30), 20 minutes (P20), 5 minutes (P5),

1 minute (P1), and 30 seconds (P0.5). Remember that we express the values in minutes, so 30 seconds is expressed as 0.5, for half of a minute.

Figure 4.2 shows how these peak power values can be seen in a single workout. This figure tracks an athlete conducting the 30-minute time-trial test, with the details shown in Figure 4.2b. Note that we can look not only at peak power, but we can also track peak paces for these same durations. In Figure 4.3, you can see the peak 20-minute pace highlighted for the same test.

You may notice something very interesting about Figure 4.3 and the P20 for pace as compared with Figure 4.2. Even though they are from the same file, the P20 values for power and pace don't line up perfectly. In fact, the P20 for pace lies

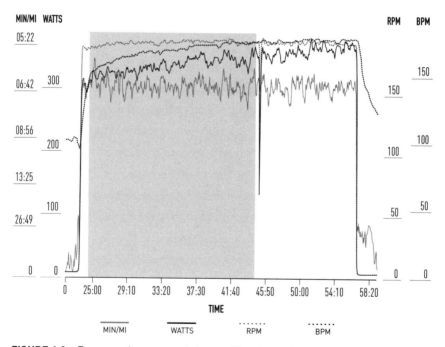

FIGURE 4.3a Power and pace graph from a 30-minute time trial test, with the peak 20-minute pace highlighted

in the first 20 minutes of the test, while the P20 for power lies in the last 20. As I mentioned earlier, just because power is rising doesn't mean pace is increasing as well. This is a consequence of running efficiency, which we will address more thoroughly in the next chapter. For now, remember that the power meter is measuring power usage in more than one plane: the plane that moves you forward, and the plane or planes in which you generate lateral and vertical movements.

We can also see peak power values over multiple sessions, or many dates, across many durations. Figure 4.4 demonstrates a mean max power curve (MMPC) for the past 90 days of this athlete's training.

Duration	Distance	TSS
20:00	3.07 mi	29.2

Work	403 kJ	IF	0.95
NP	336 W	VI	1.00
Pa:Hr	6.20 %	El. Gain	--
Grade	--	El. Loss	--
VAM	--	w/kg	4.67

	MIN	AVG	MAX	
Power	295	336	375	w
Heart Rate	145	167	175	bpm
Cadence	186	192	197	rpm

Peak Pace

☐ Entire Workout	08:50 min/mi	
☐ Peak 10:00 min	06:34 min/mi	
☐ Peak 12:00 min	06:34 min/mi	
☑ **Peak 20:00 min**	**06:35 min/mi**	
☐ Peak 30:00 min	06:35 min/mi	
☐ Peak 01:00 h	08:38 min/mi	

FIGURE 4.3b 30-minute time trial power and pace data

The MMPC displays the best average power (mean maximal) for different durations. Duration is displayed on the x-axis of the graph, while watts are displayed on the y-axis. Remember, as duration increases, intensity decreases, so every athlete's graph has a curve of some shape. How steep of a curve and how high it starts depends on the athlete, and upon the athlete's strengths and weaknesses.

Remember the example of the sprinter versus the distance runner in terms of power outputs? An MMPC for those runners would show that the sprinter would have a much higher watts value on the left (shorter durations), with a steeper curve dropoff than the distance runner. The sprinter would see higher values for the shorter durations, but lower values than the distance runner for the longer durations. Simply by looking at the curve of the graph we can see that the athlete in Figure 4.4 is more of a distance runner than a sprinter; the peak power values are not very high in the shorter durations. Figure 4.5 helps show what a sprinter's power curve might look like, with a steeper drop from the shorter durations.

Another analysis benefit of peak power outputs is that they correspond to the common training measurements of oxygen usage. For example, peak power values of 30 seconds or less would represent anaerobic capacity. Six minutes (P6) would represent VO_2max (maximal volume of oxygen consumption). An hour (P60) would represent lactate or anaerobic threshold. Two hours (P120) would represent aerobic economy. If you target these values in your training sessions, you will know that you are training more effectively when you see them improve.

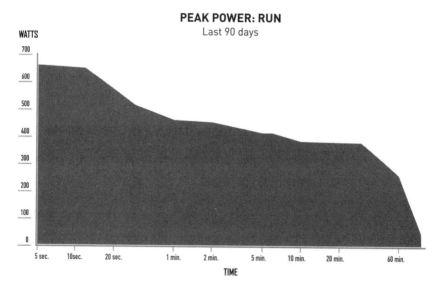

FIGURE 4.4 Mean max power curve for all run power data from the past 90 days

If you don't know exactly where to place the specific intensity or IF figures in your training for a target event, you can use the appropriate peak power duration you want to improve that is representative of your race goals. If you're trying to break 2 hours for the half-marathon, P120 is a key value for you to monitor and improve in your training, since it is specifically 2 hours. If you are trying to break 90 minutes for the half-marathon, you will likely want to target P90 improvement. We will discuss more of this in Chapter 7, on tracking season progress.

Variability Index

You surely already know this, but how you pace an event has a lot to do with how intense it is. That seems obvious, but we all know that a lot of runners

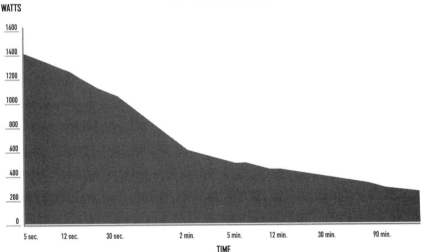

PEAK POWER: RUN

FIGURE 4.5 An example of what a sprinter's power curve might look like, with a steep drop from the power outputs in the shorter durations as compared to the longer durations

don't have the experience to pace themselves. GPS wrist units have helped many runners improve their pacing, but if the race is on a rolling course (to choose but one example), pacing isn't as simple as just holding a certain speed. Evenly paced performances, or negative splits in a race (running the second half faster than the first), have proven over time to be the most effective strategies for distance races. One study looked at 66 world records performed in the 5,000- and 10,000-meter runs on the track, from 1921 to 2004, and found that in 65 of them, the last kilometer was the fastest or second fastest of the race (Tucker, et al. 2006). In brief: Pacing matters, especially as goals get higher.

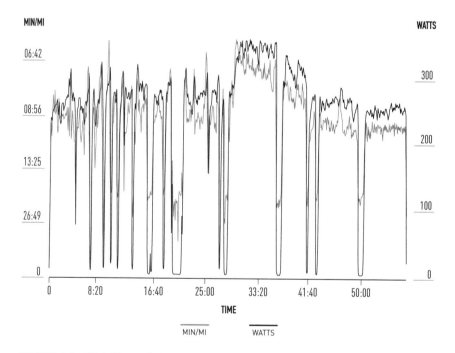

FIGURE 4.6a High VI graph from a track workout

Of course, those events are run on a track, where there are no hills or descents to contend with. Uphills and downhills challenge pacing skill. If you've ever raced uphill and downhill on a course, you know how the rolling terrain can make a slow pace feel like a death march at times.

Variability Index, or VI, gives us a representation of how steady, or how variable, a runner's power output is over the length of a session, interval, or race. It's derived from a simple equation that just compares Normalized Power (NP) and average power (AP). The equation is:

$$VI = NP/AP$$

From Chapter 3, you'll remember that Normalized Power gives us a value that is most representative of the metabolic cost of an effort. If you were to race on a flat course where you maintained a perfectly steady pace, or close to it, your average power and Normalized Power would be the same, and you'd get a VI of 1.00.

On the other hand, if you were to run a very hilly course, or were to undertake a fartlek workout with a lot of surges of high intensity, and then follow those efforts by easy bouts of running, you would see a great deal of variance in your power output files. This would yield a VI that is higher than 1.00, as NP would be greater than AP. Figure 4.6 shows a track workout conducted by an athlete where the NP is 273, and the AP is 244.

Duration		Distance		TSS
58:01.81		6.19 mi		74.0

			IF	0.88
Work	849 kJ		IF	0.88
NP	273 w		VI	1.12
VAM	3.20			

	MIN	AVG	MAX	
Power	0	244	379	w
Heart Rate	75	155	187	bpm
Cadence	0	173	201	rpm
Speed	0.00	6.40	10.6	mph
Pace	00:00	09:22	05:40	min/mi

FIGURE 4.6b High VI data

This 29-watt difference represents a 12 percent variance between the two, delivering a VI of 1.12.

This isn't surprising when you look at the file's power data; there you see big surges in power, along with some low valleys where the runner was allowed to rest and recover between intervals, producing zero power.

If you look back at the 30-minute test file in Figure 4.2, though, you can see the VI is 1.00. In that example, the athlete paced perfectly. If there were surges, they were limited in number and size.

If you've been using a power meter on your bike, you've surely seen very high VI values in your cycling power files. On the bike, riding with a pack of other cyclists is crucial for success in racing, so there tend to be big surges of power to stay with the group. Also, cyclists can coast at zero watts and get pulled along by the group, or just sit on the bike on long downhills, not pedaling at all. Runners can never coast at zero watts, so VI values are not likely to be as high for runners as we commonly see in cycling power files, unless you're doing a lot of intense stop-and-go running, as with intervals on a track.

One other way a runner might see a high VI value would come from a performance where the athlete paced so poorly that the early power outputs couldn't come close to being sustained later in the workout. This would surely be the result of a poor workout or race performance by the athlete, so I am hopeful you don't see many of those situations.

More often, if a power file shows a high VI, it likely means the session was intense, with alternating periods of high power outputs and low power outputs.

Pacing is an important skill, as it helps conserve energy for best performances in distance running, and VI can be a great tool to understand how intense a session was and how well the runner handled the job of pacing. We will use the VI metric again, in Chapter 9, as part of post-race analysis.

Summary

The two most important values in distance running when training with power are rFTPw and rFTPa. These represent the functional threshold value for power and pace respectively: the best power output or pace an athlete can hold for one hour.

Simple field tests can help you find these values. Even simply reviewing a collection of power files can lead to ways to estimate them. Keeping your rFTPw value current is critical, as many other metrics will be based on this value.

Your rFTPw gives you a baseline for intensity. You can then compare your NP with rFTPw to get Intensity Factor. You can also compare NP with AP to get a better understanding of the variance of the session, or what we call variability index.

Peak power outputs for durations of time also help athletes understand intensity. You can use these values to monitor training response and identify some race specificity demands.

5 Power for Efficiency

Have you ever been coached to change your run form? Have you been given a tip on what you can do to make yourself faster through a few simple changes to body position or foot strike? If your answer is "yes," then in most cases these tips have been given to help you with your efficiency as a runner.

In Chapter 4, I briefly touched on efficiency and how we can track it with power data. If you have an exercise science background, you'll probably be quick to correct me and state that the traditional definition of efficiency is the work completed per the energy expended, or energy out divided by energy in.

For the purposes of this book, however, the concept of efficiency coupled with power data is different. In our case, we're defining efficiency as how much speed you're getting for the watts you're producing. After all, getting more speed for the same energy output is exactly what becoming a more efficient distance runner is all about.

Dr. Andrew Coggan, a pioneer in training with power for cycling, prefers the word "effectiveness" when discussing the relation of speed per watt. I like that term too, but in our case we are trying to maximize the usefulness of a new tool, and using that new technology to measure what we could not measure in the past. We also have been using the term "efficiency factor," or EF, in training metrics for running and cycling for a few years now, comparing power outputs with heart rate (which is not a measure of energy). So for the purposes of this book—and also because the training community has already adopted the term—I will use the term "efficiency" to describe the speed for watts relationship. If you want to use "effectiveness" instead, that's fine too.

So how efficient are you in your running? How many of the watts you're producing are actually helping to move you forward? Can we limit or reduce whatever power you're producing that isn't effectively helping you run forward? Can we transfer some of it to helping you run faster?

Cycling power meters were developed to measure the work rate, the power actually applied to the pedals to move the bike forward. Note that this does not mean the cyclist's body isn't doing any other work on a bike; it

Getting more speed for the same energy output is what becoming a more efficient runner is all about.

means that the bike's power meter can measure only the work that is applied specifically to it. In some ways, this makes the job of going faster easy: Produce more watts and you're a faster cyclist. But in some ways, this method of measurement reveals a limitation of the technology. Competitive cyclists could certainly learn a lot about themselves if they could see how efficiently they produce those watts. They might find flaws in their pedaling technique or discover that they have a poor bike position. But a cycling power meter cannot measure any expenditures of energy that the rider might be wasting through extraneous body movements; it can only report how much power is flowing from the pedals through the drivetrain.

Fortunately, that's not the case with our running power meters, and it's one of the huge advantages this tool provides. Sure, measuring all the power your body produces does complicate the data a bit. But I hope the metrics in this chapter make it easier for you to track your efficiency and monitor the effect of the changes you make in your running technique or training approach. With your power meter, you can see your fitness improve in ways that are much more subtle than those you can interpret from your speed and HR data.

I want to reiterate what I mentioned in Chapter 3: First and foremost, use the power meter to get to know yourself better. If you want to maximize the data you get out of your power meter, you must first use it to learn about your tendencies, as well as your current level of efficiency, so you can work to improve. Then you can use the power meter to dial in training intensities via power zones, and monitor your efficiency to determine when you are training effectively versus when you might be overreaching. If you take this approach, training with a power meter will bring impressive gains to your racing and experience.

How Watts Lead to Speed

Will the most efficient runner win the race each time? No; the person who is first across the finish line will win. It's that simple: The winner is the fastest person from point A to point B, the runner who has built up the best combination of fitness and speed. Fitness is simply an ability to tolerate stress, and in this case, that stress is the work rate the runner can hold. But the ability to translate that work rate into speed becomes the key factor for performance. One can be inefficient and still beat an efficient runner; the less efficient runner can still have enough fitness to maintain a higher speed—even inefficiently. Inefficient runners can be fast, despite the fact that they could be more efficient (and thus even faster).

However, there comes a point where an athlete will reach the maximum work rate he or she can produce for a given time. At that point, the only way to run faster is to maximize how much of the power being generated can be applied to running faster—becoming more efficient, in other words. Where that point lies, and at what speeds or intensities, is applicable to the specific athlete and his or her goals. For example, someone might not be able to hold the work rate required to run fast for a 5K, but can hold a good work rate for the marathon.

Most observers think that elite marathoners don't care about being efficient beyond the time needed to cross the line. Ideally, they will cross the finish

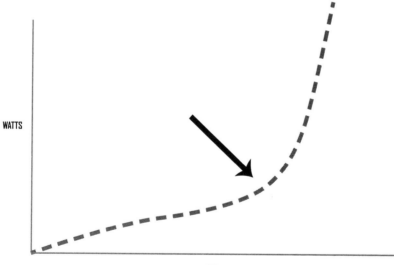

FIGURE 5.1 Watts versus speed

line at 100 percent of the potential speed they can maintain for the event. But remember, the faster they go, the less time they are on the course, and the higher the intensity they can hold.

You might think sprinters have no general concern for efficiency beyond race distance or race time. But once they hit their maximal watts, can they make changes to get another tenth or hundredth of a second faster?

Let's look at it graphically. Figure 5.1 shows how as watts increase, speed also increases. No surprise there, right? But note that the challenge is this relationship is not linear; instead, it is exponential. This means there comes a point where a lot more watts are required to go the same unit of speed faster than before. The arrow in Figure 5.1 shows where the relationship begins to change from linear to exponential.

Figure 5.1 intentionally doesn't contain any specific units for speed because it applies to all ability levels, regardless of speed of the athlete. In other words, the same relationship holds true for all runners, in all disciplines. The only thing that changes is at what speed this exponential relationship takes place for each runner. The point at which the relationship changes exponentially (where the slope of the graph changes greatly) is the point at which the athlete needs a lot more watts to go faster.

The demand for a major increase in watts to generate modest additional speed occurs for a number of reasons. The first is tied to momentum: Each step requires launching the body forward from a nearly stopped point, with the foot planted on the ground and absorbing a lot of the forward motion into the ground. Only a little momentum is carried forward by the runner from one step to the next. Obviously, the foot-strike pattern of the runner can affect this, but in general, there is a significant loss of forward momentum with each step that must be generated anew with each stride.

A second reason involves the vector, or direction, of the forces applied to and returned from the ground with each foot strike. These directional forces are not returned in a perfectly horizontal and forward plane. Instead, there is a loss of power incurred by all return forces that do not apply directly forward. In order to generate an increase in speed, every step to accelerate must produce more force than the one before it.

Cadence must increase as well. However, cadence can only go so fast, as contact time on the ground can never reach zero.

And of course, the faster we go, the more fatigue we accumulate, using energy systems that aren't sustainable for anything but short durations. This leads to breakdown in the high-force, high-speed movements, decreasing efficiency—that is, decreasing our ability to convert watts into speed through the application of our movements into horizontal power. Figure 5.2 helps illustrate this relationship of speed and efficiency.

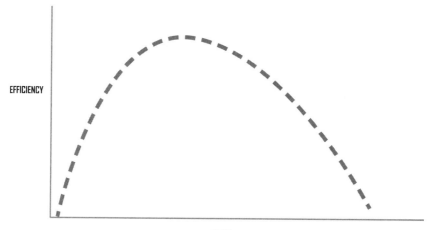

FIGURE 5.2 Efficiency versus speed

Figure 5.2 displays a feeling we've all had, the sense that although we're trying our utmost to maintain a speed or intensity, we're moving through sludge and getting nowhere. There comes a point of breakdown where we just can't help ourselves, despite our best efforts to go harder or faster.

The ability of an athlete to delay the onset of the decline in efficiency in Figure 5.2, or to delay the exponential increase in watts relative to speed in Figure 5.1, should be a central focus in daily training. Improving your efficiency as a runner yields major gains in speed and endurance.

You will notice in Figure 5.2 that runners are inefficient at both slower and faster speeds alike. There is a range of speed where each individual runner is most efficient; the goal of training should be to push this optimum zone further, building similar efficiency at higher speeds. After all, it doesn't take much change in slower speeds to become more efficient in running; the challenge is to find these gains at higher speeds.

Of course, to become a more efficient runner, you need to understand which factors affect efficiency and how you can address them in your training. As you will see, there are some that you can address easily, some not so easily, and others—sorry to say—not at all.

Factors Affecting Efficiency

Your efficiency as a runner has a number of factors and variables. As you might guess, many are biomechanical. But there are other factors that can affect the body's ability to translate watts into speed. Some of these are within your control as a runner, and some are not.

I don't intend to use this book to teach you specifically how to run efficiently, nor what techniques you should use. Many different techniques have been used successfully; you can find them in training books or can learn with a coach. I do think it is important, however, for distance runners to use a power meter to find out how the techniques they use affect their efficiency. And of course, the power meter will also reveal how other factors within their control, apart from technique, can affect their efficiency as well.

BIOMECHANICAL AND MUSCULOSKELETAL CONSIDERATIONS

Biomechanics, or the physics of running and the body's ability to maximize those physics with movements, is the most obvious factor that comes to mind for most athletes seeking efficiency. One example you might be familiar with is foot strike: hitting the ground with your heel first or hitting with your forefoot first each result in a different level of efficiency. But there's much more to biomechanics and efficiency than that: There are many variables, besides the movements of a few joints, that can affect the body's ability to be efficient.

Body Mass

Body mass is a clear determinant of efficiency. A given force production and cadence speed are effective only relative to the mass of the runner. Take the same forces and apply them to two different runners, one at 150 pounds, another at 200 pounds, and you will see a huge difference in speed per watts, even if the athletes have the same biomechanics. This difference boils down to watts per kilogram, a metric we will discuss shortly.

Going uphill with higher body mass requires more force production to move the body and overcome the effect of gravity. The effect from gravity increases as the incline of the hill increases, requiring more vertical power outputs to lift the body off the ground. Again, watts per kilogram make a big difference.

It's not just total body mass that affects efficiency; the location of mass on the body and the effect of gravity on that mass can greatly influence efficiency of movement. If you're skinny and short, you may have an efficiency advantage over a runner who is skinny and tall because you have shorter limbs to move. If you are overweight, the location of the weight on your body can affect your posture when you run, and thus your efficiency as well.

Even if you are not overweight and only carry a lot of lean mass, that mass can affect how you move. For example, an athlete with broad shoulders and a lot of upper-body muscle mass may incur more fatigue over time because she has to work harder to support the higher positioned mass than someone with more mass in his legs, lower to the ground.

For many runners, body mass is something they can positively address, and a power meter can help show the benefit of this change. The improvement would be recorded in an increase in distance traveled for a given power output—more work accomplished for the same input, in other words.

Flexibility

The flexibility of the muscles affects the body in numerous ways. For example, a lack of flexibility can reduce stride length. It can also affect posture. If an athlete has tension in areas of his hips and the supporting musculature, it can affect how his hips are aligned and how forces are applied during running. Tension can actually cause the body to fight itself, and not allow the full range of motion needed to maximize efforts.

On the other hand, excessive flexibility of the soft tissue around the ankles and through the lower leg might not allow the joint to load and rebound the foot off the ground quickly enough to create both speed of cadence and force production from the foot pushing off the ground. One key to success in running lies in how quickly the foot gets off the ground during the foot strike. A lot of this comes from the storage and release of elastic energy in the muscles, much like a spring loading and extending. The more flexibility you have in the key muscles of your lower leg, the less elastic energy those muscles hold, and the less quickly you are able to spring off the ground after landing the foot. This slows you down and is an example of when excessive flexibility is not helpful.

Shoes and Insoles

Shoes are not musculoskeletal, but they can certainly affect biomechanics, since they are where runners contact the ground. The shoe is the first and last thing to touch the ground with every step you take. Shoes affect your run efficiency and biomechanics because of the type of support they do or do not provide.

You may be a barefoot or minimalist runner who does not even wear shoes. Recently we saw a huge surge in minimalist shoes and barefoot running, and it had a lot to do with the idea that shoes (mostly negatively) affect the biomechanics of running, . Do shoes positively or negatively affect your running power? That's up for debate and largely dependent on the particular mechanics of your stride, but keep in mind that what you put under your feet can affect your power outputs and ability to maintain them as well as speed from these outputs.

Shoes can also be affected by insoles, orthotics, and other support products specific to your gait and needs as a runner. Find the right movement support in a shoe and you are likely to find yourself improving your speed per watt.

NEUROMUSCULAR CONSIDERATIONS

The ability to run involves more components than simply body structure. It also involves the relationship between the brain and the muscles.

Neuromuscular Pathway

The neuromuscular pathway is the connection between the brain and muscles through the nerves; it delivers messages from the brain, telling the muscles what to do. You have synapses that fire when the brain tells them to, transferring the message from the brain to the muscles, telling them the movements they need to conduct and support.

This pathway of neural signals and the ability of the muscles to receive the signals is something that is developed over a long period of time. The more experience the body has in sending and receiving the messages, the less likely there is to be an issue with the messaging system. This is why experienced runners tend to have better efficiency than newer runners. It takes many years of experience to develop the movement patterns needed for efficient movement during running.

For example, it is not uncommon to see a young, scrawny athlete who is tall and lanky struggling to connect the movement pattern of running. These athletes often struggle to run efficiently.

Beginning runners usually struggle with neuromuscular efficiency because they lack experience with the smooth movement pattern needed to develop the coordination to run efficiently.

You can identify neuromuscular inefficiencies with a 3D power meter by monitoring the percentage of watts you produce in the horizontal plane as compared with the lateral and vertical planes.

For example, if you produce 40 percent of your watts in horizontal power, then 60 percent came from other planes, and that 60 percent is not necessarily helping you to move forward. This example is especially true of runs on a flat course, where horizontal power is more important than vertical power or lateral power.

Fatigue

As we have noted earlier, once a certain intensity is reached, the ability to sustain efficient movement patterns is limited. This is due mostly to musculoskeletal fatigue at the time of the high-intensity efforts. But it is also possible for an athlete to suffer from fatigue before running even begins. Carry-over of fatigue from previous training sessions can greatly affect an athlete's ability to move efficiently. Though this fatigue could be musculoskeletal, it could also affect the ability of the brain to send the signal to the muscle, making it neuromuscular fatigue.

Injury

Much in the way that fatigue can affect a muscle group's ability to move and produce force effectively for running, so too can an injury affect the chain of movements through those muscle groups. Injured muscles try to protect themselves from further injury by limiting their movements. This inevitably affects efficiency. In fact, a power meter can tell us the effect of an injury beyond what we normally can see or even feel. More on that later in this chapter.

PHYSIOLOGICAL CONSIDERATIONS

In addition to the structural and neurological factors that affect efficiency, there are differences in human physiology among runners that must be considered.

Gender and Age

Your gender and your age can also affect your efficiency as a runner. If you're female, you are statistically more likely to carry greater fat mass than a male. As noted above, body mass and its location can affect efficiency of run movements.

Females also have a different Q-angle than males. This is the angle of the femur bone from the hip to the knee joint, viewed from the front. Women tend to have wider hips, increasing the femur's angle medially as it approaches the knee. Males tend to have less of an angle, creating a more vertically straight path of the femur from the hip to the knee. These differences affect force distribution in running or similar movements. These could just as easily be classified as musculoskeletal and biomechanical differences, but the differences in males and females are definitely physiological as well.

Age can also affect efficiency, as the need for additional recovery as athletes get older may be evidence of poor efficiency. Also, we know performance declines as athletes age, and efficiency is part of performance.

Conversely, younger athletes have been shown to have poor running efficiency, requiring higher outputs of power for a given speed when compared with adults (Schepens, et al.).

Temperature

Your efficiency changes with temperature. Your body may have to spend more energy heating itself in cold temperatures, while cooling itself in hot conditions can be an even bigger challenge. In general, the higher the temperature, the harder it is for the body to produce the same power output. Can you counteract this effect in your training? Yes, you can! Many athletes train in conditions that are similar to those they will face on race day for this specific adaptation purpose.

PSYCHOLOGICAL CONSIDERATIONS

Much of athletic performance comes from the mind. When athletes are motivated, confident, and clear in their focus, they can maximize performance potential. The desire to push oneself constantly in training, and the ability to dig deep in competition and push beyond perceived limits are traits shared by many successful athletes—endurance athletes in particular.

From an efficiency perspective, a runner's ability to focus on how well he or she can execute the movements of running in a technically proficient manner while under duress and fatigue comes from mental strength and toughness. Do the athlete's thoughts wander when fatigue clouds the mind? This happens to every athlete, but the point at which it occurs varies from athlete to athlete. With a clear mind, and an ability to focus consistently during deep fatigue, an athlete can greatly improve efficiency.

So can you improve your efficiency? Absolutely! Yes, there are some things in the above—your age and gender, for example—you can't change, but training has been shown to improve efficiency in runners. Beginning runners will likely see larger relative gains in efficiency, especially in the early stages of their training. Experienced runners need to have a more focused approach on their training and technique in order to continue to improve efficiency.

Metrics for Monitoring Efficiency

What can you monitor to make sure you are getting more speed per watt? There are a number of metrics that I think all distance runners should monitor throughout their training. I have created some, and others are standard metrics in wide use. These metrics will quickly reveal whether your efficiency is maintaining, improving, or dropping, and they will also help you make sure that you aren't showing signs of injury or overtraining.

Of course, in this lengthy discussion of the factors affecting efficiency, you may assume that speed per watts is the Holy Grail of every training session. That's not the case, however, and this is critical to clarify: I am not saying you should *always* see more speed for the watts you produce. Remember, in a race we don't care who is the most efficient runner; we care about who is the fastest! So in using these metrics, keep in mind the many ways you can see improvements in your fitness:

- More speed per watt: the ratio of how fast you go for the watts you produce.
- Fewer watts for a given speed: Though you might not be able to show an increase in speed, if you can hold your goal pace or whatever pace you're doing at a lower wattage, this indicates that you've increased your biomechanical efficiency; you are getting more output, pace, or speed from a lower work rate.
- Increased speed and increased watts: This item may surprise you, given this chapter's emphasis on efficiency. But remember that the speed at which you run is what determines your performance. Higher speeds generally require more watts. If you can sustain more power, and you see an increase in the speed you run, then that is improvement!
- Same speed, same watts, and lower heart rate: Heart rate, an input metric, can help you understand how hard your body is working to sustain a certain pace and power. Even if you aren't seeing much improvement in your watts or your speed, but you are seeing a lower heart rate to produce them, then that is a good sign that you are getting fitter.

If you are not seeing any of these trends in your training, then you need to address your training strategy. This isn't to say you can't have a bad workout once in a while, as no one will always improve every session. But look at the trend of what your training is showing, and make a decision about whether you need to rest more, train more, or simply change the training intensity you're focusing on.

Does this mean your EI should be 1.0? No, not necessarily; the value is entirely individual, but I created the metric because for the majority of runners it probably won't be too far off. Of course, the value of the watts will depend on whether you use a 2D or 3D power meter. If you use a 2D meter, your watts will be lower for the same speed, so the quotient, which is your EI value, will be higher than if you use a 3D meter.

You can put EI to work for you to monitor your ability to translate your watts into speed in real time. To do so, my recommendation is to use this as a rolling 30-second average of EI during a run, a calculation I call the rolling EI, or rEI. When you look at your head unit, you will see an average of the previous 30 seconds. The unit should take the current second and average it with the samples from the previous 29 seconds to display the efficiency of the watts produced.

Why use a rolling 30-second average? Excellent question. If the time frame you select for this calculation is too short, any small change will skew the EI you are actually achieving. In order to get a reliable reading of EI, you need to normalize the data over a short period of time, and 30 seconds seems to work best. Chances are you will also check your head unit once or twice a minute, and the 30-second rolling data capture will give you a good idea of how efficiently you have been running between those glances at your wrist.

I also suggest that in the post-workout analysis, athletes look at the EI for the entirety of the workout, what I call total EI. Tracking this value for similar workouts—easy paced runs, recovery runs, longer endurance efforts, race pace sets for a 5K on the track, for example—will help you see whether you are improving fitness or efficiency, or both. If you see a sudden negative change in the relationship—your watts increase without an increase in pace—you may need some recovery days, or you may need to focus on the technical aspects of your running gait (you may be allowing some inefficient movements to slip into your running form). On the other hand, if your watts increase and your pace improves as well, the ratio may not be better but you are going faster, which is a key training response we want to see.

Some users—especially those with experience of using power in cycling—might think this calculation should compare Normalized Graded Pace and Normalized Power. If you usually train on the same courses, and they are loops (you finish where you started), there is little reason to normalize the pace and the power since uphills will be matched by downhills, and vice versa. Also, unlike cycling, there is no coasting in running, nor a way to tuck into a pack of runners and draft to reduce watts by 50 percent or more, compared with being on the front. Generally speaking, there is nowhere near the variance of power outputs among runners in a race or training session, compared with cyclists.

Again, this EI metric is best used in comparing workouts of similar goals, such as easy runs only, or tempo runs only. This way you are comparing apples to apples, and there is no reason to normalize the data (you've already normalized it by isolating similar workouts).

EFFICIENCY INDEX AT FUNCTIONAL THRESHOLD (EI@FT)

We've spoken about the importance of functional threshold power and pace in terms of determining your potential as an athlete. I believe one of the best barometers of efficiency can be found in the relationship between these two values, your rFTPa and rFTPw, or what I call your Efficiency Index at functional threshold (EI@FT). This ratio gives us your speed per watt at your functional threshold power. It is expressed as:

$$EI@FT = rFTPa/rFTPw$$

In this equation, your rFTPa units are in meters per minute (m/min), so you will need to convert your pace to those units if your software won't do it for you. Your rFTPw is in watts. Keep track of this ratio. As an aerobic endurance athlete, the ability to get more speed per watt is key!

What is an ideal value for EI@FT? The answer depends on whether you're using a 2D or 3D power meter to determine your rFTPw, because the device will raise or reduce the denominator of the fraction, greatly affecting the product that the calculation spits out. Also, how good of a runner you are will affect

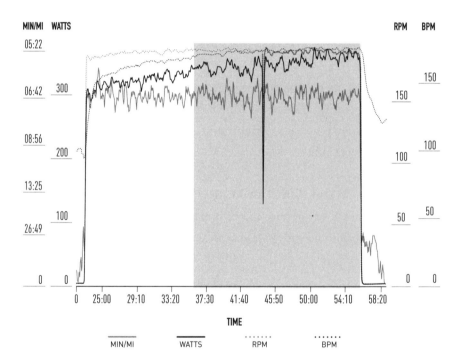

FIGURE 5.3a 30-minute time-trial on November 4, highlighting the last 20 minutes (P20 watts)

the numerator, affecting the overall value. Your focus should be on the trend of this value over time. Is it improving to a larger number, with more speed per watt at threshold? This tells you how your training is going.

Let's use the athlete from Chapter 4, who did the original FTP tests shared there, to see how he was doing in terms of improving his efficiency. Let's look at the 30-minute TT he did in early November, and compare it with how he did in the test in mid-December, about five weeks later.

Test 1: 30-Minute Time Trial, November 4

Duration	Distance	TSS
20:00	**3.05** mi	**32.4**

Work	**424** kj	IF	**1.00**
NP	**354** w	VI	**1.00**
Pa:Hr	**1.75**%	El. Gain	--
Grade	--	El. Loss	--
VAM	--	w/kg	**4.90**

	MIN	AVG	MAX	
Power	0	353	387	w
Heart Rate	170	175	177	bpm
Cadence	172	193	198	rpm
Speed	6.03	9.15	11.4	mph
Pace	09:57	06:33	05:15	min/mi

Peak Power	
☐ Entire Workout	236 w
☐ Peak 10:00 min	362 w
☐ Peak 12:00 min	358 w
☑ **Peak 20:00 min**	**353 w**
☐ Peak 30:00 min	346 w
☐ Peak 01:00 h	257 w

FIGURE 5.3b 30-minute time trial data, November 4

Figure 5.3a shows the 30-minute time-trial test for rFTPw and rFTPa, conducted on November 4. This is the same as Figure 4.2.

In this test, the athlete ran the final 20 minutes at a 6:33 min/mile pace (4:04 min/km), which equates to 245.70 m/min. The average power for this was 353 watts. To calculate his EI@FT, we take his speed in meters per minute and divide it by the average watts for that 20 minutes:

$$245.70/353 = 0.69 \text{ m/min per watt}$$

Remember the speed per watt is the key value we want to track, and the speed in this case is expressed in meters per minute.

After this test, the athlete trained for a month, focusing on very easy running and very intensive shorter speed and anaerobic work. The athlete did a lot of plyometric work, and efforts of running at 30 seconds to 1 minute very hard, with relatively long recoveries. There was no work done at all near his threshold pace or his threshold watts. Everything was either well above it or well below it.

Test 2: 30-Minute Time Trial, December 12

About five weeks after the initial 30-minute time-trial test, the athlete conducted another one so he could evaluate the training response for his functional thresholds (Figure 5.4a).

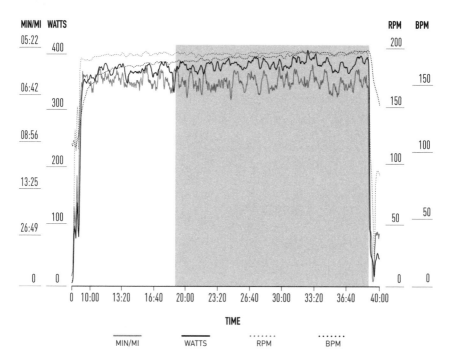

FIGURE 5.4a 30-minute time trial on December 12, highlighting the last 20 minutes

In this test, the athlete shows improvement in pace, which is excellent. In the last 20 minutes, the athlete is now running 6:07 min/mi (3:48 min/km), which equates to 263.11 m/min. The average power for his last 20 minutes was 383 watts. Again, to calculate his EI@FT, we take his speed in meters per minute and divide it by the average watts for those 20 minutes:

$$263.11/383 = 0.69 \text{ m/min per watt}$$

Duration	Distance	TSS
20:05	3.28 mi	38.0

Work	462 kJ	IF	1.08
NP	383 W	VI	1.00
		w/kg	5.32

	MIN	AVG	MAX	
Power	360	383	414	w
Heart Rate	166	171	176	bpm
Cadence	157	195	201	rpm
Pace	14:40	06:07	05:00	min/mi

Peak Power

☐ Entire Workout	307 w	
☐ Peak 6:00 min	387 w	
☐ Peak 10:00 min	385 w	
☐ Peak 12:00 min	385 w	
☑ **Peak 20:00 min**	**383 w**	
☐ Peak 30:00 min	378 w	

FIGURE 5.4b 30-minute time trial data, December 12

This is excellent news, because the athlete saw his threshold pace go up, his threshold watts go up, and he maintained the same relative efficiency. Some might look at the 0.69 value staying the same and think this is not an improvement, but clearly when the athlete is going faster and producing more watts *and* getting the same speed-per-watt ratio at his FTP values, this is excellent news!

The more your races are dependent on rFTPw and rFTPa, the more important the EI@FT value becomes to track and improve.

KILOJOULES PER KILOMETER (KJ/KM)

If you recall, kilojoules (kJ) is the amount of actual work completed.

Power is a work rate, and the work rate you hold for a given time tells you the amount of work actually accomplished.

I believe it is important to track the kJ/km at functional threshold (FT). This is the total work accomplished to cover the distance of 1 kilometer at threshold. Since we have set the distance definitively, we can look at the amount of kJ required by the athlete to cover the distance at that intensity. I know many might think that the runner's goal is always to lower the kJ/km, but in fact it depends on the individual athlete and what he or she is training for, how fast the athlete is running, and what the trend of the data shows.

For example, an elite 5K runner might find her kJ/km are increasing as she trains, but she might also find that she is getting faster and the ratio of speed per watt is staying consistent or getting better. This is a case where it is perfectly fine for an athlete to see an increase in kJ/km.

If we take our previous example of the athlete in Figures 5.3 and 5.4, we can calculate the kJ/km by taking the kJ for the last 20 minutes (listed in both Figures 5.3 and 5.4), and then divide it by the distance covered in the last 20 minutes, converted to kilometers instead of miles (1.6 × distance in miles). With these conversions, the athlete's kJ/km at FT were:

November 4 kJ/km = 84.99

December 12 kJ/km = 86.40

These results show that the athlete increased the actual amount of work completed per kilometer, because he is going faster, not because he is being inefficient, as we proved with the EI@FT analysis.

How important is this metric? Honestly, the verdict is still out. Power meter technology is still very new, and we're learning more about it each day, but I do think kJ/km could be more important than EI@FT, especially for comparison purposes, as kJ/km can help us see changes in economy. For example, the rFTPa for our example athlete improved by 6.62 percent (6:33 to 6:07), and rFTPw improved 7.84 percent. These improvements happened while EI@FT stayed the same at 0.69, but the kJ/km increased by only 1.67 percent. So even though power at rFTPw went up, the work accomplished to increase the speed was only increased by 1.67 percent to get the improvement. In this case, I believe the kJ/km figure is at least as useful for analysis as the EI@FT number, if not more so. Note, too, that if the runner maintained the same kJ/km at a faster pace, then that would also signify an improvement in running economy.

It is possible for runners to see a decrease in kJ/km if they are able to get more speed per watt to the point where less time is spent generating power for the distance of 1 km. But note that would require a large increase in speed per watt.

WATTS PER KILOGRAM (W/KG)

Remember when we normalized the data for two different runners in Chapter 3? We used watts per kilogram (w/kg), looking at the power of the athletes relative to their mass. As we saw, bigger athletes can produce more power than smaller athletes, but watts per kilogram tell us a lot more about the projected performance of the athlete. W/kg at rFTPw is probably one of the best indicators of potential performance, especially if the course is quite hilly or rolling, where the ability to overcome gravity becomes more important.

What is a good w/kg value for you to shoot for? I don't have a single answer for that, for a few reasons. First of all, a 2D power meter will give lower values than a 3D meter because the 2D doesn't calculate lateral power. So the type of power meter you use makes a difference in the number. Second, the technology is still new, and we don't yet have a good baseline of target values for different goals or skill levels (and once we do, we'll need them for 2D and 3D meters). I can say with certainty, though, the tougher the course and the longer the race, the more important a high w/kg value becomes, because body mass has a big influence on efficiency. Also, if you and another runner have an equal EI, your w/kg becomes more important in the competition against that athlete.

W/kg plays a significant role in your potential to perform, but remember that your ability to translate watts into speed is the most important aspect of your performance.

El or w/kg?

To further illustrate the role of w/kg and running efficiency, let's look at three different athletes who conducted the 3/9 Test. Table 5.1 shows the pace in min/mile outputs and power in the intervals of three different athletes (including the runner whose workouts we looked at in prior chapters for this test). It also shows what their averages were for both, along with their w/kg readings.

Let's first examine the EI of the three athletes, specifically looking at their speed per watt. You'll notice Athletes 1 and 2 have similar EI, at 0.68

TABLE 5.1 Results of Three Different Athletes Doing the 3/9 Test, Their w/kg, and EI

	3-Min Pace	3-Min Power	9-Min Pace	9-Min Power	Avg Pace	Avg Power	Mass	W/kg	EI
Athlete 1	5:23	437	5:57	399	5:40	418	72.0	5.81	0.68
Athlete 2	5:26	426	6:06	381	5:46	404	87.0	4.64	0.69
Athlete 3	4:49	405	5:40	363	5:14	384	72.7	5.28	0.80

and 0.69. These athletes have approximately the same ability to translate the watts they produce into speed. Both of them produce more watts than Athlete 3, and yet Athlete 3 is significantly faster. This is why Athlete 3 has a significantly higher EI than the other two. (I should also point out that Athlete 3 completed this test at 7,000 feet, so at sea level he would likely perform even better; this is an anaerobic test that can be greatly affected by altitude.)

Let's compare Athlete 1 with Athlete 3. Both have similar w/kg, but Athlete 3 is actually bigger, with 0.7 kg more mass than Athlete 1. Athlete 3 produces fewer watts as well, so Athlete 1 has a better w/kg ratio. But Athlete 3 is still

The tougher the course, the more important a high w/kg value becomes.

faster, by quite a bit. His EI is 0.80 to Athlete 1's 0.68, and that difference of 0.12 equates to about an 18 percent better ability to translate the watts produced to speed. So even though Athlete 1 is lighter and can produce more watts, he must address his EI in his training.

Now let's compare Athlete 1 and Athlete 2. Again, both have similar EI values at 0.68 and 0.69. But Athlete 1 is 15 kg lighter, a difference of almost 21 percent! Athlete 2 is just slightly slower than Athlete 1, and watts produced are only slightly lower, which is why the EI is so similar, but the w/kg figure is significantly lower for Athlete 2. Athlete 1 is faster, and the reason is likely the w/kg difference between the two. If Athlete 2 could bring his mass down closer to Athlete 1's, it is reasonable to think his EI would improve significantly. At that point, he would very likely be faster than Athlete 1.

So Athlete 1 needs to improve his EI, while Athlete 2 needs to improve his w/kg (which will likely improve his EI). Athlete 3 needs to improve his w/kg as well, as he has a strong EI.

Monitoring Injury and Recovery

As discussed earlier in this chapter, injuries can affect the body's ability to perform. But what if you could get a deeper view of just how much an injury affects your performance? What if you could use your EI to determine when an injury might be about to come on? Or perhaps you're compensating right now with a hamstring injury, or a calf injury, or something similar. Even though

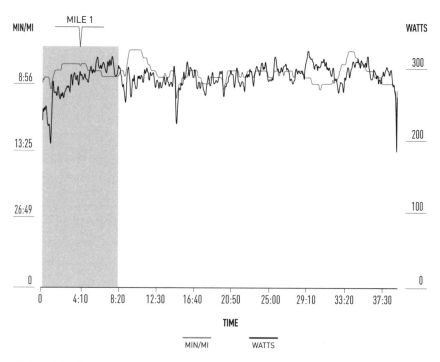

FIGURE 5.5a Run power graph for athlete in Kona, pre-injury

you may think that tight calf isn't really bothering you, the power meter can help you see whether that is really true. If there is anything a power meter can do that makes it worth your time and investment, its ability to monitor for injuries—both potential injuries and current ones that you are working to overcome so that you can return to form—makes it worth its weight in gold. The fact you're reading this book and looking for a way to make your training better indicates that this is exactly the type of insight you're looking for.

Here is an example of how a power meter can help you monitor for injury and recovery. Figure 5.5 shows a healthy athlete running a course in Kona. Figure 5.6 shows this same athlete, two days later, after falling and injuring himself between the two sessions. The injury was to his quadriceps and knee, on one leg. Both of these runs were easy, not intended for intensity.

Both of these files highlight the first mile. Again, these are from the same athlete, running the same course, a couple days apart, at the same basic effort. In Figure 5.5, the athlete is uninjured and is running normally. He runs the first mile at 8:25, and 281 average watts. In Figure 5.6, he runs the same course two days later, and runs slower, 10:20 for the first mile, but at nearly the same average watts, 273! That's nearly 2 minutes per mile slower, and yet only 8 fewer watts. This athlete was using a 3D power meter, so it's clear there were a lot of wasted movements in vertical and lateral planes—wasted power outputs that did not help the athlete. He was compensating so much, limping along,

Duration	Distance	TSS
8:25	1.00 mi	8.8

Work	142 kJ	IF	0.81
NP	285 w	VI	1.01
El. Gain	39 ft	Grade	0.4 %
El. Loss	20 ft	VAM	86 m/h
VAM w/kg	0.42		

	MIN	AVG	MAX	
Power	178	281	327	w
Speed	6.49	7.14	7.38	bpm
Pace	09:15	08:24	08:08	rpm

FIGURE 5.5b Run power data, pre-injury

that the quality of the run was not very good. He ended up running about 9 minutes slower for the same 4.6-mile course.

Of course, you don't need a power meter to tell you that you are running slower. A $2 wristwatch could tell you that. But only the power meter can reveal that this athlete produced roughly the same number of watts even though he took 9 more minutes to finish the run. For this athlete, that wattage readout should serve as a flashing red warning light.

What is the potential for this type of feedback in your running career? Could a sudden negative change in efficiency potentially signal an injury coming on? Could a negative change in speed per watt help us see compensation

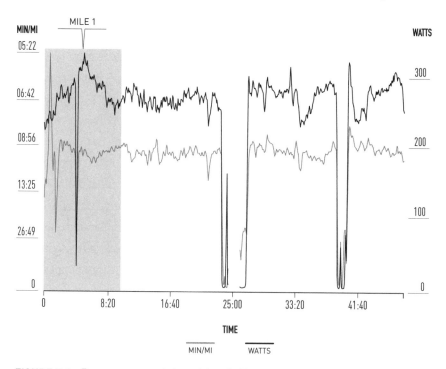

FIGURE 5.6a Run power graph for athlete in Kona, post-injury

in movements, or over time help alert us that an injury is coming, or that the athlete hasn't healed 100 percent?

Or could it tell us you need more recovery before you can begin another hard session? Perhaps you dug too deep; with an inefficient running style, putting in another hard session could risk injury. Short of a coach with a sharp eye watching you run and recognizing small changes in your gait, this type of feedback has never before been available. Many runners can't be honest with themselves about injuries. Most of us downplay them and rush back to training too quickly, or just brush them off as a bad day.

These are all potentially injury-preventing or recovery-promoting uses of your new power meter. How can you maximize this tool and use it to foresee things like this for yourself? The key lies in collecting data on every run, getting to know yourself better, following and tracking what you're doing, all so you can know your own training and training response trends. Once you have these data in hand, any changes in the trends—outliers in the data— will be clear, alerting you to some of these possibilities.

Duration	Distance		TSS
10:18.67	1.00 mi		10.4

Work	169 kJ	IF	0.79
NP	278 w	VI	1.02
El. Gain	--	Grade	-45.9 %
El. Loss	2425 ft	VAM	--

	MIN	AVG	MAX	
Power	0	273	343	w
Heart Rate	0	131	142	bpm
Cadence	0	171	181	rpm

FIGURE 5.6b Run power data, post-injury

Summary

The fastest runner wins the race, but at some point, every athlete wants more speed per watts produced. Generally speaking, the higher the speed, the more watts required. At some point this relationship becomes exponential, with a much greater amount of watts required for a small increase in speed.

Running efficiency is influenced by many factors, some of which are within our control, and some not. Beginner and novice runners will see the biggest gains in efficiency, while experienced runners will need a more focused training approach to improve speed per watt.

The metric for speed per watt is called Efficiency Index, or EI, and is calculated as meters per minute divided by average watts.

Comparing rFTPw and rFTPa values becomes one of the most important metrics for monitoring performance and training adaptations in running. This is called the EI@FT.

The kJ/km metric measures the amount of work required for a runner to travel a single kilometer at a given intensity.

Using these metrics, runners can monitor and track their improvements in efficiency, as well as fitness, throughout the season.

6 Power Zones

The previous chapter discussed efficiency, the factors that contribute to efficiency, and how to monitor it. That chapter had to come before this one, on power zones, because I believe it is most important for runners to focus on efficiency first and foremost. Maximizing your speed per watt is critical. But as you will see, training according to zones can be very helpful both for your targeted races or goals and also for your yearly planning.

Power Zones for Running

If you use technology, or if you've taken your training seriously, you likely have some experience with heart rate (HR) zones and training according to HR. It's a simple and effective method for training that provides a guide to intensities in different sessions according to your goals. You might even have some experience using a GPS watch and training according to pace zones, wherein the pace the athlete runs is tied to intensities that correspond to different physiological energy systems.

If you're active in cycling or triathlon, you may have used a cycling power meter and trained according to power zones. If so, you're likely eager to begin using your running power meter in the same way. Training by power zones on the bike allows you to adjust or dial in your intensities to simulate race demands and helps you make sure you are maximizing your training time by focusing specifically on what you want to improve. Zones are a great tool for that, and power zones on the bike have helped make it almost too easy. Simply watch the power meter, and if you're not pushing enough, dial up your power. If you're going too hard, decrease the watts.

But I want you to pause on the idea of jumping right into training by run power zones for a moment, as it is not as simple as that. Power meters for running are much more complex than for cycling because, as we've noted before, we are dealing with different planes of movement in running. Unlike in cycling,

Training by zones can be helpful both for targeted races and for yearly planning.

where we simply measure the force applied to the crankarm, in running we do not isolate the power reading solely to what is actually making you run at your pace. We have productive work (horizontal mostly) that we are measuring, and unproductive work (vertical and lateral) that we are also measuring.

If I hop on a bicycle that doesn't fit me, and I don't have the seat height right, or I am leaning too far forward or back on the seat, the power meter on the bike cannot tell me that I am not in a good position. It can't tell me how much power I am wasting, nor that I could get more watts with a better position. It can only give me the numbers that I apply to the bike's drivetrain. This is what makes a power meter on the bike a great and simple tool. Raise the watts, and you know you're doing better.

With a running power meter, though, I receive the power data for factors that do help me, along with the data for factors that do not help me. And though it is more complex, this extra data is also what makes a power meter for running an incredible tool compared with a bicycle power meter, because it lets me see where I am potentially inefficient in my running technique. Power produced in directions or planes that don't help me is power wasted, and the running meter can help me reduce that wasted work. So the limitation of the data in a bike power meter is a disadvantage, while the abundance of data in the running power meter is a big advantage.

If you're using a 3D power meter, you're seeing power data from three planes: horizontal, lateral, and vertical. Only the measurement of horizontal power matters on a flat course. If you're using a 2D power meter, you're seeing vertical and horizontal power but not lateral. This reduces the total power value that's communicated, but that is not necessarily a disadvantage, as lateral power is only a small portion of total power. Disregarding the lateral component means you can focus on limiting your vertical power to minimally needed levels.

If the power numbers that increase are not the ones making you faster, then you are likely training with poor technique or have other factors affecting your inefficiencies that need to be addressed, as discussed in Chapter 5. Big power numbers can be good, but efficient and effective numbers are better. Perhaps soon, as the technology continues to evolve, we will be better able to isolate the effective power we produce in order to move ourselves forward faster, much as we do on a bike. Until then, all power numbers and their value—even running functional threshold power (rFTPw) values—must be considered in the correct context, as bigger numbers are not always better.

At this point, you're probably wondering how your rFTPw number can be representative of your potential if you don't necessarily want it to get higher.

If you can hold more watts for an hour, doesn't that mean you're fitter? A good question. Yes, holding a higher work rate means you have more potential than those with a lower rate, but it doesn't mean you use that power effectively and efficiently in converting it to speed. For example, there are plenty of cars in the world with similar engines. Yet even cars with the same engine, capable of the same horsepower, don't go the same speed or have the same fuel consumption rate. This is because there is a difference in how the cars transfer energy from the engine to the road. The human body isn't much different with respect to running. How you transfer the forces and speed of the forces to move you forward is vital to your performance.

Consider this scenario: While a runner maintains the same rFTPa, and she is fitter than before, her power numbers are lower. The challenge lies in the fact that we have nearly equal opportunities to show fitness with increased power and with decreased power, based on our own individual efficiency as a runner. This is where power zones can contaminate your training if you use them blindly, without analyzing how efficiently you are training within them.

Don't get the wrong idea: You certainly can train according to power zones. However, I believe efficient runners will see more benefit from training by power zones than inefficient runners, due to the fact they will likely have less variance in terms of power data. If you are not using metrics that help you see your efficiency when running, and aren't actively addressing efficiency in your training, then training by zones will likely not be effective for you.

Have you ever done a lot of work on a big project only to realize you made a mistake early in the process and much of the work you did was wasted? Those are extremely frustrating moments. That is how training by power zones can be if you don't have good efficiency in your running. You can train at a certain zone, monitoring the watts to make sure you're training the right energy system, but if you don't have the ability to show that what you're doing is actually helping to make you faster, then you might as well not focus on power during those moments. Instead, you should focus on pace and push yourself. And in your post-workout analysis, use power data and power zones to see how your training at those intensities is going.

The golden reward of training with power, if you use it wisely, is that you'll not only train in a way that makes you stronger, but you'll also train much more effectively, transferring more of the work you do into running speed. You'll have clear evidence of the rewards (and pitfalls) of changes you make to your technique. You'll be able to recognize your markers for overtraining sooner and with more clarity, along with warning signs for potential injuries.

Can these running power zones help you to be faster? Certainly, they have the potential to create a breakthrough in training and performance. But this technology is so new that it is hard for us to say definitively that training by power zones is the best way to train. If you can use these zones to better understand how you approach training, perhaps by monitoring time in each zone, then you will find these zones to be effective for your training. You can also use them to focus on zones for racing. For now, after you have established efficient running techniques for maximizing speed per watt, I would encourage you to then experiment with some zone training as a way to fine-tune what you're doing.

What level of efficiency is sufficient? That's a great question. I can't give you a specific number or a test that will tell you that you are ready for zone training. This technology is still so new that we simply don't know yet. But I do think there are two things you can do to determine when you are ready to start focusing on training by power zones.

First, see about becoming more efficient in your easy efforts. If you can't improve efficiency by going easy when it's simple to focus on specific techniques in your running that lower the amount of power needed to maintain the same pace, it's hard to imagine that you can become more efficient when you're pushing hard and have less oxygen flowing to your brain to help you concentrate. Later on in this chapter, I will discuss further how you can monitor your time in power zones, which is the next best step before training by power zones.

Second, find where your race paces and intensities are, and chart your baseline efficiency at those intensities. Understand what cues and specifics you need to focus on to be efficient, and work to bring your EI up (speed per watt). Once you've improved this metric, and possibly plateaued, you can likely consider training by power zones.

Remember, the goal is to be as efficient as possible at the fastest speed possible. So start with slower and easier intensities, and work your way to faster and harder intensities. Monitor where the greatest breakdown in efficiency tends to happen. And first and foremost, train as you had been doing prior to acquiring your power meter and gather data about yourself, learning where you stand. This information gathering should last a minimum of three months, in my opinion. After that initial period, you should have a good idea of your EI at different intensities. Even after that period, it might be best to train *with* power, not necessarily *by* power. Power data is much more helpful than just establishing zones, so don't get hung up on zones as if they are the only way to improve or use power as a runner. That's just not the case.

This chapter assumes you've been using the power meter initially to recognize your tendencies and efficiency indexes to make sure you're ready to maximize the work you do, and that you are now ready to begin training with power zones. If that's not you, I encourage you to train for better efficiency first.

Defining Power Zones

So what are power zones exactly? Power zones are discrete ranges of intensity, with different energy systems being mostly used within each range. I stress "*mostly* used" because no energy system is 100 percent in use or out of use. As a corollary, training at one intensity can have effects on other energy systems and their development, even when those systems are not the focus of training. For example, a beginner who goes out to do some easy running will find his ability to run a 5K will greatly improve over time, even if he hasn't done any intensity training specific to a 5K. The fact that he has developed his basic aerobic fitness carries over to anaerobic efforts as well. I will discuss this in more detail soon.

In Chapter 4, we defined intensity through power, so it makes sense that power zones would further define intensity. We highlighted Intensity Factor, or IF, which is the quotient of the Normalized Power of a workout divided by rFTPw. The same is true for power zones, where we base the range of watts in each zone upon a percentage of rFTPw.

Those from a cycling or triathlon background are probably familiar with Dr. Andrew Coggan's power zones. He developed seven power zones for cycling, based on an athlete's FTP. I have adopted his style and the number of zones, and modified the ranges to better represent the demands of running based upon my experience in coaching runners of varying abilities. I have developed the zones with the help of 3D power meters. Although I do not have enough experience to confirm these zones for 2D meters, I have no reason to think they won't be accurate, since they are based on a percentage of rFTPw. Table 6.1 shows the power zones, the name of each zone, the percentage of rFTPw they represent, and the general time range one could sustain in such a zone.

Table 6.2 shows how these zones break down for our athlete with a 383 rFTPw from the earlier chapters. You can see in the table that the ranges are simple to follow; stay within the ranges and you'll maximize the time spent focused on those training systems or goal intensities. In post-workout analysis, these zones also give you a chance to go back later to see the breakdown of time spent in each zone. You can do this for a single run or for the past training block. More on that shortly.

Let's look more closely at each of these zones and determine what they actually represent from the standpoint of training intensity.

ZONE 1: WALKING/RECOVERY (80 PERCENT OR LESS OF rFTPw)

This is the lightest and easiest zone of training. The amount of intensity in this zone is defined as 80 percent or less of rFTPw. Though this might seem high to those with experience using a cycling power meter, it really isn't. Running uses such large groups of muscles that the range between easy and threshold watts is not as great as in cycling power zones. For all runners, this zone would include walking and light jogging, like warm-ups and easy recovery paces. For

TABLE 6.1 Power Zones and Percentage of rFTPw

Zone	Training Intensity	% of rFTPw	Time
1	Walking/recovery	‹81	3+ hours
2	Endurance	81–88	2–3 hours
3	Tempo	89–95	1–3 hours
4	Threshold	96–105	1 hour
5	High intensity	106–115	20–45 min
6	VO$_2$	116–128	2–18 min
7	Anaerobic capacity/peak power	129+	‹2 min

slower to moderately quick runners it might even include some easy to moderate base training intensity, as there is some aerobic development that can happen in this zone. Athletes should be able to sustain this intensity for quite a long time, theoretically over the course of many hours, although it is not likely to be used or needed for that long.

ZONE 2: ENDURANCE (81–88 PERCENT OF rFTPw)

This zone is a moderate aerobic training intensity. Dr. Coggan commonly calls Zone 2 "endurance," a term I like because it effectively describes what is happening. This intensity is specific for developing aerobic endurance in runners. It is more intense than Zone 1, and therefore has stronger likelihood of aerobic development, but is not so hard that an athlete can't have a conversation while running. Slower to moderately quick runners might find this zone to be in line with their marathon intensity, as it can be sustained for a few hours.

TABLE 6.2 Sample Power Zones for Runner with 383 rFTPw			
Zone	Training Intensity	% of rFTPw	Watts
1	Walking/recovery	‹81	0–306
2	Endurance	81–88	307–337
3	Tempo	89–95	338–364
4	Threshold	96–105	365–402
5	High intensity	106–115	403–440
6	VO$_2$	116–128	441–490
7	Anaerobic capacity/peak power	129+	491–5,000

ZONE 3: TEMPO (89–95 PERCENT OF rFTPw)

Most runners have done a tempo run at some point in their running careers. Most know this type of effort is above moderate aerobic endurance intensity, and not one that could be or is advised to be sustained for many hours. Faster runners would likely find this similar to their marathon intensity, while slower runners might find it to be more in line with their half-marathon intensity.

ZONE 4: THRESHOLD (96–105 PERCENT OF rFTPw)

Remember that rFTPw is the best power output that you can hold for one hour. Notice that the initial time ranges in Zones 1–3 lasted a few hours, and then just a couple hours. Now we are at about one hour, as this is the threshold zone where 100 percent of rFTPw can be found. You can train just below rFTPw and still see that value benefit. You can train slightly above it and see strong benefits too. Any race distance that requires close to one hour to complete would be highlighted in this zone. For slower runners, this might be a 10K; for elite runners, it might be as far as a half-marathon.

ZONE 5: HIGH INTENSITY (106–115 PERCENT OF rFTPw)

Zone 5 has one of the largest ranges. That may seem odd, but Zone 5 incorporates a rather wide time range for training, especially for races, interval training, or hard runs. This range begins above threshold watts and ends just around the point of VO_2max work being the main point of training. The time range to hold this intensity is somewhere between 20 and 45 minutes. If you wonder why it doesn't go closer to an hour, remember that it is above threshold, and by definition you can't really go up to an hour above your threshold. Note that the time ranges, like the zones, have a bit of overlap. You're never training just one energy system, and there isn't a draconian cutoff where 46 minutes suddenly becomes the Threshold Zone and not High Intensity. Some of these intensities are also dependent on the athlete's ability, as better runners may be able to hold intensities longer.

ZONE 6: VO$_2$ (116–128 PERCENT OF rFTPw)

This zone is called VO$_2$ because it is where the intensities begin to focus on the body's ability to use a maximal amount of oxygen. The length of time an athlete can be in this zone varies. The ability of the runner plays a role, as does the willingness to maintain a high level of discomfort. Some athletes simply can't push themselves as hard as others, so the ability to stay in this zone for a long time has a lot to do with the individual athlete.

The general time range I would expect to see in this zone would be two minutes at the highest end of the intensity, and as much as 18 to 20 minutes for the lower percentage. You can see this covers everything from an 800-meter run to possibly a 5K, depending on the athlete. Faster athletes will find this zone to be very common in speed endurance workouts, while slower athletes might find this to be more like speed development.

ZONE 7: ANAEROBIC CAPACITY/PEAK POWER (129+ PERCENT OF rFTPw)

Your peak power—the highest output you can possibly deliver over a very short period of time (only a few seconds)—lies within in this zone. It is highly neuromuscular in its outputs, dealing with how well the brain can deliver a message to the muscles to fire quickly and effectively. These intensities are so high, and the durations so short, that you could never hold them very long. The durations in this zone range up to about two minutes, depending on the athlete, but are likely to be less.

This zone is unlikely to be used much by slower or beginning runners. The intensity is so high that it carries a lot of injury risk. Experienced or faster runners might use it for speed endurance or for speed development (commonly

TABLE 6.3 Expected Physiological/Performance Adaptations Resulting from Training at Power Zones 1–7

Adaptation	1	2	3	4	5	6	7
Increased plasma volume	•	•	••	•••	••••	•	•
Increased muscle mitochondrial enzymes	•	••	•••	••••	•••	••	•
Increased lactate threshold	•	••	•••	••••	•••	••	•
Increased muscle glycogen storage	•	••	••••	•••	••	••	•
Hypertrophy of slow-twitch muscle fibers	•	•	••	••	•••	•	
Increased muscle capillarization	•	••	•••	••	•••	••	
Interconversion of fast-twitch muscle fibers (type IIb → type IIa)	•	••	•••	•••	••	•	•
Increased stroke volume/maximal cardiac output	•	•	••	•••	••••	••	•
Increased VO$_2$max	•	•	••	•••	•••	••••	•
Increased muscle high-energy phosphate (ATP/PCr) stores						•	••
Increased anaerobic capacity ("lactate tolerance")					•	••	•••
Hypertrophy of fast-twitch fibers						•	•••
Increased neuromuscular power						•	•••

Source: Adapted from Andy R. Coggan, http://home.trainingpeaks.com/blog/article/power-training-levels.

called speed work). This trains the athlete's ability to recruit more muscle fibers and generate high force at the fastest speeds possible.

Table 6.3 further illustrates the training response crossover of these seven zones. It is based upon Dr. Coggan's seven power zones for cycling. Remember that while easy efforts can contribute to a training response for harder efforts, training response is maximized when the stimulus is specific. Table 6.3 shows which zones are most effective for the various training responses.

Using Power Zones for Training

Now that you know the definition and purpose of each power zone, let's look at how we can define what those zones and power values mean for you. Remember, power zone ranges are defined by a percentage of your rFTPw, which you can find through the tests and processes laid out in Chapter 4, with the zone breakdown illustrated in Table 6.2.

In the early stages, as you learn more about how you run, I suggest you use zones for analysis post-run; that is, use them as a tool for *post*-scription of workouts, rather than *pre*scription of training intensities, because how fast you are makes a difference in terms of the energy systems you want to target for your training. For example, some people are 35-minute 10K runners, while others are trying to break 50 minutes. In fact, some are faster than 30 minutes, while others need an hour to complete a 10K. These runners are not training in the same zone, even though they are training for the same distance.

Tables 6.4 and 6.5 show how the zones and intensities might line up for you, based on your running speed. Table 6.4 shows the zones based upon an athlete who can run a sub-35-minute 10K. Table 6.5 shows how the zones line up for a runner who needs 50 minutes or more for the same distance. As a reader of this book, it's likely that you will fall toward the faster end of these values, and some serious runners might even fall below the 35-minute 10K mark. The

TABLE 6.4 Zones and Paces for Sub-35-Minute 10K Runners

Zone	Training Intensity	Pace
1	Walking/recovery	Recovery pace, warm-up pace
2	Endurance	Base training, recovery pace, warm-up
3	Tempo	Marathon pace
4	Threshold	15K, half-marathon pace
5	High intensity	15K, 10K
6	VO$_2$	5K and shorter, speed endurance
7	Anaerobic capacity/peak power	Speed endurance, speed work

TABLE 6.5 Zones and Paces for 50-Minute-Plus 10K Runners

Zone	Training Intensity	Pace
1	Walking/recovery	Base training, recovery pace, warm-up
2	Endurance	Base training, marathon pace
3	Tempo	15K, half-marathon pace
4	Threshold	10K pace
5	High intensity	5K and shorter, speed endurance
6	VO$_2$	Speed endurance, speed work
7	Anaerobic capacity/peak power	Speed work

point here is that when you understand the time ranges, you can adjust these guidelines to meet your needs. Hopefully, you will continue to improve and see yourself get faster, and will need to adjust these for your training as you go.

When reviewing your power data from a run, one of the best things you can do is look at how much time you spent in each power zone. This will give you an idea of how well your training intensities lined up with your goals for the workout. If you hoped to work on threshold, how much time did you spend in Zone 4? Figure 6.1 illustrates one athlete's track workout with threshold intervals, Zone 4, and some high intensity intervals, Zone 5. There is a pronounced amount of Zone 1 and 2 time as well, because the athlete was recovering between intervals, as well as warming up and cooling down. There is only one second of samples in Zone 6, VO_2, and no samples in Zone 7. This is good; it shows that the athlete met the intensity goals of the workout.

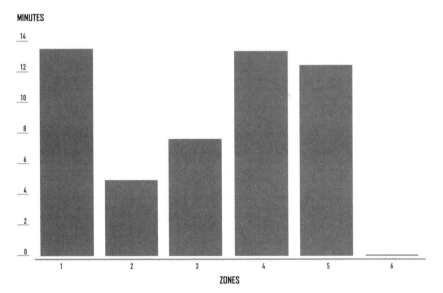

FIGURE 6.1 Sample time spent in power zones over the course of a workout

This type of intensity review is especially helpful for athletes who have no idea what their 10K or 5K pace is or should be. One of the biggest advantages of a power meter is that it helps with pacing, especially if an athlete knows what power range he can realistically hold for a certain duration. Now instead of tying his training to a pace that may not even match the energy system he actually wants to target, he can instead use these zones to see how close he is to truly representing the race demands, and can prepare specifically for the race distance (an instance of where training with power can become more prescriptive for training decisions). He can now see the paces he is capable of, and identify the paces where he needs to improve his EI. For example, if you're trying to simulate a sub-17-minute 5K pace but running in power Zones 4 and 5, you're not pushing as hard as you can, and not maximizing the training time you have available.

If you're trying to break 3:30 for the marathon, but doing high Zone 3 and 4 intensities in your goal-pace workouts, you're not likely to be able to sustain that power over the course of the race. By reviewing time spent in power zones, athletes can finish a workout with confidence that they are actually making themselves better and more likely to achieve their specific goals.

You can even see a breakdown in the amount of time you spent in a smaller range of watts (we call them bins) than the zones. For example, Figure 6.2 shows the same workout as Figure 6.1, but now in smaller bins with ranges of 20 watts. You can choose smaller or larger bins and get a clearer picture of where in the zone most of your samples fall, such as the high, middle, or low end. This could be helpful, for example, in seeing when you think you might have been a zone too high. You might have been right at the bottom end of it, which means you probably did a great job of pushing yourself in the workout.

Another potential benefit of looking at time in zones is that if you're training by effort and pace, using the power data to review afterward, you might find that the pace you ran was fast, but in a zone or bin range below what you expected. This would signify efficiency improvements in your running, which is great. The opposite could happen too, of course, where your effort is what you expect, but the zones where you spent the majority of your time were higher than you were targeting. This could signify fatigue, perhaps due to over-reaching in your training, and possibly requiring more recovery. This is a perfect example of training *with* power but not training *by* power. Initially, this is a great way to train, and you may never find the need to train specifically by power zones during a workout.

You can also review a longer term of time spent in zones or bins, such as a training block or over the course of an entire season. Because you're using power as a more precise measure of intensity than pace, you can see how hard you actually train and decide whether you trained effectively. You can also

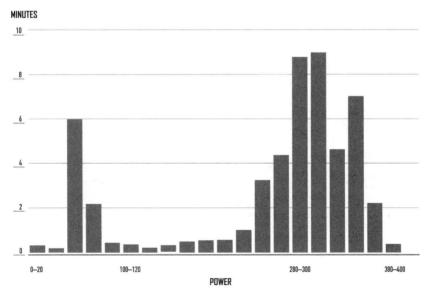

FIGURE 6.2 Breakdown of watts in 20-watt increments from workout in Figure 6.1

use it as a base point to make decisions on how to improve your training. Perhaps you're doing more intensity than you thought you were. Perhaps you're not doing enough intensity. Perhaps the intensity you're doing isn't consistent with the speed you're able to hold for the distances you're preparing for. Or perhaps there is no change throughout the different periods of the season, and you're always doing the same relative amount of intensity, across all zones. Whatever it is, this is a chance to review and let the power of data become a tool for improvement.

If you use HR zones in your training, it is important to realize they will *not* align perfectly with power zones. This means an effort in Zone 1 HR won't necessarily match Zone 1 power outputs only. For example, Figure 6.3 shows the power zones from Figure 6.1 and how they compare with Joe Friel's HR zones.

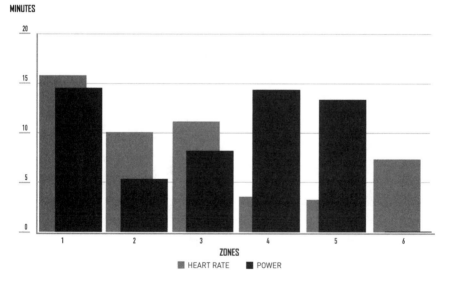

FIGURE 6.3 Comparison of the breakdown of samples for heart rate zones and power zones from a single workout

In the HR zones time distribution, you'll notice the athlete has samples of time spent in six zones, with the sixth zone being quite high, compared to having samples in only five of the power zones. This could be due to the intensity of the effort and the HR needing time to recover and drop back down during the recovery, or not having enough time to allow the HR to recover between the intervals.

You'll also notice the majority of HR samples fall in the first three zones, but the majority of power samples seem to fall in the third, fourth, and fifth zones. There are a number of factors that could contribute to this, from

Heart rate measures response and doesn't move very fast. But power represents real time.

fitness or fatigue levels to the slow response of HR relative to harder efforts or higher intensities. In that case, a shorter interval might not allow a high HR to be achieved.

A good way to think about how training by HR differs from training with power is that HR training is like looking into a rearview mirror. It will always be in response to intensity that it has been forced to adjust to, and it doesn't move very fast. Power, on the other hand, represents real time. Power is also very specific; watts are watts, and they are specific to the amount of work being produced. HR is not specific, however; it can rise through excitement or emotion, and unlike work is not tangible.

It's perfectly okay to use HR in your training, as it can play a useful role, but it is important for you to understand there isn't a fixed, proportional relationship between HR zones and power zones. One deals with the heart, the other with muscles. Heart rate zones won't change as fitness improves (or drops), but power zones will change with fitness because rFTPw will change.

Continued Monitoring for Efficiency

Again, the key takeaway from this chapter is that if you train by power zones, you should also monitor for efficiency so that you are actually getting something out of the power outputs you're generating. Training in a high power zone, but not getting faster speed from it, is not a very good use of your time or this incredible tool.

Make sure to go back and use the metrics laid out in Chapter 5 on monitoring for efficiency, and then make sure the power zones you're using in your training are effective at hitting the intensities you need in a way that will make you faster.

Summary

Runners who want to use power zones for their training should first make sure they are maximizing their efficiency in running; the first order of business is to get the most speed per watt at easy to moderate intensities.

Once runners have their rFTPw, they can establish their personal power zones, which are based on a percentage of the rFTPw value. My seven power zones start at the easiest efforts, which could theoretically be maintained for hours, and progress to durations measured in minutes to seconds. These zones signify different energy systems and different race intensities, depending on the goals and speed of the athlete. No energy system is ever 100 percent or zero percent in use, but some zones train and affect certain systems better than others.

It is best that athletes use power zones and bins first to review training, and to see how effective they were at actually hitting the target intensities they were looking for during their workouts. In addition to a single workout, this review can cover training over a longer period of time, from a short block to a full season.

Power zones can also help reveal improvements or potential regressions in efficiency, based upon the runner's target paces or intensities and how well they aligned with the target power zones.

Though HR zones can be effective as a training tool, runners should not expect them to align with power zones, due to the number of extraneous factors influencing heart rate.

7 Planning Your Training

We now have an understanding of the basic and most important metrics supplied by your power meter, along with ways to monitor for improvement. We've also established a guide to training intensities. At this point, we can move into the daily application of this technology: planning your training and making it effective throughout the year.

As I said before, the best approach to training with a power meter is pretty close to what you do in your normal training. You've purchased a power meter because you're looking for a smarter, more refined approach to your training and racing. You're looking for ways to get the most out of the training time you have and the workouts you do, and this tool will help you achieve those goals. Therefore, you should train as you normally do, but also use the data you collect to learn more about yourself and address what needs to be improved. If there is an area in training where you are falling short, use your data to track it, find ways to improve, and see how well you are addressing it.

No one knows you better than you, and that's one of the key reasons I advocate a gradual and refined approach to incorporating your power meter into your training plan. If your previous approach has been effective, there is no reason to change things dramatically. The power meter adds objective, trackable data to help you get better information.

Before we get into the detailed specifics of a training plan, let's pull back to take a wide-angle look at the elements of training. If you've studied modern training theories at all, you've heard terms like periodization, base phase, competition phase, peaking, tapering, transition phase, and more. Instead of throwing a bunch of these terms at you, I'm going to make it much more simple by breaking training into two phases, General Preparation and Specific Preparation. Some might call these Base Phase and Competition Phase, and if you are more comfortable with those terms go ahead and use them in your plan.

Very simply put, General Preparation is all about getting fitter. There's nothing complex about it: You're just building a good base of fitness so that you can leverage it for performance later in a race or goal event. Specific Preparation builds race-specific fitness on top of that base fitness. In mapping out your Specific Preparation, you choose a specific race and distance and then

Train as you normally do, but use the data you collect to improve.

match those demands in your training. As we outlined in the previous chapter, the power zone and energy systems you target should be specific to the time needed to cover the distance, so the training you do in the Specific Preparation period must be targeted at these specific zones and intensities. You also must consider the demands of the course and the temperatures or conditions the race will have.

To prepare your training for the year, you must map out your season much as you would plan for any long journey. Start by identifying your main goal race events. These are your A-priority events, the ones where you're most committed to getting the result you want. For many runners, this main target is either a marathon or half-marathon, which can include anything from a major local event to an attempt to qualify for Boston. If you're an elite, you may be looking at the World Marathon Majors, or even the Olympics or Golden League meets.

You probably shouldn't put more than three A-priority races on your calendar for the year, because the time dedicated to preparing for them, from General to Specific Preparation, including taper and recovery, doesn't allow time to maximize preparation for strong performances for more than three key races. For example, if you planned to do four marathons in a year, you would likely need to begin tapering two to three weeks out from the race, and you would need an additional two weeks of recovery post-race. That's five weeks dedicated to a race. Multiply that by four races and you are looking at 20 weeks when you will not be training to get faster. That's almost half a year! It's not hard to imagine what 20 weeks of good, consistent training could do for you. This doesn't even begin to consider the mental strain of peaking for so many major events.

Certainly, four marathons may be an extreme example, but I think you get the idea. Make too many races your goal events, and you never really get the chance to maximize your training time and opportunity to get better. The best reason to have a power meter is to get the most out of your training time, so give yourself the best chance and try to plan your season with only a few A-priority races to peak for, especially if they are marathons or similar efforts like an ultra or an Ironman.

What about races that aren't peak events? Coaches generally describe these as B-priority, or even C-priority. B-priority races still matter, of course, but not as much as the A events, and they likely require that you back off in training a little to match your performance to their stature. Your B race could be a qualifying event where you know you can do well without a peak, but don't want to enter with too much fatigue.

C-priority events are races that you can train through, without any real adjustment to your training load or structure. You might even "race tired" at these events, using them as a workout in the buildup to race day, addressing a specific need.

In Chapter 8, I will share how you can see your training graphically, including your fitness, fatigue, and race-readiness. You will be able to plan your training better and become more aware of how your training is going, so that you can make adjustments in your training before it's too late. I will even share how to fine-tune your taper and peaks, to perform at your best when it matters the most to you.

Once you have chosen your A-priority events, you simply need to place them on your calendar and then mark out the 14 weeks prior to the events. The start of that 14-week period is about the point where your training will need to change phases, from General Preparation to Specific Preparation. Remember, as you get closer to the events, you want your training to represent more specifically what the race demands will be. So your A races should always fall within the Specific Preparation phase.

If your A-priority events overlap within this 14-week window, you will have a decision to make in terms of which one is an A– and which is an A or A+ event for you. That hierarchy will help you determine where the timeline should start. If the events are very close together, and you can recover from the first one relatively quickly to be ready for the next one, you can likely use the same 14-week period for both events. Table 7.1 shows how a basic season breaks down with General and Specific Preparation phases, and one A-priority peak half-marathon.

TABLE 7.1 Annual Training Plan with One A-Priority Race

Weeks	Training Type	
1–4		Recovery
5–7		Preparation
8–37	**General Preparation Phase**	General skills and abilities
38–49	**Specific Preparation Phase**	Race-specific intensity
50–51		Taper
52		A-priority race

There are no B- or C-priority race events in this table because it doesn't matter where they fall. Your training should be based first and foremost around the A-priority event, with B and C events filled in accordingly to support the A-priority event.

You're probably asking, "Why 'about' 14 weeks? Why not a specific number of weeks?" You're starting to ask the right questions and get to the heart of training with technology like power meters. Instead of training by traditional timelines, such as 20 weeks of general base training followed by 12 weeks of specific training and a taper of 3 weeks, you can now follow your fitness more closely, making training decisions according to the numbers revealed in the data. This change allows you to train for the ideal stimulus or training stress when the timing is right for you, not just because a coach's training plan says so, or because training has traditionally been done according to specific timelines.

Nevertheless, 14 weeks is a good number to guide your planning, because the body can only take the same race-specific type of training stimulus for so long. After that, fitness starts to plateau—or worse, begins to regress. The body responds well to variety in stimulus, so weeks and weeks of a similar stimulus designed to address one specific energy system or intensity will likely show strong training response in the athlete—but only up to a point. This point tends to happen somewhere around 14 weeks for most athletes. I say most athletes, because no two athletes are the same. Long-term training history, fitness level at the start of training, injury history, weakness or physical limitations, motivation, confidence, and other factors all play a part in the training response. This is why a power meter is such an amazing tool: You'll soon know how all these variables affect you, and how your training is addressing them. If you're not addressing them effectively, you will learn that as well.

If your A-priority races are not close together, but still within the 14-week mark for the second event—let's say 10 weeks apart—then you might do close to a 14-week Specific Preparation phase into the first event followed by a short recovery and return to General Preparation. Arranging things that way will change the stimulus and return your training to maintaining your general fitness base. After that short stretch, you'd move into a short Specific Preparation phase. This type of variation, alternating the phases briefly, allows you to extend training beyond the 14 weeks and still see positive response from the specific training stimulus. How much it can be extended is, once again, highly individual. Table 7.2 shows how the season might break down with the two preparation phases and the two A-priority peak events 10 weeks apart.

I want to reiterate: I am not saying you must change from General to Specific at the 14-week mark from your peak event. I am only saying you should keep in mind where this timeline falls. As you monitor your training response and plan the next steps in your training, this timeline marker of 14 weeks out from your peak event should act as a window of opportunity. Within it, you can maximize your response to race-specific stimulus with little risk of plateauing your fitness.

You might be asking yourself, "If the timeline is usually 14 weeks, why is the General Preparation phase so much longer? Won't the training in that phase reach a plateau as well?" Excellent question. The General Preparation phase is longer because it is not designed to focus primarily on specific race stimulus for the entire period. It is instead designed to address the general limitations of the athlete. Whether we want to admit it or not, there are likely many limiters to be addressed—and the training in the General Preparation phase should vary accordingly. More on this shortly.

Now that you've set your calendar and timelines for when you're likely going to begin your General and Specific Preparation phases, we can examine

Weeks	Training Type	
TABLE 7.2 Annual Training Plan with Two A-Priority Races		
1–4		Recovery
5–7		Preparation
8–31	General Preparation Phase	General skills and abilities
32–39	Specific Preparation Phase	Race-specific intensity
40–41		Taper
42		A-priority race
43–45	General Preparation Phase	Recovery
		General skills and abilities
46–49	Specific Preparation Phase	Race-specific intensity
50–51		Taper
52		A-priority race

what the training should look like. We'll also see how you can use your power meter to monitor your training response to maximize the training you do in a way that is specific to you.

General Preparation Training: Getting Fitter

Many months before you even start training for an event, you are in the General Preparation phase of training. The first part of this phase starts at the end of your most recent Specific Preparation phase, which is immediately after you finish your race. It's a period when runners typically take time off, allowing the body to recover.

RECOVERY

Recovery is a general way of improving, and while resting and recovering by themselves won't make you fitter, they are necessary steps for most athletes, especially when coming off long, hard races like marathons, or coming off a long and large block of committed training leading into the peak event.

This period might involve zero activity for some athletes. Others might take some days off, but will otherwise remain active, albeit at a level below what anyone would consider training.

How long does this recovery period last? As long as you need it to, in order to heal up and be healthy and ready for the season ahead. This includes mental and physical preparedness. You want to be injury-free and motivated to train when you start training harder again.

PREPARATION

When you're coming back from a layoff, you start by getting yourself off the couch and doing some basic exercise routines. Depending on how long you've been idle, you should ease into training. Table 7.3 shows a basic and conservative approach to how many weeks of basic exercise you should do before you begin any serious training in the General Preparation phase. Joe Friel calls these weeks between layoff and more serious training the Preparation phase because they help you prepare for the more serious training ahead without getting injured immediately. These weeks should be very conservative, light in intensity, and low in volume, even more so if you're coming off a longer period of rest time.

You would likely begin with some easy running, with a few slightly more intense workouts here and there, and you would closely monitor how you're handling those sessions. This time period is more about building some consistency of training, rather than focusing on building fitness at any specific intensity. This would mean a lot of Zone 1 and 2 efforts, with Zone 2 likely being the highest power zone where you'd spend any substantial amount of time.

TABLE 7.3 Recommended Preparation Weeks per Weeks Off	
Weeks Off	Preparation Weeks
1	1
2	1
3	1.5
4	2
5	2
6	2.5
7	3
8+	4

GENERAL SKILLS AND ABILITIES

Once you have reached some basic building of fitness in the Preparation phase, you're ready to begin more serious training. What that training should consist of and how it should look depend entirely on your state of fitness and your abilities. In his series of Training Bibles for the endurance sports of triathlon and cycling, Joe Friel breaks down the basic athlete's training triad as shown in Figure 7.1.

The basic training triad illustrates the three most basic, general abilities an endurance athlete must have for performance. At the three points of the triangle are the three most basic abilities every runner should develop in this phase of training. These basics are aerobic endurance, muscular force, and speed skill. Let's examine each a little more closely.

AEROBIC ENDURANCE

Aerobic endurance is the ability to use oxygen to produce movement. Improvement in aerobic endurance usually signifies increased stroke volume per beat

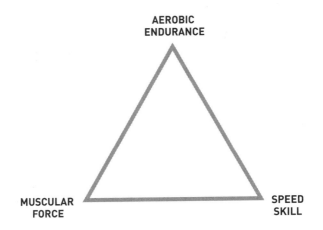

FIGURE 7.1 Joe Friel's basic training triad

of the heart, and increased capillarization to deliver more oxygen to the muscles for movement of higher intensity and/or longer duration. Basically, your heart pumps a greater amount of oxygen per beat to more of your muscles, so you can fuel those muscles to work harder.

Aerobic endurance is probably the most common training runners do. Long runs have large effects on aerobic endurance, and even easy- to moderate-paced shorter runs contribute to this ability. Runners need to be aerobically strong in order to perform well, and for many athletes this is the main focus of training. It is what has long been called long, slow distance, or LSD. It entails spending a lot of time in power Zones 1 and 2, and possibly 3.

To monitor for improvements in this type of aerobic training, runners should be comparing similar types of runs while looking at their Efficiency Index (EI, Chapter 5) for trends in the data. For example, you likely have a local loop that you like to run on a semi-regular basis. You probably run it at about the same aerobic endurance intensity. Comparing these runs and their EI values over the course of time will give you an idea on how your training is going.

It is important that you compare aerobic endurance runs only with other aerobic endurance runs. Comparing aerobic endurance runs with track interval sessions or tempo efforts does not yield apples-to-apples information. If you compare the EI of different types of workouts, you might become discouraged because you'll see that your efficiency or fitness is not improving. But a steady aerobic effort is not comparable with a track-intervals effort in terms of pace or power outputs, or in terms of judging progress. If you want to look at intervals on a track, compare it with other intervals on a track.

If one of your goals for your General Preparation phase is to develop aerobic fitness for your aerobic endurance training runs, you should strive to see at least one of these trends taking place:

Improving EI. You may see that you are not getting faster; instead you are simply maintaining the same pace in these types of runs. But is your EI improving? Are the watts getting lower for the same pace? You can also track your HR values for the same pace. If you are maintaining the same pace but seeing you are using less power to maintain it, or a lower HR, that's a strong signal of more efficient movement and aerobic fitness gains.

Maintaining EI. If your pace is increasing and you are getting faster in your aerobic endurance intensities, are you maintaining the same EI? If so, then the fact that efficiency tends to decrease exponentially as speed increases means you've helped push that point of decrease further out. You can likely hold higher intensities, especially aerobic intensities, much longer than before.

Improving speed and EI. If you're getting faster and seeing EI improve with the increase in pace, your training is outstanding! You might wonder if this improvement is even possible. Remember from Chapter 5 all the factors that contribute to efficiency. Make a few positive changes in a couple of those areas, and suddenly you could see a lot of improvement in power, pace, EI, and HR, all at the same time. In fact, it is not uncommon for novice runners to see these gains as significant training response and large gains in efficiency are widespread among runners who don't have much training history.

Your EI is the most important metric for monitoring progress in your aerobic endurance training. The more efficient you are in your aerobic endurance intensities, the better prepared you are as a runner. Aerobic endurance is the fundamental base of fitness because running is an endurance sport first and foremost.

Note that aerobic endurance training is not the only type of training runners should pay attention to. Yes, it is a basic ability that needs to be developed, but it is far from the only type of training. Muscular force and speed skill are equally important. Let's look at those next.

MUSCULAR FORCE

Muscular force is another leg in the training triad, especially throughout the General Preparation phase. Muscular force is the ability of the muscles to contract and apply a high force during movement. For running, this is generally thought of as the force you can apply to the ground in order to propel your foot up and off the ground. How important is this general ability? Remember that power is force times speed, so how much force you can produce is a major component of your power. And it needs to be trained.

The body's ability to transfer force to the ground and move forward isn't just a product of the force produced by the legs, but also the core of the body. Because the ground returns an equal and opposite force to propel the body up and forward, the body must be able to absorb that force and transfer it through the body, up the entire kinetic chain, allowing the force to be concentrated forward. Channeling this power requires core strength in the body. The core in this instance refers to the region from your shoulders to your knees, where the majority of the mass of the body is located. Without proper core strength, the ability to convert the force produced into movement can't be maximized.

Muscular force can be developed in the weight room, via squats and other leg-strengthening exercises, as well as through core-strength exercises. It can also be developed in high-force running movements, such as hill work, where gravity adds to the resistance of the body's propulsion. Another type of high-force movement can be developed in sprints and surges. Coincidentally, these sprinting movements combine high speed and high force, which is the definition of peak power. In fact, Zone 7 in Chapter 6 is exactly this combination of high speed and high force, which is the peak power output an athlete can produce.

Remember also that a force applied must consider who is applying it. By this I mean the size of the individual. If you recall the efficiency considerations from Chapter 5, w/kg is a number that shows the number of watts produced per mass of the athlete. If you lose some unneeded mass but keep force production constant, the value of that force increases. You've improved your watts per kilogram, and therefore your efficiency.

Can a power meter show you that your muscular force has improved? Yes, it shows up in your w/kg; an increase there reflects the change in your force production. If your cadence hasn't changed but your power has increased, your force production must have improved. Is producing more watts better if there is no increase in training pace? I don't believe so, as speed per watt is still the most important aspect of running and power. Remember, if you're not getting faster, you should at least be seeing improvements in your EI that confirm you are running more efficiently. If you're seeing a drop in your EI without an improvement in pace, your training response is going in the wrong direction.

Does this mean you should see an improvement in EI after every workout? It would be great if that could happen, but it is more likely that there will be days when you might be slow and sluggish. It is likely this fatigue will show up in your data as higher watts with poor speed. Managing and monitoring fatigue with your power meter is one of the main topics we will discuss in Chapter 8.

So high-speed and high-force movements can build power specifically, because power is force times speed. The third general ability athletes should work on in this phase is speed of movement, or what Friel calls speed skill.

SPEED SKILL

Speed skill training is designed to improve efficiency of movement. Sound familiar? How fast can you move? Think of the Tasmanian Devil cartoon you watched when you were a kid. He would turn his legs at an extremely high rate, but he also spun away a lot of energy that could have been moving him forward faster instead. The ability to put one foot in front of the other as fast as possible is an example of speed. But how well does that move you toward the finish line? That's where the skill aspect comes in.

Again, with power encompassing force and speed, your ability to move at a high rate of speed is a skill that improves power. Remember that being able to coordinate movements quickly and effectively, from the brain to the working muscles, is part of what creates running efficiency.

Speed is the most precious resource a runner can have, so it is arguably the most important skill you should train. Even if you find that you can't improve your speed skill, you should at least work to maintain it.

How fast a runner can go is also a key indicator of potential. If you can't maintain high speed, your power will be limited. In general, as speed increases, watts increase, with watts eventually increasing at an exponential rate. At what speed the exponential increase of watts occurs is entirely dependent on the athlete and his or her ability to transform the watts produced into speed. But if the runner's max speed is limited, then the ceiling of power and pace is limited as well. We know this exponential increase is likely to happen sooner for slower athletes. The faster the athlete, the faster the speed at which the exponential increase begins to happen. This means that as you can hold better speeds, your potential ability to be efficient at slower speeds increases. Once again, we are talking about EI. We want to identify the point at which the watts required to produce more speed are so high that the speed per watt diminishes exponentially.

The ability to reach a higher speed can also help an athlete overcome a comparatively low EI value. Remember, efficient runners don't win races—the fastest runners do. The higher the speed at which you are efficient and the longer the distance of the race, the better for you. But it doesn't matter if I am more efficient if the athlete I am competing against is so much faster that he can cover the distance before efficiency becomes an issue. He doesn't need to be as efficient as me if he is that much faster.

One of the easiest ways to improve your speed skill is to increase the cadence at which you can run for sustained periods. In general, the slower the cadence, the slower the athlete. When the foot is planted on the ground, the athlete is not moving forward. Again, the speed of the force applied is part of the equation of power. If the cadence is slow, the speed of the force is slow.

We saw in Chapter 3 that a cadence of 90 rpm, or 180 spm, is a minimum target. If you can't hold that cadence for an aerobic endurance run, you likely need to address it in your training. It is one of the best and easiest ways to improve your power output and performance in general.

Figure 7.2 shows an athlete who, in the initial weeks of using his power meter, sees a clear relationship between his EI and his cadence. The higher his cadence, the better his EI becomes.

This analysis identifies a specific speed skill for this athlete to work on. He would address it in his General Preparation simply by trying to hold a higher cadence, first in his aerobic endurance runs then in his harder efforts. If the athlete cannot hold a higher cadence in lighter, aerobic endurance efforts, it will be difficult for him to hold it during higher intensity efforts. So the correct approach is to start working on cadence in the lighter efforts, then focus on maintaining an improved technique at all running speeds and intensities.

Once the athlete reaches a plateau, wherein EI no longer improves with cadence increases, or the cadence flattens out, he can move on from training this speed skill. The other option is to change his training stress if he is not happy with the level of cadence he has reached.

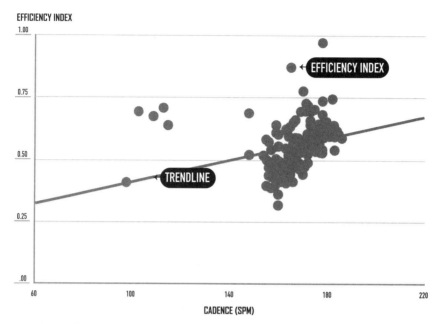

FIGURE 7.2 EI versus cadence: The higher the cadence, the higher the EI. This athlete needs to raise his cadence in all runs.

From Basic to Advanced Abilities

The evaluation and training areas above cover simple ways to identify and address your general abilities. Once your general abilities are strong, you've laid a solid foundation for your race-specific fitness training.

Does this mean runners should only train those three abilities in the General Preparation phase? No, not at all. But those abilities need to take priority before moving on. If the abilities aren't strong and polished at the basic, lower intensities, it is hard to believe they will get any better at harder intensities.

You may have already mastered some of these abilities. In that case, you need only maintain them in your training while you focus on improving the others. Perhaps your speed skill is fine, with high cadence, but your force production or aerobic endurance just isn't good enough to race well. In all cases, your power meter will help focus your efforts by showing which training methods are most effective for you.

Figure 7.3 shows the complete triad of training from Friel. Once the three main abilities are addressed satisfactorily, athletes can move on to the more advanced qualities of muscular endurance, anaerobic endurance, and sprint power.

You'll notice that the general abilities are on the points of the triangle, while the advanced abilities are on the sides, showing the connection between the general abilities. That is, muscular endurance is the combination of aerobic endurance and force, anaerobic endurance is the combination of aerobic endurance and speed skill, while sprint power is the combination of muscular force and speed skill.

Let's look into these three advanced abilities, starting with the lowest intensity and moving to the highest.

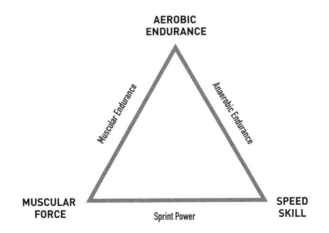

FIGURE 7.3 Joe Friel's complete training triad

MUSCULAR ENDURANCE

Muscular endurance is the combination of aerobic endurance and force, as illustrated in Figure 7.3. It is the ability to apply a relatively hard force for a long time. Muscular endurance training efforts typically fall in the Zone 3 to 4 ranges, the Tempo and Threshold zones. Tempo efforts, where you hold an intensity and force for a long period, can last up to three hours. Threshold efforts, where you hold a high intensity for about an hour, train muscular endurance as well.

How can you use a power meter to improve muscular endurance? The best way is to track how your EI is trending in efforts or intervals designed to improve muscular endurance. What is your power output, and what is the relationship of pace to that output? If you're improving your pace and either maintaining or improving EI, your training is going well. If your EI is decreasing, that may not be bad if the change is small and you are happy with your pace increases.

ANAEROBIC ENDURANCE

Anaerobic endurance is the combination of aerobic endurance and speed skill. These efforts are not all-out sprints (that's sprint power), but near-maximal efforts that address the aerobic capacity of the athlete, or what we commonly refer to as VO_2max.

How can you use a power meter to judge whether you're improving your anaerobic endurance? If you recall from Chapter 6, Zone 6 is called VO_2. It tends to run from 2 to 18 minutes. The amount of time an athlete records in this zone is indicative of how well he or she is addressing anaerobic endurance in training. If EI isn't improving, despite the athlete clearly working in this zone, there is likely a need to change training stimulus.

Much as with muscular endurance, if there are intervals you're doing consistently, tracking EI and other efforts designed to address your anaerobic endurance can give you clear guidance as to how your training is going.

SPRINT POWER

You might think sprint power isn't necessary for you, and you could be correct. This type of training is represented by Zone 7, and as I wrote in Chapter 6, there is a lot of risk in it. Many strained muscles and other injuries have resulted from Zone 7 training. However, this is a high-force, high-speed movement, so your sprint power has a direct carryover into the max power you can produce. The higher the max power you can produce, the higher the ceiling you have as an athlete.

How can you use a power meter to see improvement in your sprint power? Since these efforts are very short in duration, EI doesn't work as well. You can probably best see the results of this training by looking at your peak power outputs from each individual session, for durations of 2 to 30 seconds. The mean max power curve helps illustrate top performances for all durations recorded, which makes it a great tool for tracking. You can also just isolate these durations for peak outputs and track them, as seen in Figure 7.4.

Figure 7.4 shows the trend of an athlete's peak power outputs for each week, for 5 seconds, 12 seconds, and 30 seconds. This graph selects the highest outputs for each of those durations in a 7-day span. The upward trend shows this athlete's peak power outputs are improving each week, meaning the training response is going very well.

Specific Preparation Training: Race Preparation

Specific Preparation usually begins somewhere around 14 weeks prior to a key, A-priority race. However, it is possible for an athlete to never even enter this phase of training. If the General Preparation training is going well, with consistent improvement in the general abilities, there is no reason to rush into the Specific Preparation phase. This situation is more likely with novice runners, as experienced runners probably won't see continuous improvement to race-specific intensities in the General Preparation phase.

In this period, the training sessions that are intensive in nature should mimic the intensities of the A-priority race. This doesn't mean the athlete will run at race intensity every day, but that on the days where harder efforts are scheduled, these workouts should be designed to address race intensity or race

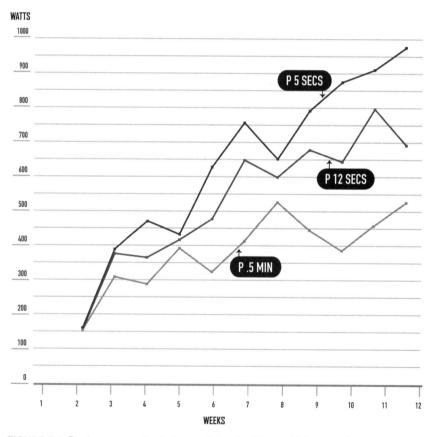

FIGURE 7.4 Peak power outputs by week for 5-, 12-, and 30-second durations

demands. In Chapter 6 we discussed power zones and how they might line up according to race events or distances, depending on the speed of the athlete. These zones and the intensities can help signify how an athlete can prepare specifically for a race event.

Let's take the example of an athlete trying to run a 3:30 marathon. The duration of this race effort tells us that it must be a sub-threshold-intensity effort. If the athlete is trying for a 3:30 marathon, he or she would want to train and race in Zone 3, the tempo zone.

If the athlete is conducting race-intensity tempo runs, which are designed to prepare specifically for the race, then the tempo runs should be conducted at goal pace for a 3:30 marathon. A post-run review will show how effective the runner was at keeping the effort in Zone 3. If the tempo effort was mostly Zone 4, but less than an hour, then the runner is unlikely to be able to sustain that effort for more than an hour. In that case, the pace needs to be reassessed and the question asked as to whether it can actually be accomplished on race day.

If the IF for the tempo run was 1.00 or greater for more than an hour, this is not possible. The runner likely needs to retest for a more accurate rFTPw.

If the tempo-run effort was mostly in Zone 2, the runner can likely go faster, and definitely harder, than the 3:30 pace or intensity. How well he or she can translate an increase of watts into speed is entirely based on efficiency.

If the target marathon is on a very hilly course, then these tempo runs should be conducted on a hilly course, with the hills simulating the ones seen on the racecourse. A hilly course might make it more difficult to stay consistently in Zone 3, but the average and Normalized Power values should still end up being in the Zone 3 range.

A more advanced way to use a power meter to prepare for a marathon is to monitor for Zone 3 watts during the tempo run, instead of goal pace. Doing so allows the runner to see what pace equates with that effort. While staying in Zone 3 watts, the runner can try to focus on changes in run technique and form to increase the speed to a faster pace while maintaining power in Zone 3. Monitoring watts during training is essentially a way of working in the moment to improve EI.

This approach is probably even more race specific than a simple tempo run, because every runner who pushes hard in a race will face a point where technique and form will begin to break down. At this point, watts will be produced that are not effectively turned into speed. The athlete might be maintaining the same watts while going slower, or even worse, slowing down with watts also decreasing; the athlete at this point is too broken down to maintain the same EI even at slower paces.

Again, I want to stress that in-the-moment monitoring is an advanced way of using a power meter during run training and racing. As I mentioned in Chapter 6, it is best for those just beginning to use a power meter for running to use it mostly in post-run data analysis to see how effectively they met

 Metrics from the power meter can be used to show progress toward training goals.

the goals of the workout. Monitoring for an improved EI, potential injuries, extreme fatigue from over-reaching in training, and seeing how well pace tracks wattage outputs is best done post-workout. Running according to a power zone is most effective if you have proven you can run efficiently while doing so.

I would only suggest this advanced monitoring during a session for those with a lot of experience using a power meter: those who have been paying attention to the watts during training and post-workouts. You must have confidence in the accuracy of your rFTPw value and have a keen knowledge of what technical cues you need to focus on to maintain an excellent EI value at race intensity. If you do not have that confidence, you should train by pace, not watts.

The main purpose of using a power meter is specificity: knowing the exact type of training you need to target, from specific energy systems to improvements in efficiency at those intensities. The specific pacing you can actually execute, the ability to have a clear picture of how efficiently you can run at that pace and of how effective your training is at improving that specific intensity and pace, is the golden feedback from a power meter you've never had before.

TAPER

Once you are about two to three weeks out from your peak event, it is time to consider tapering. The goal of a taper is to shed fatigue while maintaining fitness so you have maximal potential for the best performance you are capable of.

There have been many studies showing that maintaining race-specific intensity while reducing training volume is highly effective at creating great performances. Since we can use a power meter to dial in specific intensity, you can now taper more effectively. If you're seeing your EI improve over the course of intervals and efforts during the taper, you know you're responding well to the taper, and ready to perform well. In Chapter 8 I will discuss how you can dial in your taper to a specific number. Once you know which number works best for you, your confidence in your taper will skyrocket, especially if your training has confirmed that you have effectively prepared for the specifics of what you will need to execute in the race.

Tracking Season Progress

The power meter's measurement of power and pace gives us a clearer indication of how our training is going than we can get with pace alone. Tracking the progress of power and pace through the season provides an even better view of training response, either confirming or rejecting the training decisions you're making.

There have been days in your training, I am sure, where you have gone in expecting a great result and instead finished the workout disappointed or upset with the pace you achieved, not close to what you were targeting. With your power meter, you can see the process of performance, not just the result. You can begin to judge your training and training response in a much more meaningful way.

TAKE INVENTORY

The first step to tracking progress for the season is to take inventory of your fitness at the beginning of the season. This involves nothing more than a few weeks to a month of collecting training data to see what your numbers tell you. Over time, perhaps a season or two, as you use a power meter more and more, you can reduce this data-collection time to just the length of the Preparation phase at the start of General Preparation.

This inventory period also includes testing for rFTPw and rFTPa, and identifying your EI@FT. Tracking the trend of these values as the season progresses can be done in many training software suites, and displayed graphically over time for easy assessment.

These three metrics are most indicative of your performance potential, and should have your attention no matter the distance you're training for. Plan to test for these metrics every four to six weeks, so you can monitor your progress. The longer your race distance, the more important your EI@FT will be.

IDENTIFY THE KEY METRICS

The next step in tracking your progress for the season is to identify the specific durations that pertain to your goal event. For example, our 3:30 marathoner would want to look at the following to see if his training is working:

P120. The peak power output for two hours, which will likely come from longer, aerobic endurance runs. It could also come from tempo-run efforts or whatever training sessions you design over that duration. But an athlete preparing for an effort over two hours should see power, as well as pace, improving for two hours. This should be monitored regularly, and improvement should be seen in the General Preparation and Specific Preparation phases. If General Preparation is going well, you should see gains transfer to your specific goals, even without specific preparation. This is why the General Preparation phase is so important; even though it isn't specific, it still contributes greatly to your race fitness.

EI for long runs. How many watts are you turning into speed during longer efforts? If there is a pace where EI dramatically changes, working at that pace for a better EI might translate to better performance. If your EI in aerobic endurance runs is not good, going faster and harder likely won't produce a better EI in the race.

Training time in Zone 3. In the Specific Preparation phase, are you training according to your goals for the session? With a 3:30 marathon goal, your race intensity efforts should be distributed within Zone 3. If the zones don't match up with the systems and intensities you're trying to target, then you need to either reassess your rFTPw, your goals, or your training paces. If you're continuing to run Zone 3 in your tempo-run efforts and the pace in those tempo runs is improving, you know your training is going very well. If it's getting slower for the same power output, you likely need to reassess your training structure and schedule more recovery.

Overall, once you've identified the goals of your training, whether to address a weakness like sprint power, or intensity or pace for a goal event and goal time, the way to track progress is to identify the key metrics related to it that signify specific preparation. Are those metrics improving? If they are, then you know you're well prepared. If they are not, then there is something that needs to be addressed in training. You may need more rest. You may need to focus more on your training if you haven't been consistent with it.

If I were to train to run a 10K in less than 30 minutes, I would track a duration or interval I identify as important in my training, such as 30-minute peak power and peak pace. You might find something else to identify in between, perhaps some intervals of a certain length that correspond with durations you're doing in training. For example, if I were trying to run 2K repeats on the track, I would identify and track the EI and pace in each of those intervals over the course of weeks, to see whether I am progressing in response to the training.

The key to improvement is to identify the metrics related to your goals in training and track them. If they are improving, you're doing things right. If they are plateauing or regressing, it's time to reassess.

Summary

We can divide the season into two parts, General and Specific Preparation. General is focused on overall abilities, while Specific is designed to mimic the peak race demands.

Most runners need to address the general abilities of aerobic endurance, force, and speed skill before working on race intensities. After the general abilities have a solid foundation, it's time to focus on other abilities like muscular endurance, anaerobic endurance, and sprint power. Once you are within about 14 weeks of your peak A-priority race, your training should begin to shift to race specificity, as long as you have completed good progress on the general and advanced abilities.

Metrics from the power meter, as well as some from pace, can be used to show progress toward training goals. Monitoring these goals can give an athlete or coach a good indication of the effectiveness of their training decisions.

8 Advanced Training for High Performance

In the previous four chapters, you've seen how you can use a power meter to get more insights into your training, pacing, efficiency, weaknesses, and strengths. These are all simple and easy ways to tell whether you're improving or not, and will give you clear guidelines on how to make training decisions that make sense for you. But there is even more you can do with power data—some pretty advanced things, in fact.

If you're new to power technology, this chapter may contain more than you need to know about using a power meter right now. But the higher you set your goals, the more important the concepts in this chapter will become. If you're a beginning runner, or if you want to merely use a power meter to gain insights on your efficiency and monitor a few similar metrics, that's fine, and the concepts in this chapter probably aren't necessary for you. But if you have some serious goals and A-priority events on your calendar, I would encourage you to try the advanced data tracking here.

Once again, I want to stress that runners who want to use power data for more advanced training should first make sure they are efficient, with a fair ability to translate the watts they produce into speed. More on that will come later in the chapter.

Training Stress Concepts

As I've said before, fitness is really just an ability to tolerate stress. The harder you go, or the faster you go, the more stress you put into your body. In fact, training in general is stressful. Intensity is stressful.

Your run fitness is determined by your ability to tolerate a fast pace and high power output, to deal with the stronger and more forceful contractions of the muscles, and to handle the forces the body must absorb as each foot strike hits the ground. If you can't tolerate these stressors, you'll slow down as your body breaks down biomechanically. The longer you can tolerate these movements, the stronger and more fit you are. With running fitness defined as the ability to tolerate stress and breakdown, it's almost as if running is all about punishing yourself. (And some might think running is exactly that!)

Another stress factor in training and racing arises from the duration of the session or event. Compare a 5K you might run with a strong race effort to a similar effort for a marathon. The length of time you spent running in the marathon, even if at a slower pace and lower power, will almost certainly require more recovery time than your 5K effort, barring injury. This is just the nature of running and its weight-bearing demands.

Even a 30-minute run at a nice and easy pace at Zone 1 power (Recovery) will have a very different effect on the body than the same pace maintained for two hours. You might be able to run an easy two hours, but I doubt you would choose to do so the day before your biggest and most important race of the year. You know it would affect your performance greatly. This is why you probably do a light, short jog the day before a major event, maybe with a few surges or accelerations. Nothing major, just enough to stay sharp.

Duration matters in running, perhaps more than in other sports. You could do an easy swim for an hour, or ride your bike with your family for an hour, and you would feel much different afterward compared with a 1-hour easy run. Even though the run might be easy, it taxes the body more than most activities.

Throughout this book, we have shown how we can measure and define intensity much more specifically with power than with other measurement methods. So it makes sense that if we can define and measure intensity, as well

Fitness is really just an ability to tolerate stress.

as track the duration of this intensity, we should be able to define and measure stress in our training. We can, and we call this Training Stress Score, or TSS.

How hard you go and how long you go are the variables of training that affect training stress. We refer to this combination as the workload of a training session. Workload can increase or decrease as intensity and duration rise and fall.

With the advent of the power meter, we have values for both of these components. How hard is measured by your power meter in watts. How long is the simple measure of time we have always used in run training. With these workload values, we can score a workout based on how much stress it brings to our bodies. This is the Training Stress Score. TSS was developed by

Dr. Andrew Coggan for cycling; it's another of his pioneering metrics of training with power. But TSS also applies to running power data.

After you've collected the appropriate data from your power meter, the calculation for TSS is straightforward:

$$\text{TSS} = [(\text{workout duration in seconds} \times NP \times IF) / (rFTPw \times 3{,}600)] \times 100$$

As you can see, the components are all based on intensity or duration. In this equation, 3,600 represents the number of seconds in an hour, to account for the duration aspect of training. You surely noticed that our old intensity friends NP, IF, and rFTPw from Chapter 4 are in the equation as well. Once again, intensity matters.

Let's look at an all-out effort of 1 hour. This is your rFTPw by definition. If you run all-out for an hour, you should have an NP equal to your rFTPw (if not, your rFTPw value is incorrect). Let's say you have a 350w rFTPw, and you do 350w as an NP for 1 hour. Your IF is 1.00. (Remember that IF equals NP/rFTPw.) Let's plug these into the TSS equation. First let's define the variables:

$$\text{Workout duration} = 1 \text{ hour effort} = 3600 \text{ seconds}$$

$$\text{Athlete's } rFTPw = 350$$

$$NP = 350 \text{ for the effort}$$

$$IF = 1.00$$

$$\text{TSS} = [(\text{workout duration in seconds} \times NP \times IF) / (rFTPw \times 3{,}600)] \times 100$$

$$\text{TSS} = [(3{,}600 \times 350 \times 1.00) / (350 \times 3600)] \times 100$$

We can cancel the two 3,600s and 350s on the top and bottom of the fraction, and we get:

$$TSS = (1.00) \times 100$$

$$TSS = 100$$

This gets us to our baseline for TSS. When an athlete does a one-hour all-out effort at functional threshold, the TSS is 100. An athlete can't have a TSS higher than 100 for an hour, as this is the definition of functional threshold. That is, you can't go harder for an hour than the best you can do for an hour.

As you work with TSS, you will see how it helps give you a clearer picture of intensity and the training stress associated with that intensity. To show how TSS is accumulated based upon different efforts and durations, I have broken it down in Table 8.1 according to what would be accumulated in each of the

TABLE 8.1 Approximate TSS per Time in Zones

Zone	TSS per Minute	TSS per Hour
1	‹1.0	‹60
2	1.1–1.4	65–88
3	1.5–1.6	89–95
4	1.6–1.7	96–100
5	1.8–1.9	N/A
6	1.9–2.2	N/A
7	2.2+	N/A

power zones from Chapter 6, per minute and per hour. The TSS you accumulate per minute and per hour, based on the time you spend in different power zones, helps you begin to understand the differences in training stress that the varying intensities of the different power zones create. You probably noticed that Zones 5 through 7 don't have any values of TSS per hour. Again, this is because these zones represent intensities that are above functional threshold, and functional threshold is an all-out one-hour effort. The values above Zone 4 can't have a per-hour TSS because they can't be sustained for an hour.

Now that you understand the basics of TSS and have a sense of what an effort means in terms of a score of training stress on you, let's see how these equate to different race distances. Table 8.2 shows the estimated TSS values for a runner racing different distances and time ranges. (Note that this table was compiled with a 3D power meter; a 2D meter's numbers might vary slightly.)

TABLE 8.2 TSS Range per Race Distance Based on Speed

5K	Sub 15 Min	Sub 18 Min	Sub 20 Min	20+ Min
	~30	32–35	35–38	38+

10K	Sub 30 Min	Sub 35 Min	Sub 45 Min	50+ Min
	~55	60–65	70–80	90+

Half-marathon	1:00–1:10	1:10–1:20	1:30–1:45	2+ hrs
	~100	110–125	140–160	165+

Marathon	Sub 2:20	Sub 2:45	Sub 3:30	4:30+
	190–210	230–250	260–280	270+

Table 8.2 gives you an excellent snapshot of the relative training stress on the body for different events. It can greatly help you gauge how much recovery you might need after a race, relative to a race distance you know well.

For example, if you usually require about three days of recovery from a hard 5K race, you can see in this table that a half-marathon would likely impose more than three times the training stress on the body as the 5K. That's because the body's response to training stress isn't linear, where one TSS point is only one additional unit of stress reaction from the body. The greater the TSS, the greater the need for recovery. This could translate into more than nine days of recovery from a half-marathon effort.

The greater the stress on the body, the more the runner is at risk of injury and physical breakdown. Figure 8.1 shows the exponential relationship of injury risk and TSS.

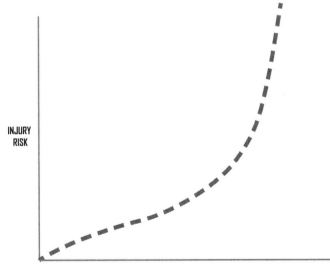

FIGURE 8.1 The risk of injury rises with TSS

How does training duration affect TSS and recovery? If you are training according to zones, much of your specific race training is determined by the speed you can run. Since TSS is a score based on intensity and duration, this means that TSS scores actually rise for slower athletes who will be out on the course for a longer amount of time.

Of course, the winner and the last-place finisher are rarely ever running the same relative intensity. Nevertheless, if you are in the front to middle of the pack, you might be in the same power zone as the leader, or very close to it. But your duration is going to be greater. That means your TSS will be higher.

You might wonder: If slower runners have a higher TSS, do they need more recovery than faster runners? Excellent question. The answer is yes. To return briefly to the concepts in Chapter 5, remember that your ability to translate watts into speed not only helps you to be faster for less work, but it can also help you recover quicker from hard efforts. After all, the faster you are, the less time you spend running hard. A relatively small increase in intensity can lead to a better opportunity for quick recovery. In fact, it is generally true that the fitter you are, the better you can handle training stress, and the quicker you can recover.

For example, let's say that you are racing another runner at nearly the same pace, and you finish within a couple seconds of each other. With most other things being relatively equal, if one of you is running at a higher EI, that person will likely recover more quickly from the effort. The exact amount will depend upon the amount of difference in the EI and the length of the race.

As mentioned briefly above, perhaps the most valuable aspect of Table 8.2 is that the ranges listed will give you an idea of the TSS you are aiming for. As you enter your Specific Preparation phase, you can design workouts around these TSS values to prepare for your A-priority races. For example, the TSS you are likely to record in a 10K if you run faster than 35 minutes is about 60. To better prepare for the event, design your workouts to get close to 60 TSS in the main set. When you are doing intervals, for example, such as 3 × 2 miles or 10 × 1 km, you want to get the total of the hard portions of your workout to equal about 60 TSS. (These values wouldn't include warm-up and cool down, just the main set.)

As you work with TSS, you will find the ranges can guide you in all your training decisions. If you are recording a greater TSS in your training, you're likely going to need more recovery than you wanted from the workout. If your TSS is too low, you are likely not training specifically for the event.

Take the previous example: If you ran 5 × 2 miles and your TSS was 80, you've done too much, and you are probably going to need another day or two of recovery, instead of quickly bouncing back and getting in another quality training session to stimulate more fitness.

On the other hand, if you ran the 3 × 2 miles and only had a 40 TSS, you didn't run hard enough to represent race demands. Although you may recover very quickly, you lost an opportunity to deliver the correct amount of stimulus to maximize your training time.

Let me say though, I don't advise putting in marathon-level TSS scores regularly to try to prepare for a marathon, nor even the same for a half-marathon. But these TSS guidelines give you an idea of how much load a 5K, 10K, or half-marathon workout should carry in its main set, in order to have the specificity to prepare you effectively.

Another thing to keep in mind about Table 8.2 is that while it lists a range of TSS scores for some common time frames for racing these distances, you may not fall exactly into the ranges listed. In fact, since I haven't listed all the possible times, it's likely that you might be between them. But Table 8.2 should give you a good idea of the stress you're training for. You might find yourself under these ranges if your EI is high enough that you can run at lower watts for these speeds and paces. As you compare the values in Table 8.2 with your own scores, you can get a sense of how well your EI stacks up. It should always be your goal to be the fastest you can be to move yourself up into the lowest end of these ranges.

Periodization with Power

Intensity and duration are two of the most important aspects of training. The third and final aspect is frequency. Frequency is simply a measure of how often the training stress is accumulated for an athlete. It doesn't matter if you're just training for fun, trying to win the Boston Marathon, or going for the Olympics in track and field; the only aspects of training are how hard you train, how long you train, and how often you train.

FREQUENCY OF TSS

Volume is probably a term you've heard or used a lot to describe the level of training you're doing. Volume is simply frequency of workouts times the duration of the workouts:

$$\text{Volume} = \text{Frequency} \times \text{Duration}$$

You'll notice that intensity is missing from that equation. This is the reason that volume itself is not a good indicator of training quality, despite its popularity among runners for quantifying training. If you are training by volume, you are chasing the wrong numbers.

Frequency is probably one of the hardest aspects of training to determine properly. There are many different philosophies in the world of distance running, ranging from the high-volume Lydiard model to the opposing models of low volume/high intensity, and everything in between. It's hard to know what your training should look like.

With the advent of TSS, however, we can now see how intensity, duration, and frequency interplay to create your fitness, no matter what training philosophy or model you follow. You can use TSS to figure out what stimulus works best for you, and you can confirm that by monitoring how you respond to it.

So far we have looked at TSS from a single session, where intensity and duration have been defined. Since we were considering a single workout, frequency had a value of one. But let's begin to look at TSS on a more frequent basis.

FITNESS AND CHRONIC TRAINING LOAD (CTL)

If you had a run on Monday of about 30 minutes, and finished with a TSS of about 35, our power zones and TSS charts would indicate this workout fell into a Zone 1 or 2 effort—an easy run. On Tuesday you do a hard workout that gives you a total TSS of 80, and on Wednesday you do another easy 30 minutes for a 35 TSS. You now have a total of 150 TSS for the three days. The average TSS for those three days, then, was 50 TSS per day (TSS/d). Does 50 seem like a hard and taxing TSS average? Well, it depends on the TSS you average regularly in your training.

Remember when we said fitness was just an ability to tolerate stress? This is where we want to see how well you can handle the stress your training is giving you. We want to get some idea of what your fitness is in order to better understand how you can handle this stress value. If we take a longer look at your past TSS scores over time, we will get a good idea of how an average of 50 TSS compares.

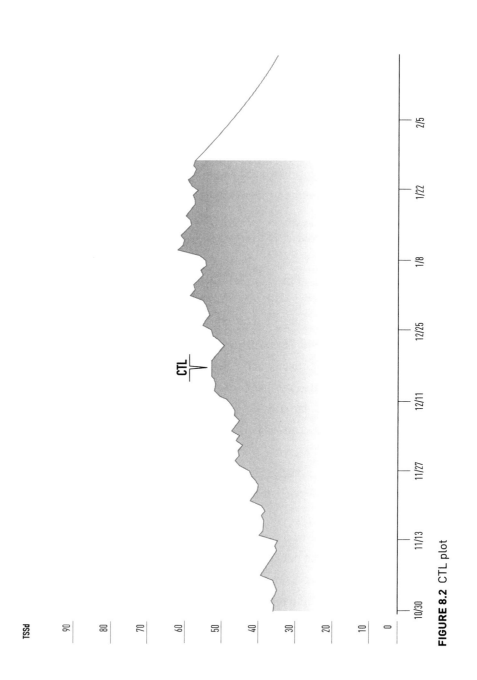

FIGURE 8.2 CTL plot

How far back should we look for data? Excellent question. Six weeks usually gives us a pretty good idea. The previous 42 days usually have the most bearing on current fitness.

When we take a rolling 42-day average of TSS per day, we get a numerical look at the level of stress you are used to handling on a daily basis at your current fitness level. This average value is called the Chronic Training Load, or CTL. We call it this because it represents a long-term training load that you have been able to sustain. CTL takes the TSS from the current day and averages it with the 41 days previous to get a TSS/day value over that entire period. Figure 8.2 shows the plotting of CTL over many weeks. You can see that the CTL value increases over time as the athlete is steady and consistent in his training. This makes sense, as the athlete's ability to tolerate stress increases as his fitness increases. This is why CTL is also commonly referred to or regarded as "fitness." As CTL increases, fitness increases.

FATIGUE AND ACUTE TRAINING LOAD (ATL)

In the example above, when we compared the 50 TSS average over three days to the athlete's long-term TSS average—his CTL—we were actually looking at how the short-term average of stress might challenge the athlete beyond his current fitness level, or his current TSS average per day over the long term. When we compare a short-term average of TSS/day with a long-term average, we get a sense of how fatigued the runner might be if subjected to those short-term changes in TSS averages.

For example, let's say an athlete has a CTL of 60 TSS/day. He then does a seven-day block of training where he averages 120 TSS/day. This average for a seven-day period is double what he was used to for the previous six weeks, and signifies a lot of fatigue. If you're unsure of this claim, I would challenge you over the course of a week to double the amount of training stress you've aver-

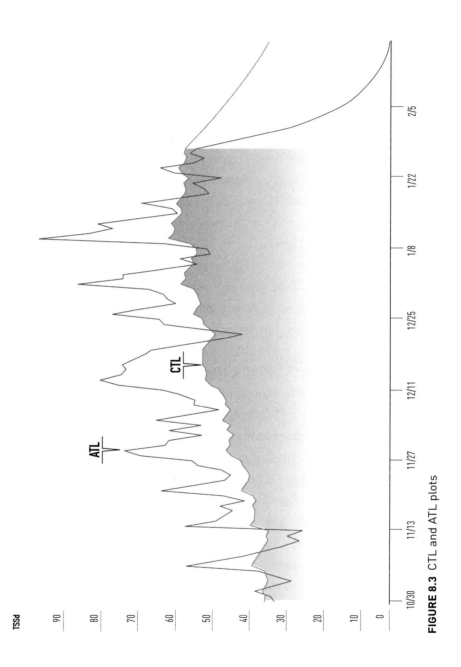

FIGURE 8.3 CTL and ATL plots

aged for the past six weeks, and tell me you don't feel fatigued. I can promise you that if you're doing serious training, it will definitely fatigue you greatly.

When we look at this short-term average, we are looking at an acute amount of training stress. A standard period of acute training stress is seven days. This seven-day average for TSS scores is called the Acute Training Load, or ATL. The ATL value is highly representative of the fatigue level of the athlete. Figure 8.3 shows how this ATL looks when plotted on a graph with the CTL from Figure 8.2. You can see how the large increases in ATL stimulate increases in CTL. Again, you must create fatigue to get fitness, so ATL must increase for CTL to increase. The peaks and valleys of ATL also help signify how training goes in cycles. There are blocks that create fatigue, followed by a period of recovery before the next block.

TRAINING STRESS BALANCE (TSB)

CTL and ATL are averages of TSS per day. One is long term (CTL), while the other is short term (ATL). Since these are both numerical values of the same units of TSS/day, we can compare the two to get a good idea of how the athlete is doing. For example, if our athlete has a CTL of 65 TSS/day, and her ATL is 100 TSS/day, this means she has been subject to an increase of 35 TSS/day, which is more than a 50 percent increase. That's a big jump. If you don't believe me, feel free to add a 50 percent increase to your training and let me know if you'd be ready to step on a start line for a race.

The difference between your CTL and ATL—the difference between your fitness and fatigue—can give us a good idea of how race-ready you are. It can show us whether you are under a training load that's much greater than what you are used to. The example above of 100 for ATL and 65 for CTL, for example, represents a negative training stress balance: –35. Over the previous seven days, that runner was subjected to TSS loads that were well beyond her normal

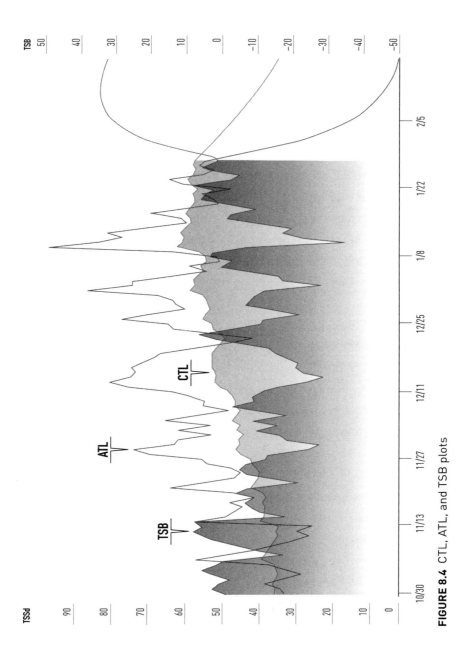

FIGURE 8.4 CTL, ATL, and TSB plots

workload. If, on the other hand, she had recorded the same CTL of 65 TSS/day and had an ATL of 50 TSS/day over the course of seven days, the difference would be +15 in favor of fitness relative to fatigue.

The difference in training stress is called training stress balance, or TSB. When the runner has little fatigue over the short term compared with fitness, there is usually a positive TSB. If the athlete is under a lot of training with heavy workload, TSB is likely to be negative. Figure 8.4 shows how TSB looks when plotted on our graph of CTL and ATL.

Training stress balance is probably best described as an indicator of whether you are rested and race-ready. If your TSB is positive and your fitness is high, you're ready to do well in a race. This may sound like an obvious and not terribly valuable conclusion, but this is where understanding the amount of training load you are subjecting yourself to is important to know. For example, you might be extremely fit and in sub-2:20-marathon fitness. The day after you run that sub-2:20 marathon, though, your fitness is still high—but you are not race-ready at all. You've got too much fatigue to perform at any level. Just walking down stairs the day after a marathon might be tough.

Sometimes you can race well while showing a negative TSB. A C-priority race might not be a problem. You might have a B-priority race where you could show up with a negative TSB, or a slightly positive value. For your A-priority race, though, you will definitely want to have a positive TSB.

Training stress balance helps us better understand the effect of the training decisions we make, and how they can determine performances in the future. More on using TSB for tapering shortly.

Analysis and Performance Management

The combination of CTL, ATL, and TSB gives us a better picture of the load you are under, how you are responding to it, and when you are ready to perform at your best. These metrics help us manage performance on a daily basis. In some cases, they can even predict how you are going to perform. When we combine the three metrics into the same chart or graph, we call it the Performance Management Chart, or PMC. Figure 8.4 is a PMC where you can see how the relationship between the three metrics helps show training response and recovery, and the potential to perform well at a specific date.

You might also notice that beyond the shaded area of the PMC, there are points on the graph for the next 21 days of training. You can see that during this period, the values for CTL and ATL plummet, while TSB rises. That is because there are no values for the dates in the future, which begins at the edge of the shaded area. This is what your PMC would look like if you stopped training entirely for 21 days. We will get into how this 21-day insight into the future can be put to use when we discuss tapering and peaking later in this chapter.

PMC ENHANCEMENTS

If we were to pinpoint the 10 best performances of your season, would you be able to mark them on a calendar? Would you know when you had your top-10 power-output days? Where on the calendar should you mark your top-10 run paces? The answers might surprise you. It's likely that most of your best performances happened during a specific intensive run workout you did with your friends on a regular basis. I have seen many athletes have their best performances in practice or training, and never in a race. To see that trend would be incredibly useful information for identifying a need to change your training routine or approach.

TOP 10S FOR POWER

Knowing the peak power outputs for durations you focus on in your training can enhance your PMC. The trend of the data of top-10 power outputs for 6 minutes would be good to know if the VO_2 zone training time you were focusing on was beginning to pay off with a positive trend. We would refer to this as the top-10 P6 values.

Looking at the trend of the best 30-minute power outputs is also a good data set to watch, because most runners will have a large number of 30-minute samples to examine. There aren't many serious runners who conduct a lot of runs under 30 minutes. The trend of this value, therefore, is probably highly indicative of your fitness and how it evolves.

Figure 8.5 shows the PMC for the runner we used in the previous figures, with the P6 and P30 power outputs for the previous 90 days (again, the 21-day future period is shown as well, without values). You'll notice that the values have jumped considerably in the past four weeks, with 15 of the best 20 total outputs happening in this short stretch. They show a definite positive trend of higher outputs, which is excellent.

TOP 10S FOR PACE

As I mentioned at the outset, the fastest runner wins the race. Top-10 power outputs show the potential to have great performances, but where did the actual best performances in terms of pace fall? Figure 8.6 shows the trend of pace for these values. You can see that the P6 value is on a very clear and strong surge of improvement, while P30 top samples are also improving in the recent times.

You can also see that both the P6 and P30 for pace have a concentration of top performances within the past four weeks. This is the positive trend that the athlete wants to see. If you were doing 1-hour tempo runs at your marathon goal pace and saw your pace improving and your P60 values improving, you would know your training decisions were sound. If you were to find the paces were getting slower, you would probably need to consider more rest and recovery.

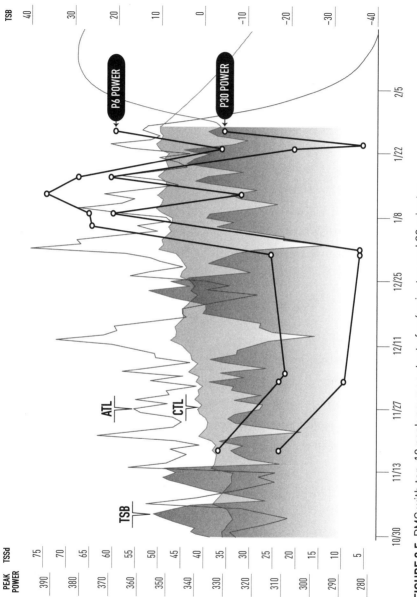

FIGURE 8.5 PMC with top-10 peak power outputs for 6 minutes and 30 minutes

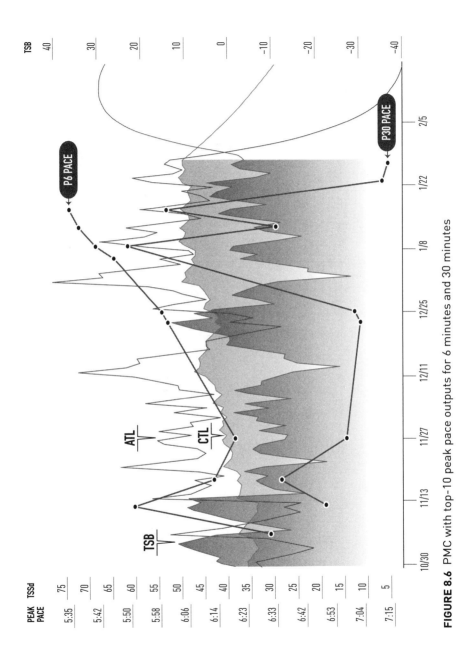

FIGURE 8.6 PMC with top-10 peak pace outputs for 6 minutes and 30 minutes

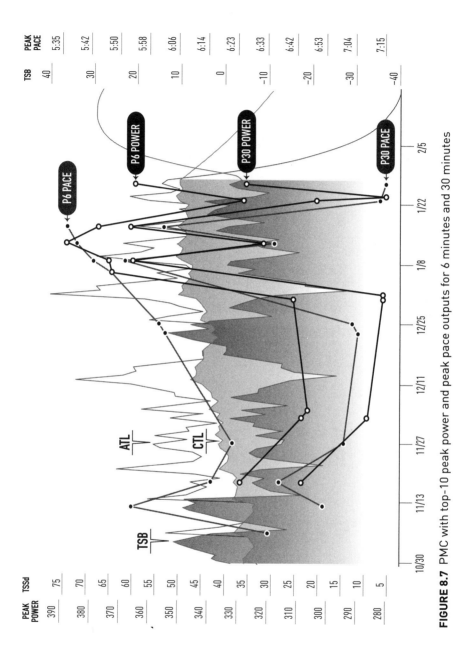

FIGURE 8.7 PMC with top-10 peak power and peak pace outputs for 6 minutes and 30 minutes

Since we have spoken so much about the speed per watt a runner can produce, you may be wondering if the power and pace top-10 values coincide. Let's see how these two P6 and P30 values look when we overlay them on the PMC in Figure 8.7.

In Figure 8.7, nearly every top-10 power output coincides with a top-10 pace output. And as the power values increase, pace values increase as well. This shows a good EI value. That is, the athlete getting a good amount of speed per watt produced.

If you record and review these values regularly, you will probably come across cases where some top-10 power outputs don't correspond with top-10 pace values. Conditions such as headwinds and hills can cause this disconnect. Remember, a power meter is a better measure of intensity than pace precisely because pace is subject to these types of variables in terrain or weather.

TOP 10S FOR EI

If your training analysis software supports it, it is useful to highlight your top-10 runs for a selected length or distance that have a peak EI value. For example, if we wanted to see your EI values for runs of 90 minutes or longer, we could highlight the best 90-minute EI, call it a P90 EI, and see if the trend of this EI value is improving. This would be especially useful to check when you are targeting better EI for those durations, whether in the General or the Specific Preparation Phase. Whatever the focus of your training, look at the related durations and output metrics so you can receive feedback on the training response. If you want to review a recent trend in EI values, as opposed to a longer-term range throughout your General or Specific Preparation periods, you can do so simply by looking at a shorter time range within your PMC.

All peak outputs of pace, power, and EI can also be tracked easily in most analysis software programs, even outside of a PMC. If your software doesn't have this EI option, you might have to do the math yourself. Find the points where your peaks of power and pace overlap and record them for comparison purposes later.

MONITORING FOR BREAKDOWNS

When you look at these PMCs or other charts that record top performances of pace and power, you can begin to see trends in your training load—whether it is too much, not enough, or just right. You can look at the PMC during post-season analysis too, to look for trends in the days prior to when you may have become injured or sick.

Where were your plateaus in performance? Where were the regressions? Why did the regressions happen? Was it due to injury or to overly aggressive training? What were the EIs in the runs prior to this breakdown or plateau? Was there a sudden decrease in EI that could have signaled possible breakdown? What can you see that may have been a signal prior to the plateau or breakdown?

Seeing the load of ATL, or finding a specific negative TSB value you achieved prior to an injury, can tell you with great specificity how much load is too much or too risky. This can be critical information. Athletes and coaches always seek to deliver the right amount of stimulus at the right time in order to achieve the biggest gains in fitness over a specific length of time. As you examine your training response over time, you can design a training program most suited to your strengths, weaknesses, and individual training response.

MONITORING FOR BREAKTHROUGHS

When your top performances for a certain duration skyrocketed in their improvement, what type of training were you doing? What was the training structure and how did it compare with prior weeks and months? What about the training that preceded the surge? Did it help lay the foundation for the big jump in fitness and performance?

Few things can bring you more confidence than seeing your best performances of the year happening in the recent and current time frames. When you can have the data to show how you are doing historically compared with other times, or can easily see a steep positive trend, it is hard not to be excited about your training and feel confident that it is preparing you effectively.

TAPERING AND PEAKING

One of your main training goals is to peak for your A-priority events. You want to maximize the preparation you've done while dialing in your taper right down to a number. The power meter's technology can do that for you.

When you taper for a race, you're usually cutting back on volume (reducing frequency and/or duration) and resting more. You are going to lose some fitness when you taper, because you're no longer stressing your body. Fitness is the ability to tolerate stress, so lower stress means lower fitness. The tradeoff, of course, is that you are betting that the rest will make up for the small loss of fitness.

You can delay the loss of fitness with the right dosage of stress, meaning a dose that is specific to what you're preparing for. To do this, you have to make sure you include intensity. You can maintain a CTL fairly well with workouts that are targeted at a decent TSS score. To do this while reducing duration, you can keep the frequency while maintaining a midlevel amount of intensity. If you cut back on intensity, though, you really lose CTL, which is fitness. Specific intensity is what you want; if you are tapering for a marathon, you don't want to suddenly start doing all-out 400-meter repeats on a track. That would not be the right stress.

How much stress is enough, and how much is not enough? What is a reasonable amount of CTL to lose? The first rule I would suggest is to maintain your training frequency but reduce the duration. Doing so will reduce volume, but allow you to maintain sharpness.

The second rule I would suggest is to lose no more than 10 percent of your CTL, no matter what race distance you are tapering for. This 10 percent

TABLE 8.3 Taper Plan Example		
	TSS	**Workout Notes**
Monday	0	Rest
Tuesday	40	Easy run
Wednesday	80	Race-specific workout
Thursday	40	Easy run
Friday	0	Rest
Saturday	70	Race-specific workout
Sunday	40	Easy run
Monday	0	Rest
Tuesday	30	Easy run
Wednesday	50	Race-specific workout
Thursday	30	Easy run
Friday	0	Rest
Saturday	20	Pre-race workout
Sunday	N/A	Race

guideline covers the period from the start of your taper (which is likely your peak) to race day.

If you plan to use a two-week taper, you can dial in the taper to hit a specific CTL and TSB in the PMC. The PMC in the earlier figures in this chapter displayed a time frame of the past 90 days, plus the next 21 days. That is why the trace lines suddenly drop beyond the shaded area; it represents the future. This 21-day window into the future is for designing your taper, getting it to a number that works for you.

If your training software can display a PMC like this, you can plan the taper by day and by TSS to see where your CTL and TSB values will end up. Table 8.3 provides a basic example of how you could plan a two-week taper by TSS. Plug

PMC can help you better understand training response and dial in the right stimulus at the right time.

these values into your PMC and you will see what your taper plan actually yields numerically in terms of TSB and CTL loss.

So what is a good TSB to achieve? What is an acceptable CTL loss? These are questions that must take race distance into consideration, as well as athlete individuality.

Table 8.4 provides some TSB ranges a runner might look to achieve, depending on the distance and priority of the event. These ranges are guidelines meant as a starting point. If you race well without a taper, you can use these to stay below the guidelines. If you tend to overtrain or not feel sharp for your races, you might need to be above or at least on the higher end of these guidelines.

You probably noticed in Table 8.4 that marathons are not considered B- or C-priority events. Marathons are just too long and taxing to enter in anything less than top fitness. I don't consider a marathon to be anything but an A-priority event. In general, tapering is probably best left for A-priority events as a whole, but I have provided some guidelines for B-priority events in Table 8.4, should you feel a desire to taper slightly for those distances.

You'll likely also notice in Table 8.4 that as the distance of the race increases, the TSB guideline range increases with it. This is because the longer the event, the more your performance will be affected by residual training fatigue. In this case, more rest and recovery is generally needed in the taper.

Once you plan out your taper, you can later go back and review how it went. If you felt it wasn't perfect, you can tweak the numbers to attempt another strategy, or just better dial in the one you have. When you find a successful taper strategy, you can now set it up by numbers, and execute it effectively for each A-priority race. If you feel the taper you have is perfect

TABLE 8.4 Guidelines for CTL Loss and TSB Values for A-, B-, and C-Priority Races

Race Type	A-Priority		B-Priority		C-Priority	
	CTL Loss	TSB	CTL Loss	TSB	CTL Loss	TSB
5K	<5%	5–10	0%	(–20)	N/A	(–30)
10K	<5%	10–15	<2%	(–15)–(–5)	N/A	(–20)
Half-marathon	<7%	15–20	<5%	(–5)–0	N/A	(–10)
Marathon	<10%	20–25	N/A	N/A	N/A	N/A

for you, you can have a lot of confidence that you have executed it perfectly each time you step on the start line.

Lastly, although this book is about power meters for running, I want to mention that everything in this chapter based on rFTPw and power data for TSS can also be calculated with rFTPa and pace data. If you're not sure you want to use a PMC based on TSS scores from power data, you can instead use pace data. Which one is better or more effective? The technology is still so new that I don't have that answer for you, and I think a lot of it might be personal preference. But the great thing about this technology is that you now have a lot of options and information to do what works best for you to perform well at your biggest races.

Summary

Fitness is an ability to tolerate stress. Now that we can mathematically define intensity and duration, we can use the two metrics to define training stress to a number. We call this number Training Stress Score, or TSS.

TSS tracking allows us to understand the runner's fitness and fatigue levels to create the Performance Management Chart, or PMC. Using the PMC, we can track trends of recent performances and highlight peak outputs. We can also use the PMC to better understand training response, and dial in the right stimulus at the right time, to perfect your training approach.

The PMC can also help you dial in the perfect taper based upon the race distance you are focused on.

9 Power for Racing

To this point, everything we have discussed has been about training. We've talked about the general concepts and the specifics of training, outlined the important metrics you should track and gather during workouts, and looked at how to use that data to discover your tendencies and needs in order to create a better training plan. Now let's talk about racing.

I have always believed that there are six keys to performance on race day. The first three are preparation, preparation, and preparation. You can show up on race day with a great attitude and a perfect race plan, but preparation for your key events is what makes the difference, especially as you set your goals ever higher. As we'll see a little further on, you must prepare physically, prepare mentally, and prepare technically.

The last three keys to performance are execution, execution, and execution. To meet your expectations for your race, you need to execute physically, execute mentally, and execute technically. Your training is worth little if you don't show up to the starting line with the determination to execute a great performance. Run the first mile of a 5K race a lot faster than goal pace, and you've likely sacrificed your chance at a great performance. Get overly excited in the first 10 miles of a marathon, and you might be walking the last few miles. Ignore your nutrition needs in a long race, and you might not be able to finish.

In short, you can't train randomly and hope on race day that things will somehow come together for you to run perfectly. Hope is not a strategy for high performance.

Since 50 percent of my beliefs about performance deal with race day, I am definitely guilty of not devoting 50 percent of this book to race day itself. In my defense, though, I also believe that race-day execution is learned through the preparation phases, especially in Specific Preparation (see Chapter 7). If you commit to the lessons and experiences of your training, and are confident in your preparation, you will likely be able to handle the execution on race day. And as you get more experience in using your power meter in both racing and

Race-day execution is as much about confidence as it is about skill.

training, you will get better at your race execution. Execution is as much about confidence as it is about skill. Pay attention to the data in your training and you will be confident on race day, able to execute a plan you believe in.

There is much to learn initially about yourself and your power numbers as you begin racing with power, and your best opportunity to learn and be prepared is to gather data with your power meter to assess your strengths, weaknesses, and tendencies. So just as you did when you started to use your power meter in training, you should collect your race data but not react to it during your first races with your power meter. Trying to create a strategy based entirely on power data during a race when you don't yet know how your race efforts equate with your power output and the courses you compete on will likely cause a series of mistakes and setbacks. So use your power meter for every race, but don't react to your power numbers until you have been able to study a handful of race downloads to identify trends, needs, and goals.

Now, let's talk about racing and race day.

Race Preparation

At the beginning of this chapter I spoke about the importance of preparation when it comes to race day. Every workout you do to build toward your key events must embrace three specific goals: a physical goal, a mental goal, and a technical goal. These preparation goals may overlap, but you should make all three a part of every session you do. If you are to race well, you must train with purpose.

Of course, you can't just decide on race day to apply these skills to your racing. You need time to learn these skills, and that's why pursuing these three goals in your daily training is so important. I believe that 80 percent of your race preparation and execution is set before race day even arrives. The last 20 percent has to come under the pressure of a race and its unpredictable situations, where you prove that you can execute what you have practiced. Handling race atmosphere comes with experience. Luckily, your power meter can help you in your preparation, as well as enhance your learning from your races.

PHYSICAL GOALS

Each training workout commonly has a specific physical goal. The workouts you undertake are intended to support the physical training response you'll use on race day. Your physical goal for a workout might be a general skills or abilities session, or it might be some kind of specific preparation. On other days, your physical goal will be a rest day, scheduled to permit recovery from the previous stimulus so you can be well rested to achieve the maximum training response for the next session.

When you set a physical goal, you understand that the workout you're undertaking has a physical purpose to get your body to adapt to a certain training stress. That is why you're choosing to do that workout in one specific way. Your power meter will help you verify that your workouts target the specific zones related to your race.

MENTAL GOALS

A mental goal for a workout is sometimes less common, and it's often overlooked by athletes. A mental goal deals with factors of mental approach and skill that the athlete has recognized and needs to improve. It can be a need to focus on certain skills late in a hard run effort (in which case it overlaps as a technical goal as well), or building confidence throughout a workout, thinking positively instead of negatively. It could be pacing skill, working on patience and holding back early in a workout. It may involve visualizing what the race will be like, perhaps even conducting workouts on the race course to learn what to expect. A mental goal could include practicing strategies for different parts of the course.

I have even seen athletes do workouts entirely by feel, never looking at a watch or head unit. Later, in the post-workout analysis, they can see how their perceptions matched or missed the goals of the workout. This is an excellent method for enhancing your mental approach and building confidence in your ability to read and understand the right intensities for your goal events. Too often, athletes get caught up in looking at a watch during a workout or race, worried they are going too hard or too fast, not confident they can hold it even if their perceived exertion tells them they can. This dependency on an external system can be crippling. If you have done everything right in your training, when race day comes you should be able to ask more of your body and fitness than you ever have before. Holding yourself to numbers can restrict this opportunity. Having a strong mental sense of perceived exertion and confidence in your plan is key to strong race performances.

I have seen many successful athletes focus on giving themselves positive talk and affirmations when running. The ability to be positive with yourself is a skill that must be honed. Your power meter can be part of this process: Seeing your fitness improve in your daily data review will help you gain confidence.

TECHNICAL GOALS

The third goal is to improve technical skills. This is where your power meter is an invaluable tool, allowing you to measure and see the benefits from any technical change you make. If you run with a slow cadence, for example, you may know that you need to work on bringing your cadence up, but how do you know if a quicker cadence is actually helping you? Your power meter will reveal an increase in EI, or an increase in watts and pace, delivering value far beyond what a watch can show you.

RACE NUTRITION

If you're racing less than two hours, chances are you need few to no calories during your race. But in-race nutrition is a technical skill that will come into play in a longer event like a marathon. This isn't a book on race nutrition, and in any case I don't have your personal data to help you figure out your nutritional plan. However, your power meter data can help you see where the nutritional strategies you test in training are or aren't working. For example, it is not uncommon to see a breakdown in technique over the course of efforts of two hours or more. You may see increased power output but no gain in speed, or you may see a decrease in both power and speed. Race-day nutrition could help prevent these breakdowns. The art of race nutrition is a technical skill you must learn and perfect based on your own individual needs, tastes, strengths, and weaknesses. Be sure to record and analyze your pre-workout

Set some basic targets to hit before and during the race.

and in-workout nutrition (write it down in your training log), and then square it up with your power meter data to help you figure out where your nutritional strategies are strong and where they might be lacking.

One word of warning though: No nutritional strategy can make up for poor pacing. Otherwise, whoever ate the most would win. You can't suddenly run a zone higher than you've trained just because you've decided to increase the number of calories you take in during a long race. Test your nutritional strategies and logistics during training, and see how the data supports or doesn't support it.

Power Data for Racing

I mentioned in Chapter 7 that using your power meter to control your training is an advanced skill that requires knowledge and experience. Using a power meter for your racing is no different. In fact, it's probably even more advanced, because your racing experiences will be much more limited than your training experiences. If you plan to execute a strategy based on the power meter, you need to make sure your plan is fully in line with your capabilities and potential. This is not easy to do, especially in your early days or even months of using your power meter.

Whether or not you plan to design a strategy around your power meter, I think it is important in your pre-race planning to set some basic targets to hit before and during the race. These metrics would include

- The CTL you plan to have the day before race day (compare this with your peak CTL at the start of your taper);
- The TSB you will have on race day;
- The TSS you expect to have for this race;
- The IF you expect to have for this race;
- Your expected EI for this race;
- Your expected VI for this race;
- The power zones you will hit for most of the race, broken into percentages; and
- Your anticipated peak power output for durations of 12 seconds and less.

Once the race is over, you can assess how well you hit the targets. If you exceeded them, what does this tell you about your planning, preparation, and expectations? What if you fell short? What do the numbers say about your execution on race day? This is key information to take away from a race.

EI

The training you do at race intensity should give you a good idea of the EI you can expect to hold at your race efforts and paces. If you find your EI improves in your 5K efforts (or other race distances), you can be confident your training is giving you the results you've been seeking.

If you can monitor your predetermined EI during the race (especially on a rolling 30-second average) and stay at or above it, you will know you're executing the race fairly well. This is especially true if you are knocking out your goal paces at a higher EI than expected—that is to say, you find you are holding your speed with fewer watts than you produced in training at that pace. This may sound like a dream race, but in fact recording better efficiency during a race is not unusual; it generally results from a combination of a great taper and great technical execution during the race.

Post-race, compare your total actual EI with your total predicted EI. That will give you an idea of how well your training lined up with your race performance.

Comparing your EI@FT with your total race EI can also give you an idea of how efficient you are at efforts above or below your functional thresholds. You can also begin to track the trend of this comparison to the fitness gains in your training. The EI values at different intensities can help you find your own personal efficiency curve at different paces.

SOFTWARE TOOLS

Software programs have been and will continue to be developed to help analyze training and to plan pacing at specific races based on the course profile, wind, and climate conditions; you can find a list of these and other training analysis programs in Appendix B. As of the time of this book's publication, the race-pace planning software does not yet incorporate power outputs for running, since power meter technology is so new. Precise outputs would also be greatly dependent on each runner's EI. But the pacing software does use paces matched to the variables of the courses and conditions, which can help you dial in your training.

There are additional applications and EI recording and analysis software available for your head unit. These and many other applications will continue to be developed; current ones are listed in Appendix B.

Post-Race Analysis

Whether you have a great race or an awful race, you can always learn something when you review data after the event. If it was a great race, you have a clear picture of how a successful performance looks in a power file. It can serve as a model for the specificity in your training and can guide your future training decisions with a plan for what to do next time, or do even better.

If you had an awful race, there is also a lot you can learn to make sure your next race has a different result. It can be hard to review a performance that was well below expectations, but studying the contributing factors for such a performance can help you avoid them next time.

My advice is to look at the following key metrics in your post-race analysis:

- NP
- IF
- VI
- TSS
- EI
- CTL the day before race day
- TSB on race day
- Your w/kg during the race
- Power zone distributions
- Point in the race where your power and/or pace dropped off.

To help illustrate the important metrics I look at when analyzing race files, we will use a power file from a half-marathon. Figures 9.1a, 9.1b, and 9.1c show the details of a half-marathon race for a runner using a 3D power meter. Note

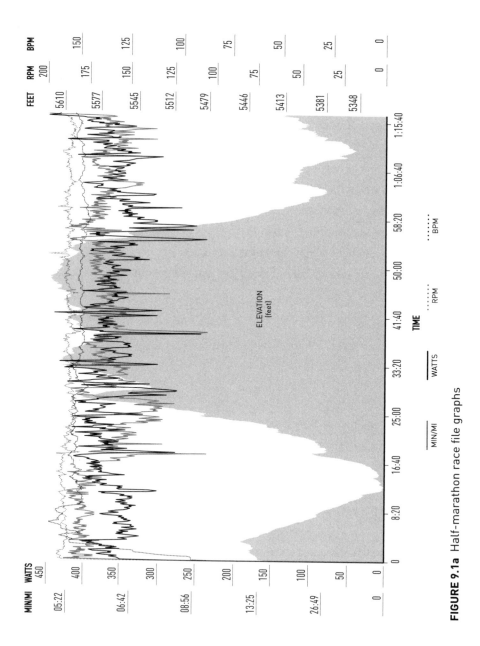

FIGURE 9.1a Half-marathon race file graphs

that the file says the race length was 12.8 miles; I am not sure how accurate the course or the GPS was, but the race was listed as a half-marathon! Anyway, this athlete ran 1:16:59 for the distance.

You'll notice the course was not flat; in fact, it started at 5,400 feet (about 1,650 meters). The course climbed to just over 5,600 feet, and dropped at its lowest point to 5,300 feet. The athlete saw power increase on the climbs, even though his pace decreased. The opposite happened on the descents. Minimum power during the race was 224w, while the maximum was 462w, which occurred in the sprint to the finish.

NP

The athlete's Normalized Power for the event was 362w, which is only 2w higher than the average power for the whole race.

Duration	Distance	TSS
1:16:59	12.8 mi	120.8

Work	1662 kJ	IF	0.97
NP	362 W	VI	1.01
		El. Gain	541 ft
		El. Loss	551 ft
		w/kg	5.15

	MIN	AVG	MAX	
Power	0	360	462	w
Heart Rate	84	149	166	bpm
Cadence	0	188	207	rpm
Pace	00:00	06:00	04:50	min/mi

FIGURE 9.1b Half-marathon race file data

IF

Intensity Factor is the quotient of NP and rFTPw. The rFTPw for this athlete was 372w, so the IF for this race effort was 0.97. This makes sense, because this race was about 17 minutes longer than an hour. The runner's effort was close to a Zone 4 threshold effort (362 watts falls in the lower end of his Zone 4 range with his rFTPw of 372), and he did an excellent job of running very close to threshold for the effort.

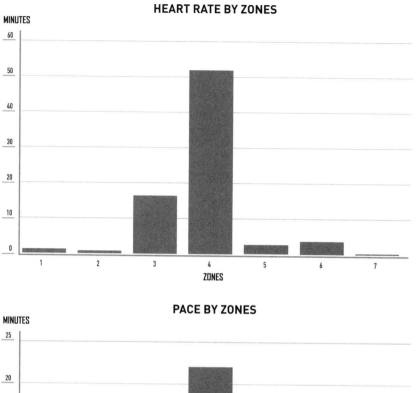

HEART RATE BY ZONES

MINUTES

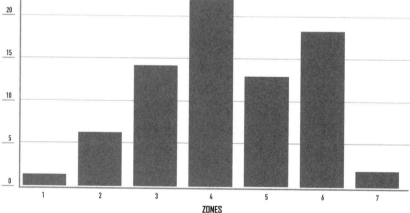

PACE BY ZONES

MINUTES

FIGURE 9.1c Half-marathon race file distributions

POWER BY ZONES

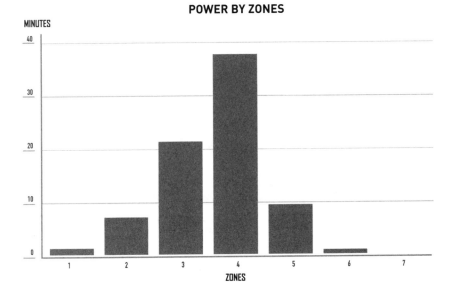

POWER DISTRIBUTION CHART

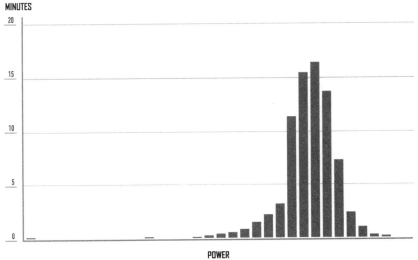

FIGURE 9.1c Continued

VI

Remember that VI compares average power with Normalized Power to give us an idea of how surges or harder efforts compared with the other efforts. The runner recorded a VI of 1.01, which shows the race was quite well paced, in terms of variance of the outputs.

TSS

The runner recorded a TSS of 120.8, which falls into the 110 to 125 TSS range listed in Table 8.2 for this distance. If the race had traveled the full half-marathon distance, he still would likely have finished within this range, but closer to the higher end.

EI

His pace was 6:00 per mile, which translates to 268.22 m/min. To get EI, we divide the m/min by the average watts of 360. This yields an EI of 0.75. How good is this value? Well, his EI@FT value is 0.77, so this race performance is below it. Shouldn't his race EI be better than EI@FT, since the race effort is below rFTPW and rFTPa? Potentially, yes, but the course considerations, the elevation, and individuality of the athlete may have affected the effort and EI.

Either way, the 0.75 EI value for workouts in Zone 4 is quite useful for judging future training and race performances. Also in terms of planning, the more you track your race EI values over different race distances, the better picture you will assemble of your personal EI curve at different paces and power outputs.

CTL AND TSB

What was this athlete's CTL the day before the race? How does it compare with CTL at the start of the taper? He treated this race like a glorified training run,

with no loss of CTL coming into the event. So there was no taper, and TSB was
–0.5. All races are based on goals, and using this as a training run means the
numbers from it could almost certainly be even better with more TSB. The CTL
loss and TSB guidelines listed in Table 8.4 show that the runner approached
this race as a B-priority goal.

W/KG

How do we interpret the recorded w/kg value of 5.15? By itself, this value
may not mean much, but keeping track over time of how mass affects performance can be a great tool. You might find that a certain w/kg yields a better
EI at race intensity. That analysis can help with your diet planning and weight
management.

POWER DISTRIBUTIONS

Which power zones are most represented in the race data? Looking at those
will help you identify the specific training needs and demands of the race.
In Figure 9.1c, we can see the athlete spent about 50 percent of the race in
Zone 4, right around threshold. This was clearly the most represented zone
for the samples.

The next most represented zone was Zone 3, the Tempo zone. This represented about 27 percent of the samples. Given the downhill portions of the
course, it makes sense that the efforts below Zone 4 would be fairly high.

The third most represented zone was Zone 5, High-Intensity, at about
12 percent of the samples. You might expect an athlete of this speed to run
a half-marathon largely in Zone 4 (Threshold), but this racecourse clearly
demanded efforts above threshold. When you anticipate a similar situation in
your pre-event planning, be sure to address it in your race-specific training by
planning and monitoring your efforts above threshold.

In total, Zones 3, 4, and 5 represented close to 90 percent of the race. If your race-specific workouts meet this distribution, you're training quite specifically.

If you look at Figure 9.1c, in the power distribution chart you can see the samples form a pretty good bell curve. This spread of power is usually indicative of a well-paced effort, as most of the samples for the race are concentrated heavily in a narrow range. The athlete was able to stay in that small range for most of the race, signifying good pacing.

WHERE DID POWER AND PACE DROP OFF?

This file has no big drops in power, nor in pace, which represents a good performance. If drops were present, they might point to pacing errors, which could be revealed by comparing the early EI with the later EI, as well as by examining IF and VI values. A coach or athlete could also use the point where the pace and/or power dropped off to better understand where training for the event fell short. It would identify an intensity duration that the athlete needs to address in training. Perhaps the runner lacks the aerobic endurance or muscular endurance to sustain the effort. Perhaps the athlete's tempo runs weren't long enough to support his goals. And of course, if the runner comes into the race with a very low or negative TSB, it is possible he is simply carrying too much fatigue to perform to his potential.

Summary

Performance on race day is all about preparation and execution. Your training needs to address the specifics of physical preparation, mental preparation, and technical preparation, ideally on a daily basis. This is training with purpose.

In the days before the race, make it a practice to predict the values of the key metrics for the race. This exercise will solidify your knowledge of your perceived exertion and abilities. Post-race analysis should include a review of all key metrics, starting from the initiation of the race taper to the EI for the race itself.

Post-race analysis can help you learn what race specificity looks like so that you can plan your training during your specific preparation period. Make it a point to review each race performance, comparing your race data with your race-specific workouts. Doing so will give you a huge advantage in identifying the specific demands of the events you're preparing for, and judging the effectiveness of your training.

POWER-BASED SPECIFIC PHASE TRAINING PLANS

In Chapter 7, I laid out how to break the season into General and Specific preparation. Because General Preparation is dependent on individual needs, I have written these plans to focus on the 14 weeks of your Specific Preparation phase. They are designed to prepare you for your A-priority race. The training plans, in order, are as follows:

- Sub-16-minutes 5K plan
- Sub-18-minutes 5K plan
- Sub-32-minutes 10K plan
- Sub-40-minutes 10K plan
- Sub-1:20 half-marathon plan
- Sub-1:40 half-marathon plan
- Sub-2:30 marathon plan
- Sub-3:30 marathon plan

Context is important when using power-based training because runners have different needs, EI values, strengths, and weaknesses. If you choose to use one of these plans, feel free to make changes as necessary, but maintain the balance of stress and recovery. Don't shove many tough days together.

Make sure the first week of training is not a big jump in intensity (TSS) or volume from your General Preparation. If it is, either cut it back or try to plan ahead in your General Preparation to be ready when the second phase arrives.

To take full advantage of the power meter's ability to record intensity, most plans are based on time in zones. Some intervals, however, are prescribed as a distance to help define the stress for a specific race distance and time.

In each plan, the first week includes conducting the rFTPw and rFTPa tests discussed in Chapter 4. Once you have your rFTPw value, set your zones according to Chapter 6. Continuously monitor your watts at race pace, your paces at race intensity, and your EI value for race-specific efforts.

Each page in the plans covers one week of training, with supplementary notes where necessary. In addition, please note the following throughout the plans:

Second run of the day. On days that call for two runs, the first run should be done in the morning and the second in the afternoon or evening. The second run should be an easy jog in Zones 1–2. Don't overdo it.

Envelope run. This run is all about pushing the envelope of pace for a given level of watts. The goal is to go faster without increasing your wattage output, which means focusing on efficiency. Use this run to find the technical cues that will reduce watts, increase speed, and improve EI. Think smooth, think rhythm, think body position, putting all your energy into moving forward and eliminating extraneous movement.

Goal-pace tempo run. For this run (half-marathon and marathon plans only), see Chapter 6 for details on the zone breakdowns. Your goal pace should fall into the zone that corresponds with your goal speed over the distance. If you find you are spending a majority of your time in Zones 5 and 6, then you need to reassess your goal pace or your rFTPw. You also need to focus on improving your EI.

WEEK 1 Sub-16-Min 5K Plan, 14 Weeks Specific Phase

MON Time: 1:10	**3/9-min Stryd test:** Warm up 15 min, preparing for hard effort at the end; conduct a 3-min interval at maximal effort; recover with 5-min walk, 10 min easy jog, 5 min walk, 5 min easy jog, 5 min walk (30 min total); conduct a 9-min interval at maximal effort; cool down 10–15 min easy. *Follow the protocol for this test and estimating rFTPw and rFTPa per Chapter 4.*
TUES Time: 0:40	**Easy run/walk:** Zone 1–2 power run. Run 40 min as 4 min run at Zone 2, 1 min walk at Zone 1. Repeat for the duration of the run.
WED Time: 0:40	**Easy run/walk:** Zone 1–2 power run. Run 40 min as 4 min run at Zone 2, 1 min walk at Zone 1. Repeat for the duration of the run.
THURS Time: 1:00	**30-min test:** Warm up 15 min, preparing for a hard effort at the end. Start a 30-min time trial (best effort) on a flat road or track collecting power data (pace and HR data as well if possible). Cool down 10–15 min easy.
FRI Time: 0:40	**Easy run/walk:** Zone 1–2 power run. Run 40 min as 4 min run at Zone 2, 1 min walk at Zone 1. Repeat for the duration of the run.
SAT Time: 0:00	**Day off:** Actively focus on recovery today: (1) stay off legs all you can; (2) watch nutrition closely (healthy carbs, lean protein, good fats); (3) stretch; (4) drink when thirsty. Other common recovery aids include massage, napping, elevating legs, and compression wear.
SUN Time: 1:00 Time: 0:30	**Easy run/walk:** Zone 1–2 power run. Run 40 min as 4 min run at Zone 2, 1 min walk at Zone 1. Repeat for the duration of the run. **2nd run of the day:** Easy Zone 1–2 jog.

Total time: 6:10

WEEK 2 Sub-16-Min 5K Plan, 14 Weeks Specific Phase

MON Time: 0:40	**Easy run/walk:** Zone 1–2 power run. Run 40 min as 4 min run at Zone 2, 1 min walk at Zone 1. Repeat for the duration of the run.
TUES Time: 0:40 Time: 0:30	**Easy run/walk:** Zone 1–2 power run. Run 40 min as 4 min run at Zone 2, 1 min walk at Zone 1. Repeat for the duration of the run. **2nd run of the day:** Easy Zone 1–2 jog
WED Time: 1:00	**Cruise intervals:** Warm up 15 min, building intensity through the warm-up, starting at Zone 1, then the last min at zones 4–5. Then do 3 × 8 min, build to Zone 5–6 (3 min recoveries). Monitor pace, trying to be faster for the same power output. Cool down to make 1 hour at Zone 1–2.
THURS Time: 0:40	**Easy run/walk:** Easy Zone 1–2 power run. Run 40 min as 4 min run at Zone 2, 1 min walk at Zone 1. Repeat for the duration of the run.
FRI Time: 1:00	**Envelope run:** Start easy in Zone 1–2 for the first 10–15 min, then work to a moderate pace on the edge of comfort/discomfort. Look at the power zone you are in, likely Zone 3–4. Stay in that zone, but find a way to go faster. Push that envelope, trying to be quicker without raising your watts. It's a balance of trying to hold or increase speed with technique. Focus on your rhythm, cadence, forward lean, soft foot strike, relaxation, eyes and head position. Last 10 min should be easy Zone 1–2 running.
SAT Time: 1:00	**Cruise intervals:** Warm-up 15 min, building intensity through the warm-up, starting at Zone 1, then the last min at zones 4–5. Then do 3 × 8 min. Build to Zone 5–6 (3-min recoveries). Monitor pace, trying to be faster for the same power output. Cool down about 15 min. Zone 1–2.
SUN Time: 1:00 Time: 0:30	**Easy run/walk:** Zone 1–2 power run. Do this as 5 min run at Zone 2, 1 min walk at Zone 1. Repeat for the duration of the run. **2nd run of the day:** Easy Zone 1–2 jog

Total time: 7:00

WEEK 3 Sub-16-Min 5K Plan, 14 Weeks Specific Phase	
MON Time: 0:40	**Easy run/walk:** Zone 1–2 power run. Run 40 min as 4 min run at Zone 2, 1 min walk at Zone 1. Repeat for the duration of the run.
TUES Time: 1:00	**VO₂ intervals:** Warm up well for about 15 min, building from Zone 1–2 to Zone 3–5. Then do 5 × 3 min at your 5K goal pace. Take note of the power zone you are in at that pace. Try to be more efficient, to get more speed per watt while running. Take a 3-min recovery interval as 1 min walk at Zone 1, 2 min easy jog at Zone 2. Afterward do a 15-min easy Zone 1–2 power cooldown. *You may do this as 5 × 1K on the track if you prefer.*
WED Time: 1:00	**Envelope run:** Start easy in Zone 1–2 for the first 10–15 min, then work to a moderate pace on the edge of comfort/discomfort. Look at the power zone you are in, likely Zone 3–4. Stay in that zone, but find a way to go faster. Push that envelope, trying to be quicker without raising your watts. It's a balance of trying to hold or increase speed with technique. Focus on your rhythm, cadence, forward lean, soft foot strike, relaxation, eyes and head position. Last 10 min should be easy Zone 1–2 running.
Time: 0:30	**2nd run of the day:** Easy Zone 1–2 jog
THURS Time: 0:40	**Easy run/walk:** Zone 1–2 power run. Run 40 min as 4 min run at Zone 2, 1 min walk at Zone 1. Repeat for the duration of the run.
FRI Time: 1:10	**VO₂ intervals:** Warm up well for about 15 min, building from Zone 1–2 to Zone 3–5. Then do 6 × 3 min at your 5K goal pace. Take note of the power zone you are in at that pace. Try to be more efficient, to get more speed per watt while running. Take a 3-min recovery interval as 1 min walk at Zone 1, 2 min easy jog at Zone 2. Afterward do a 15-min easy Zone 1–2 power cooldown. *You may do this as 6 × 1K on the track if you prefer.*
Time: 0:30	**2nd run of the day:** Easy Zone 1–2 jog
SAT Time: 1:20	**Easy run/walk:** Easy Zone 1–2 power run. Do this as 7 min run at Zone 2, 1 min walk at Zone 1. Repeat for the duration of the run.
SUN Time: 0	**Day off:** Actively focus on recovery today: (1) stay off legs all you can; (2) watch nutrition closely (healthy carbs, lean protein, good fats); (3) stretch; (4) drink when thirsty. Other common recovery aids include massage, napping, elevating legs, and compression wear.

Total time: 6:50

WEEK 4 Sub-16-Min 5K Plan, 14 Weeks Specific Phase

MON Time: 0:40	**Easy run/walk:** Zone 1–2 power run. Run 40 min as 4 min run at Zone 2, 1 min walk at Zone 1. Repeat for the duration of the run.
TUES Time: 1:10	**3/9-min Stryd test:** Warm up 15 min, preparing for hard effort at the end; conduct a 3-min interval at maximal effort; recover with 5-min walk, 10 min easy jog, 5 min walk, 5 min easy jog, 5 min walk (30 min total); conduct a 9-min interval at maximal effort; cool down 10–15 min easy. *Follow the protocol for this test and estimating rFTPw and rFTPa per Chapter 4.*
WED Time: 0:40	**Easy run/walk:** Zone 1–2 power run. Run 40 min as 4 min run at Zone 2, 1 min walk at Zone 1. Repeat for the duration of the run.
THURS Time: 0:40	**Easy run/walk:** Zone 1–2 power run. Run 40 min as 4 min run at Zone 2, 1 min walk at Zone 1. Repeat for the duration of the run.
FRI Time: 1:00	**30-min test:** Warm up 15 min, preparing for a hard effort at the end. Start a 30-min time trial (best effort) on a flat road or track, collecting power data (pace and HR data as well if possible). Cool down 10–15 min easy. *Follow the protocol for this test and estimating rFTPw and rFTPa in Chapter 4. Now you should begin to see a good relationship between the 3/9 test and the 30-min test. To avoid the 30-min test for the rest of the plan, focus on using the 3 min.*
Time: 0:30	**2nd run of the day:** Easy Zone 1–2 jog
SAT Time: 0	**Day off:** Actively focus on recovery today: (1) stay off legs all you can; (2) watch nutrition closely (healthy carbs, lean protein, good fats); (3) stretch; (4) drink when thirsty. Other common recovery aids include massage, napping, elevating legs, floating in water, and compression wear.
SUN Time: 1:00	**Envelope run:** Start easy in Zone 1–2 for the first 10–15 min, then work to a moderate pace on the edge of comfort/discomfort. Look at the power zone you are in, likely Zone 3–4. Stay in that zone, but find a way to go faster. Push that envelope, trying to be quicker without raising your watts. It's a balance of trying to hold or increase speed with technique. Focus on your rhythm, cadence, forward lean, soft foot strike, relaxation, eyes and head position. Last 10 min should be easy Zone 1–2 running.
Time: 0:30	**2nd run of the day:** Easy Zone 1–2 jog

Total time: 6:10

WEEK 5 Sub-16-Min 5K Plan, 14 Weeks Specific Phase

MON Time: 0:40	**Easy run/walk:** Easy Zone 1–2 power run. Run 40 min as 6 min run at Zone 2, 1 min walk at Zone 1. Repeat for the duration of the run. *This 7-min sequence won't divide evenly into 40, so you will finish on a run. Walk a few minutes after.*
TUES Time: 1:00	**Fartlek:** Run of surges. Warm up well for about 15 min, building from Zone 1–2 to Zone 3–5. On rolling course, run 1–2-min pickups at faster than 5K pace (Zone 6–7), with recoveries at Zone 1–2 as long as you feel you need between the surges. Form! Cadence! Use the last 10 min to cool down with easy Zone 1 running/walking.
WED Time: 1:00	**Envelope run:** Start easy in Zone 1–2 for the first 10–15 min, then work to a moderate pace on the edge of comfort/discomfort. Look at the power zone you are in, likely Zone 3–4. Stay in that zone, but find a way to go faster. Push that envelope, trying to be quicker without raising your watts. It's a balance of trying to hold or increase speed with technique. Focus on your rhythm, cadence, forward lean, soft foot strike, relaxation, eyes and head position. Last 10 min should be easy Zone 1–2 running.
Time: 0:30	**2nd run of the day:** Easy Zone 1–2 jog
THURS Time: 0:40	**Easy run/walk:** Zone 1–2 power run. Run 40 min as 6 min run at Zone 2, 1 min walk at Zone 1. Repeat for the duration of the run. *This 7-min sequence won't divide evenly into 40, so you will finish on a run. Walk a few minutes after.*
FRI Time: 1:00	**12 × 400:** Warm up well for about 15 min, building from Zone 1–2 to Zone 3–5. Then, on track, run 12 × 400 at 5K goal pace, with 1 min recovery between. Monitor the power zone in which you run these. They should be in Zone 6, some Zone 7. You might see more Zone 7 later in the workout as you begin to break down. If you are in Zone 7 the whole time, review how realistic your goal pace is or whether your rFTPw is too low. Cool down for 15 min, easy Zone 1–2 jogging and walking. *If you don't have a track, do the intervals on the road, using a GPS, for 0.4 km/0.25 mile.*
Time: 0:30	**2nd run of the day:** Easy Zone 1–2 jog
SAT Time: 1:10	**4 × 1 mile:** Warm up well for about 15 min, building from Zone 1–2 to Zone 3–5. Find a flat stretch and run 4 × 1 mile (or 1.6 km) at Zone 5. Do *not* go above Zone 5. Stay in Zone 5 with 3-min recovery jog at Zone 1–2 between each. Cool down for 15 min, easy Zone 2 jogging and Zone 1 walking.
Time: 0:30	**2nd run of the day:** Easy Zone 1–2 jog
SUN Time: 1:15	**Easy run/walk:** Zone 1–2 power run. Do this as 7 min run at Zone 2, 1 min walk at Zone 1. Repeat for the duration of the run. *The run/walk portions won't divide perfectly, so you will finish with a run. Walk a few minutes after.*

Total time: 8:15

WEEK 6 Sub-16-Min 5K Plan, 14 Weeks Specific Phase

MON Time: 0:40	**Easy run/walk:** Easy Zone 1–2 power run. Run 40 min as 6 min run at Zone 2, 1 min walk at Zone 1. Repeat for the duration of the run. *This 7-min sequence won't divide evenly into 40, so you will finish on a run. Walk a few minutes after.*
TUES Time: 1:10	**3 × 1 mile:** Warm up well for about 15 min, building from Zone 1–2 to Zone 3–5. On flat ground run 3 × 1 mile (or 1.6km) at Zone 3. Do *not* go above Zone 3. Stay in Zone 3 with 3-min recovery jog at Zone 1–2 between each. Cool down for 15 min with easy Zone 2 jogging and Zone 1 walking.
WED Time: 1:00	**Envelope run:** Start easy in Zone 1–2 for the first 10–15 min, then work to a moderate pace on the edge of comfort/discomfort. Look at the power zone you are in, likely Zone 3–4. Stay in that zone, but find a way to go faster. Push that envelope, trying to be quicker without raising your watts. It's a balance of trying to hold or increase speed with technique. Focus on your rhythm, cadence, forward lean, soft foot strike, relaxation, eyes and head position. Last 10 min should be easy Zone 1–2 running.
Time: 0:30	**2nd run of the day:** Easy Zone 1–2 jog
THURS Time: 1:10	**VO$_2$ intervals:** Warm up well for about 15 min, building from Zone 1–2 to Zone 3–5. Then do 6 × 3 min at your 5K goal pace. Take note of the power zone you are in at that pace. Try to be more efficient, to get more speed per watt while running. Take a 3-min recovery interval as 1 min walk at Zone 1, 2 min easy jog at Zone 2. Afterward do a 15-min easy Zone 1–2 power cooldown. *You may do this as 6 × 1K on the track if you prefer*
Time: 0:30	**2nd run of the day:** Easy Zone 1–2 jog
FRI Time: 0	**Day off:** Actively focus on recovery today: (1) stay off legs all you can; (2) watch nutrition closely (healthy carbs, lean protein, good fats); (3) stretch; (4) drink when thirsty. Other common recovery aids include massage, napping, elevating legs, floating in water, and listening to music.
SAT Time: 1:10	**14 × 400:** Warm up well for about 15 min, building from Zone 1–2 to Zone 3–5. Then, on track, run 14 × 400 at 5K goal pace, with 1 min recovery between. Monitor the power zone in which you run these. They should be in Zone 6, some Zone 7. You might see more Zone 7 later in the workout as you begin to break down. If you are in Zone 7 the whole time, review how realistic your goal pace is or whether your rFTPw is too low. Cool down for 15 min, easy Zone 1–2 jogging and walking. *If you don't have a track, do the intervals on the road, using a GPS, for 0.4 km/0.25 mile.*
Time: 0:30	**2nd run of the day:** Easy Zone 1–2 jog
SUN Time: 1:20	**Easy run/walk:** Easy Zone 1–2 power run. Do this as 7 min run at Zone 2, 1 min walk at Zone 1. Repeat for the duration of the run.
Time: 0:30	**2nd run of the day:** Easy Zone 1–2 jog

Total time: 8:30

MON Time: 0:40	**Easy run/walk:** Zone 1–2 power run. Run 40 min as 4 min run at Zone 2, 1 min walk at Zone 1. Repeat for the duration of the run.
TUES Time: 1:10	**3 × 1 mile:** Warm up well for about 15 min, building from Zone 1–2 to Zone 3–5. On flat ground run 3 × 1 mile (or 1.6 km) at Zone 4. Do *not* go above Zone 4. Stay in Zone 4 with 3-min recovery jog at Zone 1–2 between each. Cool down for 15 min with easy Zone 2 jogging and Zone 1 walking.
WED Time: 0:40	**Easy run/walk:** Zone 1–2 power run. Run 40 min as 4 min run at Zone 2, 1 min walk at Zone 1. Repeat for the duration of the run.
THURS Time: 1:10	**Goal-pace run:** Warm up well for 15 min building from Zone 1–2 to zone 3–5. Then on a track or flat road, run 2 × 2 km at 5K goal pace, with 2 min recovery. Your watts should line up in Zone 6, perhaps some in Zone 7. After the second interval and 2 min rest, do 1 km at 5K goal pace. Cool down for 15 min with easy Zone 2 jogging and Zone 1 walking.
Time: 0:30	**2nd run of the day:** Easy Zone 1–2 jog
FRI Time: 0:40	**Easy run/walk:** Easy Zone 1–2 power run. Run 40 min as 4 min run at Zone 2, 1 min walk at Zone 1. Repeat for the duration of the run.
SAT Time: 1:15	**15 × 400:** Warm up well for about 15 min, building from Zone 1–2 to Zone 3–5. Then, on track, run 15 × 400 at 5K goal pace, with 1 min recovery between. Monitor the power zone in which you run these. They should be in Zone 6, some Zone 7. You might see more Zone 7 later in the workout as you begin to break down. If you are in Zone 7 the whole time, review how realistic your goal pace is or whether your rFTPw is too low. Cool down for 15 min, easy Zone 1–2 jogging and walking. *If you don't have a track, do the intervals on the road, using a GPS, for 0.4 km/0.25 mile.*
Time: 0:30	**2nd run of the day:** Easy Zone 1–2 jog
SUN Time: 1:20	**Easy run/walk:** Easy Zone 1–2 power run. Do this as 7 min run at Zone 2, 1 min walk at Zone 1. Repeat for the duration of the run.
Time: 0:30	**2nd run of the day:** Easy Zone 1–2 jog

Total time: 8:25

WEEK 8 Sub-16-Min 5K Plan, 14 Weeks Specific Phase

MON Time: 0	**Day off:** Actively focus on recovery today: (1) stay off legs all you can; (2) watch nutrition closely (healthy carbs, lean protein, good fats); (3) stretch; (4) drink when thirsty. Other common recovery aids include massage, napping, elevating legs, and compression wear.
TUES Time: 0:40	**Easy run/walk:** Zone 1-2 power run. Run 40 min as 4 min run at Zone 2, 1 min walk at Zone 1. Repeat for the duration of the run.
WED Time: 1:10	**3/9-min Stryd test:** Warm up 15 min, preparing for hard effort at the end; conduct a 3-min interval at maximal effort; recover with 5-min walk, 10 min easy jog, 5 min walk, 5 min easy jog, 5 min walk (30 min total); conduct a 9-min interval at maximal effort; cool down 10-15 min easy. *Follow the protocol for this test and estimating rFTPw and rFTPa per Chapter 4.*
Time: 0:30	**2nd run of the day:** Easy Zone 1-2 jog
THURS Time: 0:40	**Easy run/walk:** Zone 1-2 power run. Run 40 min as 4 min run at Zone 2, 1 min walk at Zone 1. Repeat for the duration of the run.
FRI Time: 1:00	**Envelope run:** Start easy in Zone 1-2 for the first 10-15 min, then work to a moderate pace on the edge of comfort/discomfort. Look at the power zone you are in, likely Zone 3-4. Stay in that zone, but find a way to go faster. Push that envelope, trying to be quicker without raising your watts. It's a balance of trying to hold or increase speed with technique. Focus on your rhythm, cadence, forward lean, soft foot strike, relaxation, eyes and head position. Last 10 min should be easy Zone 1-2 running.
Time: 0:30	**2nd run of the day:** Easy Zone 1-2 jog
SAT Time: 1:15	**Fartlek:** Run of surges. Warm up well for about 15 min, building from Zone 1-2 to Zone 3-5. On rolling course, run 1-2-min pickups at faster than 5K pace (Zone 6-7), with recoveries at Zone 1-2 as long as you feel you need between the surges. Form! Cadence! Use the last 10 min to cool down with easy Zone 1 running/walking.
Time: 0:30	**2nd run of the day:** Easy Zone 1-2 jog
SUN Time: 1:30	**Envelope run:** Start easy in Zone 1-2 for the first 10-15 min, then work to a moderate pace on the edge of comfort/discomfort. Look at the power zone you are in, likely Zone 3-4. Stay in that zone, but find a way to go faster. Push that envelope, trying to be quicker without raising your watts. It's a balance of trying to hold or increase speed with technique. Focus on your rhythm, cadence, forward lean, soft foot strike, relaxation, eyes and head position. Last 10 min should be easy Zone 1-2 running.
Time: 0:30	**2nd run of the day:** Easy Zone 1-2 jog

Total time: 8:15

WEEK 9 Sub-16-Min 5K Plan, 14 Weeks Specific Phase	
MON Time: 0	**Day off:** Actively focus on recovery today: (1) stay off legs all you can; (2) watch nutrition closely (healthy carbs, lean protein, good fats); (3) stretch; (4) drink when thirsty. Other common recovery aids include massage, napping, elevating legs, floating in water, and compression wear.
TUES Time: 1:00	**Fartlek:** Run of surges. Warm up well for about 15 min, building from Zone 1–2 to Zone 3–5. On rolling course, run 1–2-min pickups at faster than 5K pace (Zone 6–7), with recoveries at Zone 1–2 as long as you feel you need between the surges. Form! Cadence! Use the last 10 min to cool down with easy Zone 1 running/walking.
Time: 0:30	**2nd run of the day:** Easy Zone 1–2 jog
WED Time: 0:40	**Easy run/walk:** Zone 1–2 power run. Run 40 min as 4 min run at Zone 2, 1 min walk at Zone 1. Repeat for the duration of the run.
THURS Time: 1:10	**2K-2K-1K @ 5K goal pace:** Warm up well for about 15 min, building from Zone 1–2 to Zone 3–5. Then on a track or stretch of road, run 2 × 2 km at 5K goal pace, with 2 min recovery. Your watts should line up in Zone 6, perhaps some in Zone 7. After the second interval and 2 min rest, do 1 km at 5K goal pace. Cool down for 15 min with easy Zone 2 jogging and Zone 1 walking.
Time: 0:30	**2nd run of the day:** Easy Zone 1–2 jog
FRI Time: 0:40	**Easy run/walk:** Zone 1–2 power run. Run 40 min as 4 min run at Zone 2, 1 min walk at Zone 1. Repeat for the duration of the run.
SAT Time: 1:20	**16 × 400:** Warm up well for about 15 min, building from Zone 1–2 to Zone 3–5. Then, on track, run 16 × 400 at 5K goal pace, with 1 min recovery between. Monitor the power zone in which you run these. They should be in Zone 6, some Zone 7. You might see more Zone 7 later in the workout as you begin to break down. If you are in Zone 7 the whole time, review how realistic your goal pace is or whether your rFTPw is too low. Cool down for 15 min, easy Zone 1–2 jogging and walking. *If you don't have a track, do the intervals on the road, using a GPS, for 0.4 km/0.25 mile.*
Time: 0:30	**2nd run of the day:** Easy Zone 1–2 jog
SUN Time: 1:30	**Envelope run:** Start easy in Zone 1–2 for the first 10–15 min, then work to a moderate pace on the edge of comfort/discomfort. Look at the power zone you are in, likely Zone 3–4. Stay in that zone, but find a way to go faster. Push that envelope, trying to be quicker without raising your watts. It's a balance of trying to hold or increase speed with technique. Focus on your rhythm, cadence, forward lean, soft foot strike, relaxation, eyes and head position. Last 10 min should be easy Zone 1–2 running.

Total time: 7:50

WEEK 10 Sub-16-Min 5K Plan, 14 Weeks Specific Phase	
MON Time: 0	**Day off:** Actively focus on recovery today: (1) stay off legs all you can; (2) watch nutrition closely (healthy carbs, lean protein, good fats); (3) stretch; (4) drink when thirsty. Other common recovery aids include massage, napping, elevating legs, floating in water, and listening to music.
TUES Time: 1:00	**Fartlek:** Run of surges. Warm up well for about 15 min, building from Zone 1–2 to Zone 3–5. On rolling course, run 1–2-min pickups at faster than 5K pace (Zone 6–7), with recoveries at Zone 1–2 as long as you feel you need between the surges. Form! Cadence! Use the last 10 min to cool down with easy Zone 1 running/walking.
Time: 0:30	**2nd run of the day:** Easy Zone 1–2 jog
WED Time: 0:40	**Easy run/walk:** Zone 1–2 power run. Run 40 min as 4 min run at Zone 2, 1 min walk at Zone 1. Repeat for the duration of the run.
THURS Time: 1:10	**2K-2K-1K @ 5K goal pace:** Warm up well for about 15 min, building from Zone 1–2 to Zone 3–5. Then on a track or stretch of road, run 2 × 2 km at 5K goal pace, with 2 min recovery. Your watts should line up in Zone 6, perhaps some in Zone 7. After the second interval and 2 min rest, do 1 km at 5K goal pace. Cool down for 15 min with easy Zone 2 jogging and Zone 1 walking.
Time: 0:30	**2nd run of the day:** Easy Zone 1–2 jog
FRI Time: 0:40	**Easy run/walk:** Zone 1–2 power run. Run 40 min as 4 min run at Zone 2, 1 min walk at Zone 1. Repeat for the duration of the run.
SAT Time: 1:20	**16 × 400:** Warm up well for about 15 min, building from Zone 1–2 to Zone 3–5. Then on track, run 16 × 400 at 5K goal pace, with 1 min recovery between. Monitor the power zone you are running in these. They should be probably in Zone 6, some Zone 7. You might see more Zone 7 later in the workout, as you begin to break down. If you are Zone 7 the whole time, you want to review how realistic your goal pace is, or if your rFTPw is too low. Cool down after this run for 15 min easy Zone 1–2 jogging and walking. *If you don't have a track, do the intervals on the road, using a GPS, for 0.4 km/0.25 mile.*
Time: 0:30	**2nd run of the day:** Easy Zone 1–2 jog
SUN Time: 1:30	**Envelope run:** Start easy in Zone 1–2 for the first 10–15 min, then work to a moderate pace on the edge of comfort/discomfort. Look at the power zone you are in, likely Zone 3–4. Stay in that zone, but find a way to go faster. Push that envelope, trying to be quicker without raising your watts. It's a balance of trying to hold or increase speed with technique. Focus on your rhythm, cadence, forward lean, soft foot strike, relaxation, eyes and head position. Last 10 min should be easy Zone 1–2 running.

Total time: 7:50

MON Time: 0	**Day off:** Actively focus on recovery today: (1) stay off legs all you can; (2) watch nutrition closely (healthy carbs, lean protein, good fats); (3) stretch; (4) drink when thirsty. Other common recovery aids include massage, napping, elevating legs, floating in water, and listening to music.
TUES Time: 1:00	**Fartlek:** Run of surges. Warm up well for about 15 min, building from Zone 1–2 to Zone 3–5. On rolling course, run 1-2-min pickups at faster than 5K pace (Zone 6–7), with recoveries at Zone 1–2 as long as you feel you need between the surges. Form! Cadence! Use the last 10 min to cool down with easy Zone 1 running/walking.
Time: 0:30	**2nd run of the day:** Easy Zone 1–2 jog
WED Time: 0:40	**Easy run/walk:** Zone 1–2 power run. Run 40 min as 4 min run at Zone 2, 1 min walk at Zone 1. Repeat for the duration of the run.
THURS Time: 1:10	**Goal-pace run:** Warm up well for 15 min building from Zone 1–2 to Zone 3–5. Then on a track or flat road, run 2 × 2 km at 5K goal pace, with 2 min recovery. Your watts should line up in Zone 6, perhaps some in Zone 7. After the second interval and 2 min rest, do 1 km at 5K goal pace. Cool down for 15 min with easy Zone 2 jogging and Zone 1 walking.
Time: 0:30	**2nd run of the day:** Easy Zone 1–2 jog
FRI Time: 0:40	**Easy run/walk:** Zone 1–2 power run. Run 40 min as 4 min run at Zone 2, 1 min walk at Zone 1. Repeat for the duration of the run.
SAT Time: 1:20	**16 × 400:** Warm up well for about 15 min, building from Zone 1–2 to Zone 3–5. Then, on track, run 16 × 400 at 5K goal pace, with 1 min recovery between. Monitor the power zone in which you run these. They should be in Zone 6, some Zone 7. You might see more Zone 7 later in the workout as you begin to break down. If you are in Zone 7 the whole time, review how realistic your goal pace is or whether your rFTPw is too low. Cool down for 15 min, easy Zone 1–2 jogging and walking. *If you don't have a track, do the intervals on the road, using a GPS, for 0.4 km/0.25 mile.*
Time: 0:30	**2nd run of the day:** Easy Zone 1–2 jog
SUN Time: 1:30	**Envelope run:** Start easy in Zone 1–2 for the first 10–15 min, then work to a moderate pace on the edge of comfort/discomfort. Look at the power zone you are in, likely Zone 3–4. Stay in that zone, but find a way to go faster. Push that envelope, trying to be quicker without raising your watts. It's a balance of trying to hold or increase speed with technique. Focus on your rhythm, cadence, forward lean, soft foot strike, relaxation, eyes and head position. Last 10 min should be easy Zone 1–2 running.
Time: 0:30	**2nd run of the day:** Easy Zone 1–2 jog

Total time: 8:20

WEEK 12 Sub-16-Min 5K Plan, 14 Weeks Specific Phase

MON Time: 0	**Day off:** Actively focus on recovery today: (1) stay off legs all you can; (2) watch nutrition closely (healthy carbs, lean protein, good fats); (3) stretch; (4) drink when thirsty. Other common recovery aids include massage, napping, elevating legs, floating in water, and listening to music.
TUES Time: 0:40	**Easy run/walk:** Zone 1–2 power run. Run 40 min as 4 min run at Zone 2, 1 min walk at Zone 1. Repeat for the duration of the run.
WED Time: 1:10	**3/9-min Stryd test:** Warm up 15 min, preparing for hard effort at the end; conduct a 3-min interval at maximal effort; recover with 5-min walk, 10 min easy jog, 5 min walk, 5 min easy jog, 5 min walk (30 min total); conduct a 9-min interval at maximal effort; cool down 10–15 min easy. *Follow the protocol for this test and estimating rFTPw and rFTPa per Chapter 4.*
Time: 0:30	**2nd run of the day:** Easy Zone 1–2 jog
THURS Time: 0:40	**Easy run/walk:** Zone 1–2 power run. Run 40 min as 4 min run at Zone 2, 1 min walk at Zone 1. Repeat for the duration of the run.
FRI Time: 1:00	**Envelope run:** Start easy in Zone 1–2 for the first 10–15 min, then work to a moderate pace on the edge of comfort/discomfort. Look at the power zone you are in, likely Zone 3–4. Stay in that zone, but find a way to go faster. Push that envelope, trying to be quicker without raising your watts. It's a balance of trying to hold or increase speed with technique. Focus on your rhythm, cadence, forward lean, soft foot strike, relaxation, eyes and head position. Last 10 min should be easy Zone 1–2 running.
SAT Time: 1:00	**Fartlek:** Run of surges. Warm up well for about 15 min, building from Zone 1–2 to Zone 3–5. On rolling course, run 1–2-min pickups at faster than 5K pace (Zone 6–7), with recoveries at Zone 1–2 as long as you feel you need between the surges. Form! Cadence! Use the last 10 min to cool down with easy Zone 1 running/walking.
Time: 0:30	**2nd run of the day:** Easy Zone 1–2 jog
SUN Time: 0	**Day off:** Actively focus on recovery today: (1) stay off legs all you can; (2) watch nutrition closely (healthy carbs, lean protein, good fats); (3) stretch; (4) drink when thirsty. Other common recovery aids include massage, napping, elevating legs, and compression wear.

Total time: 5:30

WEEK 13 Sub-16-Min 5K Plan, 14 Weeks Specific Phase	
MON Time: 1:10	**Goal-pace run:** Warm up well for 15 min building from Zone 1–2 to Zone 3–5. Then on a track or flat road, run 2 × 2 km at 5K goal pace, with 2 min recovery. Your watts should line up in Zone 6, perhaps some in Zone 7. After the second interval and 2 min rest, do 1 km at 5K goal pace. Cool down for 15 min with easy Zone 2 jogging and Zone 1 walking.
TUES Time: 0:40 Time: 0:30	**Easy run/walk:** Zone 1–2 power run. Run 40 min as 4 min run at Zone 2, 1 min walk at Zone 1. Repeat for the duration of the run. **2nd run of the day:** Easy Zone 1–2 jog
WED Time: 1:00	**Fartlek:** Run of surges. Warm up well for about 15 min, building from Zone 1–2 to Zone 3–5. On rolling course, run 1–2-min pickups at faster than 5K pace (Zone 6–7), with recoveries at Zone 1–2 as long as you feel you need between the surges. Form! Cadence! Use the last 10 min to cool down with easy Zone 1 running/walking.
THURS Time: 0:40 Time: 0:30	**Easy run/walk:** Zone 1–2 power run. Run 40 min as 4 min run at Zone 2, 1 min walk at Zone 1. Repeat for the duration of the run. **2nd run of the day:** Easy Zone 1–2 jog
FRI Time: 0	**Day off:** Actively focus on recovery today: (1) stay off legs all you can; (2) watch nutrition closely (healthy carbs, lean protein, good fats); (3) stretch; (4) drink when thirsty. Other common recovery aids include massage, napping, elevating legs, and compression wear.
SAT Time: 1:00 Time: 0:30	**12 × 400:** Warm up well for about 15 min, building from Zone 1–2 to Zone 3–5. Then, on track, run 12 × 400 at 5K goal pace, with 1 min recovery between. Monitor the power zone in which you run these. They should be in Zone 6, some Zone 7. You might see more Zone 7 later in the workout as you begin to break down. If you are in Zone 7 the whole time, review how realistic your goal pace is or whether your rFTPw is too low. Cool down for 15 min, easy Zone 1–2 jogging and walking. *If you don't have a track, do the intervals on the road, using a GPS, for 0.4 km/0.25 mile.* **2nd run of the day:** Easy Zone 1–2 jog
SUN Time: 0:40	**Easy run/walk:** Zone 1–2 power run. Run 40 min as 4 min run at Zone 2, 1 min walk at Zone 1. Repeat for the duration of the run.

Total time: 6:40

WEEK 14 Sub-16-Min 5K Plan, 14 Weeks Specific Phase

MON Time: 0	**Day off:** Actively focus on recovery today: (1) stay off legs all you can; (2) watch nutrition closely (healthy carbs, lean protein, good fats); (3) stretch; (4) drink when thirsty. Other common recovery aids include massage, napping, elevating legs, and compression wear.
TUES Time: 0:40	**5 × 2 min at Zone 4–6:** 15-min warm-up run followed by 5 × 2 min, starting at Zone 4 for the first min, then building to Zone 5–6 in the last minute, with 2 min easy recovery jog. Easy cooldown in Zone 1–2 to make 40 min.
WED Time: 0:40 Time: 0:30	**Easy run/walk:** Zone 1–2 power run. Run 40 min as 4 min run at Zone 2, 1 min walk at Zone 1. Repeat for the duration of the run. **2nd run of the day:** Easy Zone 1–2 jog
THURS Time: 0:30	**Run with surges:** First part of the run is easy, then do 5–7 × 7-sec surges at Zone 6–7 with long recoveries, getting faster over the course of the run. Focus on forefoot strike, quick cadence, slight forward lean, and fluid motion, not forcing it.
FRI Time: 0:20	**Preview course:** Run start and finish of course. Note landmarks. Include several accelerations to race pace. Otherwise, keep power in Zone 1.
SAT	**5K RACE**

Total time: 2:40

WEEK 1 Sub-18-Min 5K Plan, 14 Weeks Specific Phase	
MON Time: 1:10	**3/9-min Stryd test:** Warm up 15 min, preparing for hard effort at the end; conduct a 3-min interval at maximal effort; recover with 5-min walk, 10 min easy jog, 5 min walk, 5 min easy jog, 5 min walk (30 min total); conduct a 9-min interval at maximal effort; cool down 10–15 min easy. *Follow the protocol for this test and estimating rFTPw and rFTPa per Chapter 4.*
TUES Time: 0:40	**Easy run/walk:** Zone 1–2 power run. Run 40 min as 4 min run at Zone 2, 1 min walk at Zone 1. Repeat for the duration of the run.
WED Time: 0:40	**Easy run/walk:** Zone 1–2 power run. Run 40 min as 4 min run at Zone 2, 1 min walk at Zone 1. Repeat for the duration of the run.
THURS Time: 1:00	**30-min test:** Warm up 15 min, preparing for a hard effort at the end. Start a 30-min time trial (best effort) on a flat road or track, collecting power data (pace and HR data as well if possible). Cool down 10–15 min easy. *Follow the protocol for this test and estimating rFTPw and rFTPa per Chapter 4.*
FRI Time: 0:40	**Easy run/walk:** Zone 1–2 power run. Run 40 min as 4 min run at Zone 2, 1 min walk at Zone 1. Repeat for the duration of the run.
SAT Time: 0	**Day off:** Actively focus on recovery today: (1) stay off legs all you can; (2) watch nutrition closely (healthy carbs, lean protein, good fats); (3) stretch; (4) drink when thirsty. Other common recovery aids include massage, napping, elevating legs, floating in water, and compression wear.
SUN Time: 1:00	**Easy run/walk:** Zone 1–2 power run. Do this as 5 min run at Zone 2, walk 1 min at Zone 1. Repeat for the duration of the run.
Time: 0:30	**2nd run of the day:** Easy Zone 1–2 jog

Total time: 5:40

WEEK 2 Sub-18-Min 5K Plan, 14 Weeks Specific Phase

MON Time: 1:00	**Cruise intervals:** Warm-up 15 min building intensity through the warm-up, starting at Zone 1, then the last min at zones 4–5. Then do 3 × 8 min. Build to Zone 5–6 (3-min recoveries). Monitor pace, trying to be faster for the same power output. Cool down about 15 min. Zone 1–2.
TUES Time: 0:40	**Easy run/walk:** Zone 1–2 power run. Run 40 min as 4 min run at Zone 2, 1 min walk at Zone 1. Repeat for the duration of the run.
Time: 0:30	**2nd run of the day:** Easy Zone 1–2 jog
WED Time: 1:00	**Cruise intervals:** Warm-up 15 min building intensity through the warm-up, starting at Zone 1, then the last min at zones 4–5. Then do 2 × 8 min. Build to Zone 5–6 (3-min recoveries). Monitor pace, trying to be faster for the same power output. Cool down to make 1 hour at Zone 1–2.
THURS Time: 0:40	**Easy run/walk:** Zone 1–2 power run. Run 40 min as 4 min run at Zone 2, 1 min walk at Zone 1. Repeat for the duration of the run.
FRI Time: 1:00	**Envelope run:** Start easy in Zone 1–2 for the first 10–15 min, then work to a moderate pace on the edge of comfort/discomfort. Look at the power zone you are in, likely Zone 3–4. Stay in that zone, but find a way to go faster. Push that envelope, trying to be quicker without raising your watts. It's a balance of trying to hold or increase speed with technique. Focus on your rhythm, cadence, forward lean, soft foot strike, relaxation, eyes and head position. Last 10 min should be easy Zone 1–2 running.
SAT Time: 1:00	**Cruise intervals:** Warm-up 15 min building intensity through the warm-up, starting at Zone 1, then the last min at zones 4–5. Then do 4 × 6 min. Build to Zone 5–6 (2-min recoveries). Monitor pace, trying to be faster for the same power output. Cool down about 15 min. Zone 1–2.
SUN Time: 1:10	**Easy run/walk:** Zone 1–2 power run. Do this as 5 min run at Zone 2, walk 1 min at Zone 1. Repeat for the duration of the run. *The run/walk portion won't divide perfectly, so you will finish with a run. Walk a few minutes after.*
Time: 0:30	**2nd run of the day:** Easy Zone 1–2 jog

Total time: 7:30

WEEK 3 Sub-18-Min 5K Plan, 14 Weeks Specific Phase	
MON Time: 0:40	**Easy run/walk:** Zone 1–2 power run. Run 40 min as 4 min run at Zone 2, 1 min walk at Zone 1. Repeat for the duration of the run.
TUES Time: 1:00	**VO₂ intervals:** Warm up well for about 15 min, building from Zone 1–2 to Zone 3–5. Then do 5 × 3 min at 5K goal pace. Take note of the power zone you are in at that pace. Try to be more efficient, get more speed per watt while running. Take a 3-min recovery interval as 1 min walk Zone 1, 2 min easy jog Zone 2. Afterward do a 15 min easy Zone 1–2 power cooldown. *You may do this as 5 × 1K on the track if you prefer.*
WED Time: 1:00	**Envelope run:** Start easy in Zone 1–2 for the first 10–15 min, then work to a moderate pace on the edge of comfort/discomfort. Look at the power zone you are in, likely Zone 3–4. Stay in that zone, but find a way to go faster. Push that envelope, trying to be quicker without raising your watts. It's a balance of trying to hold or increase speed with technique. Focus on your rhythm, cadence, forward lean, soft foot strike, relaxation, eyes and head position. Last 10 min should be easy Zone 1–2 running.
Time: 0:30	**2nd run of the day:** Easy Zone 1–2 jog
THURS Time: 0:40	**Easy run/walk:** Zone 1–2 power run. Run 40 min as 4 min run at Zone 2, 1 min walk at Zone 1. Repeat for the duration of the run.
FRI Time: 1:10	**VO₂ intervals:** Warm up well for about 15 min, building from Zone 1–2 to Zone 3–5. Then do 6 × 3 min at 5K goal pace. Take note of the power zone you are in at that pace. Try to be more efficient, get more speed per watt while running. Take a 3-min recovery interval as 1 min walk Zone 1, 2 min easy jog Zone 2. Afterward do an easy Zone 1–2 power cooldown to make 70 min. *You may do this as 6x1K on the track if you prefer.*
Time: 0:30	**2nd run of the day:** Easy Zone 1–2 jog
SAT Time: 1:20	**Easy run/walk:** Zone 1–2 power run. Do this as 7 min run at Zone 2, walk 1 min at Zone 1. Repeat for the duration of the run.
SUN Time: 0	**Day off:** Actively focus on recovery today: (1) stay off legs all you can; (2) watch nutrition closely (healthy carbs, lean protein, good fats); (3) stretch; (4) drink when thirsty. Other common recovery aids include massage, napping, elevating legs, and compression wear.

Total time: 6:50

WEEK 4 Sub-18-Min 5K Plan, 14 Weeks Specific Phase

MON Time: 0:40	**Easy run/walk:** Zone 1–2 power run. Run 40 min as 4 min run at Zone 2, 1 min walk at Zone 1. Repeat for the duration of the run.
TUES Time: 1:10	**3/9-min Stryd test:** Warm up 15 min, preparing for hard effort at the end; conduct a 3-min interval at maximal effort; recover with 5-min walk, 10 min easy jog, 5 min walk, 5 min easy jog, 5 min walk (30 min total); conduct a 9-min interval at maximal effort; cool down 10–15 min easy. *Follow the protocol for this test and estimating rFTPw and rFTPa per Chapter 4.*
WED Time: 0:40	**Easy run/walk:** Zone 1–2 power run. Run 40 min as 4 min run at Zone 2, 1 min walk at Zone 1. Repeat for the duration of the run.
THURS Time: 0:40	**Easy run/walk:** Zone 1–2 power run. Run 40 min as 4 min run at Zone 2, 1 min walk at Zone 1. Repeat for the duration of the run.
FRI Time: 1:00	**30-min test:** Warm up 15 min, preparing for a hard effort at the end. Start a 30-min time trial (best effort) on a flat road or track, collecting power data (pace and HR data as well if possible). Cool down 10–15 min easy. *Follow the protocol for this test and estimating rFTPw and rFTPa in Chapter 4. Now you should begin to see a good relationship between the 3/9 test and the 30-min test. To avoid the 30-min test for the rest of the plan, focus on using the 3-min.*
Time: 0:30	**2nd run of the day:** Easy Zone 1–2 jog
SAT Time: 0	**Day off:** Actively focus on recovery today: (1) stay off legs all you can; (2) watch nutrition closely (healthy carbs, lean protein, good fats); (3) stretch; (4) drink when thirsty. Other common recovery aids include massage, napping, elevating legs, and compression wear.
SUN Time: 1:00	**Envelope run:** Start easy in Zone 1–2 for the first 10–15 min, then work to a moderate pace on the edge of comfort/discomfort. Look at the power zone you are in, likely Zone 3–4. Stay in that zone, but find a way to go faster. Push that envelope, trying to be quicker without raising your watts. It's a balance of trying to hold or increase speed with technique. Focus on your rhythm, cadence, forward lean, soft foot strike, relaxation, eyes and head position. Last 10 min should be easy Zone 1–2 running.
Time: 0:30	**2nd run of the day:** Easy Zone 1–2 jog

Total time: 6:10

WEEK 5 Sub-18-Min 5K Plan, 14 Weeks Specific Phase

MON Time: 0:40	**Easy run/walk:** Zone 1–2 power run. Run 40 min as 4 min run at Zone 2, 1 min walk at Zone 1. Repeat for the duration of the run. *This 7-min sequence won't divide evenly into 40, so you will finish on a run. Walk a few minutes after.*
TUES Time: 1:00	**Fartlek:** Run of surges. Warm up well for about 15 min, building from Zone 1–2 to Zone 3–5. On rolling course, run 1–2-min pickups at faster than 5K pace (Zone 6–7), with recoveries at Zone 1–2 as long as you feel you need between the surges. Form! Cadence! Use the last 10 min to cool down with easy Zone 1 running/walking.
WED Time: 1:00	**Envelope run:** Start easy in Zone 1–2 for the first 10–15 min, then work to a moderate pace on the edge of comfort/discomfort. Look at the power zone you are in, likely Zone 3–4. Stay in that zone, but find a way to go faster. Push that envelope, trying to be quicker without raising your watts. It's a balance of trying to hold or increase speed with technique. Focus on your rhythm, cadence, forward lean, soft foot strike, relaxation, eyes and head position. Last 10 min should be easy Zone 1–2 running.
Time: 0:30	**2nd run of the day:** Easy Zone 1–2 jog
THURS Time: 0:40	**Easy run/walk:** Zone 1–2 power run. Run 40 min as 6 min run at Zone 2, walk 1 min at Zone 1. Repeat for the duration of the run. *This 7-min sequence won't divide evenly into 40, so you will finish on a run. Walk a few minutes after.*
FRI Time: 1:00	**12 × 400:** Warm up well for about 15 min, building from Zone 1–2 to Zone 3–5. Then, on track, run 12 × 400 at 5K goal pace, with 1 min recovery between. Monitor the power zone in which you run these. They should be in Zone 6, some Zone 7. You might see more Zone 7 later in the workout as you begin to break down. If you are in Zone 7 the whole time, review how realistic your goal pace is or whether your rFTPw is too low. Cool down for 15 min, easy Zone 1–2 jogging and walking. *If you don't have a track, do the intervals on the road, using a GPS, for 0.4 km/0.25 mile.*
Time: 0:30	**2nd run of the day:** Easy Zone 1–2 jog
SAT Time: 1:10	**4 × 1 mile:** Warm up well for about 15 min, building from Zone 1–2 to Zone 3–5. Find a flat stretch and run 4 × 1 mile (or 1.6 km) at Zone 5. Do *not* go above Zone 5. Stay in Zone 5 with 3-min recovery jog at Zone 1–2 between each. Cool down for 15 min with easy Zone 2 jogging and Zone 1 walking.
Time: 0:30	**2nd run of the day:** Easy Zone 1–2 jog
SUN Time: 1:15	**Easy run/walk:** Zone 1–2 power run. Do this as 7 min run at Z2, walk 1 min at Z1. Repeat for the duration of the run. *The run/walk portions won't divide perfectly, so you will finish with a run. Walk a few minutes after.*

Total time: 8:15

WEEK 6 Sub-18-Min 5K Plan, 14 Weeks Specific Phase	
MON Time: 0:40	**Easy run/walk:** Zone 1–2 power run. Run 40 min as 6 min run at Zone 2, 1 min walk at Zone 1. Repeat for the duration of the run. *This 7-min sequence won't divide evenly into 40, so you will finish on a run. Walk a few minutes after.*
TUES Time: 1:10	**3 × 1 mile:** Warm up well for about 15 min, building from Zone 1–2 to Zone 3–5. Find a flat stretch and run 4 × 1 mile (or 1.6 km) at Zone 3. Do *not* go above Zone 3. Stay in Zone 3 with 3-min recovery jog at Zone 1–2 between each. Cool down for 15 min with easy Zone 2 jogging and Zone 1 walking.
WED Time: 1:00	**Envelope run:** Start easy in Zone 1–2 for the first 10–15 min, then work to a moderate pace on the edge of comfort/discomfort. Look at the power zone you are in, likely Zone 3–4. Stay in that zone, but find a way to go faster. Push that envelope, trying to be quicker without raising your watts. It's a balance of trying to hold or increase speed with technique. Focus on your rhythm, cadence, forward lean, soft foot strike, relaxation, eyes and head position. Last 10 min should be easy Zone 1–2 running.
Time: 0:30	**2nd run of the day:** Easy Zone 1–2 jog
THURS Time: 1:00	**VO$_2$ intervals:** Warm up well for about 15 min, building from Zone 1–2 to Zone 3–5. Then do 5 × 3 min at 5K goal pace. Take note of the power zone you are in at that pace. Try to be more efficient, get more speed per watt while running. Take a 3-min recovery interval as 1 min walk Zone 1, 2 min easy jog Zone 2. Afterward do a 15 min easy Zone 1–2 power cooldown. *You may do this as 6 × 1K on the track if you prefer.*
Time: 0:30	**2nd run of the day:** Easy Zone 1–2 jog
FRI Time: 0	**Day off:** Actively focus on recovery today: (1) stay off legs all you can; (2) watch nutrition closely (healthy carbs, lean protein, good fats); (3) stretch; (4) drink when thirsty. Other common recovery aids include massage, napping, elevating legs, floating in water, and listening to music.
SAT Time: 1:10	**14 × 400:** Warm up well for about 15 min, building from Zone 1–2 to Zone 3–5. Then, on track, run 14 × 400 at 5K goal pace, with 1 min recovery between. Monitor the power zone in which you run these. They should be in Zone 6, some Zone 7. You might see more Zone 7 later in the workout as you begin to break down. If you are in Zone 7 the whole time, review how realistic your goal pace is or whether your rFTPw is too low. Cool down for 15 min, easy Zone 1–2 jogging and walking. *If you don't have a track, do the intervals on the road, using a GPS, for 0.4 km/0.25 mile"*
Time: 0:30	**2nd run of the day:** Easy Zone 1–2 jog
SUN Time: 1:20	**Easy run/walk:** Zone 1–2 power run. Do this as 7 min run at Zone 2, walk 1 min at Zone 1. Repeat for the duration of the run.
Time: 0:30	**2nd run of the day:** Easy Zone 1–2 jog

Total time: 8:20

WEEK 7 Sub-18-Min 5K Plan, 14 Weeks Specific Phase

MON Time: 0:40	**Easy run/walk:** Zone 1–2 power run. Run 40 min as 4 min run at Zone 2, 1 min walk at Zone 1. Repeat for the duration of the run.
TUES Time: 1:10	**3 × 1 mile:** Warm up well for about 15 min, building from Zone 1–2 to Zone 3–5. Find a flat stretch and run 4 × 1 mile (or 1.6 km) at Zone 4. Do *not* go above Zone 4. Stay in Zone 4 with 3-min recovery jog at Zone 1–2 between each. Cool down for 15 min with easy Zone 2 jogging and Zone 1 walking.
WED Time: 0:40	**Easy run/walk:** Zone 1–2 power run. Run 40 min as 4 min run at Zone 2, 1 min walk at Zone 1. Repeat for the duration of the run.
THURS Time: 1:10	**Goal-pace run:** Warm up well for about 15 min, building from Zone 1–2 to Zone 3–5. Then, on a track or flat road, run 2 × 2 km at 5K goal pace, with 2 min recovery. Your watts should line up in Zone 6, perhaps some in Zone 7. After the second interval and 2-min rest, do 1 km at 5K goal pace. Cool down for 15 min with easy Zone 2 jogging and Zone 1 walking.
Time: 0:30	**2nd run of the day:** Easy Zone 1–2 jog
FRI Time: 0:40	**Easy run/walk:** Zone 1–2 power run. Run 40 min as 4 min run at Zone 2, 1 min walk at Zone 1. Repeat for the duration of the run.
SAT Time: 1:15	**15 × 400:** Warm up well for about 15 min, building from Zone 1–2 to Zone 3–5. Then, on track, run 15 × 400 at 5K goal pace, with 1 min recovery between. Monitor the power zone in which you run these. They should be in Zone 6, some Zone 7. You might see more Zone 7 later in the workout as you begin to break down. If you are in Zone 7 the whole time, review how realistic your goal pace is or whether your rFTPw is too low. Cool down for 15 min, easy Zone 1–2 jogging and walking. *If you don't have a track, do the intervals on the road, using a GPS, for 0.4 km/0.25 mile.*
Time: 0:30	**2nd run of the day:** Easy Zone 1–2 jog
SUN Time: 1:20	**Easy run/walk:** Zone 1–2 power run. Do this as 7 min run at Zone 2, walk 1 min at Zone 1. Repeat for the duration of the run.
Time: 0:30	**2nd run of the day:** Easy Zone 1–2 jog

Total time: 8:25

WEEK 8 Sub-18-Min 5K Plan, 14 Weeks Specific Phase

MON Time: 0	**Day off:** Actively focus on recovery today: (1) stay off legs all you can; (2) watch nutrition closely (healthy carbs, lean protein, good fats); (3) stretch; (4) drink when thirsty. Other common recovery aids include massage, napping, elevating legs, and compression wear.
TUES Time: 0:40	**Easy run/walk:** Zone 1–2 power run. Run 40 min as 4 min run at Zone 2, 1 min walk at Zone 1. Repeat for the duration of the run.
WED Time: 1:10	**3/9-min Stryd test:** Warm up 15 min, preparing for hard effort at the end; conduct a 3-min interval at maximal effort; recover with 5-min walk, 10 min easy jog, 5 min walk, 5 min easy jog, 5 min walk (30 min total); conduct a 9-min interval at maximal effort; cool down 10–15 min easy. *Follow the protocol for this test and estimating rFTPw and rFTPa per Chapter 4.*
Time: 0:30	**2nd run of the day:** Easy Zone 1–2 jog
THURS Time: 0:40	**Easy run/walk:** Zone 1–2 power run. Run 40 min as 4 min run at Zone 2, 1 min walk at Zone 1. Repeat for the duration of the run.
FRI Time: 1:00	**Envelope run:** Start easy in Zone 1–2 for the first 10–15 min, then work to a moderate pace on the edge of comfort/discomfort. Look at the power zone you are in, likely Zone 3–4. Stay in that zone, but find a way to go faster. Push that envelope, trying to be quicker without raising your watts. It's a balance of trying to hold or increase speed with technique. Focus on your rhythm, cadence, forward lean, soft foot strike, relaxation, eyes and head position. Last 10 min should be easy Zone 1–2 running.
Time: 0:30	**2nd run of the day:** Easy Zone 1–2 jog
SAT Time: 1:15	**Fartlek:** Run of surges. Warm up well for about 15 min, building from Zone 1–2 to Zone 3–5. On rolling course, run 1–2-min pickups at faster than 5K pace (Zone 6–7), with recoveries at Zone 1–2 as long as you feel you need between the surges. Form! Cadence! Use the last 10 min to cool down with easy Zone 1 running/walking.
Time: 0:30	**2nd run of the day:** Easy Zone 1–2 jog
SUN Time: 1:30	**Envelope run:** Start easy in Zone 1–2 for the first 10–15 min, then work to a moderate pace on the edge of comfort/discomfort. Look at the power zone you are in, likely Zone 3–4. Stay in that zone, but find a way to go faster. Push that envelope, trying to be quicker without raising your watts. It's a balance of trying to hold or increase speed with technique. Focus on your rhythm, cadence, forward lean, soft foot strike, relaxation, eyes and head position. Last 10 min should be easy Zone 1–2 running.
Time: 0:30	**2nd run of the day:** Easy Zone 1–2 jog

Total time: 8:15

WEEK 9 Sub-18-Min 5K Plan, 14 Weeks Specific Phase	
MON Time: 0	**Day off:** Actively focus on recovery today: (1) stay off legs all you can; (2) watch nutrition closely (healthy carbs, lean protein, good fats); (3) stretch; (4) drink when thirsty. Other common recovery aids include massage, napping, elevating legs, and compression wear.
TUES Time: 1:00	**Fartlek:** Run of surges. Warm up well for about 15 min, building from Zone 1–2 to Zone 3–5. On rolling course, run 1–2-min pickups at faster than 5K pace (Zone 6–7), with recoveries at Zone 1–2 as long as you feel you need between the surges. Form! Cadence! Use the last 10 min to cool down with easy Zone 1 running/walking.
Time: 0:30	**2nd run of the day:** Easy Zone 1–2 jog
WED Time: 0:40	**Easy run/walk:** Zone 1–2 power run. Run 40 min as 4 min run at Zone 2, 1 min walk at Zone 1. Repeat for the duration of the run.
THURS Time: 1:10	**Goal-pace run:** Warm up well for about 15 min, building from Zone 1–2 to Zone 3–5. Then on a track or flat road, run 2 × 2 km at 5K goal pace, with 2 min recovery. Your watts should line up in Zone 6, perhaps some in Zone 7. After the second interval and 2 min rest, do 1 km at 5K goal pace. Cool down for 15 min with easy Zone 2 jogging and Zone 1 walking.
Time: 0:30	**2nd run of the day:** Easy Zone 1–2 jog
FRI Time: 1:00	**Easy run/walk:** Zone 1–2 power run. Run 40 min as 4 min run at Zone 2, 1 min walk at Zone 1. Repeat for the duration of the run.
SAT Time: 1:20	**16 × 400:** Warm up well for about 15 min, building from Zone 1–2 to Zone 3–5. Then, on track, run 16 × 400 at 5K goal pace, with 1 min recovery between. Monitor the power zone in which you run these. They should be in Zone 6, some Zone 7. You might see more Zone 7 later in the workout as you begin to break down. If you are in Zone 7 the whole time, review how realistic your goal pace is or whether your rFTPw is too low. Cool down for 15 min, easy Zone 1–2 jogging and walking. *If you don't have a track, do the intervals on the road, using a GPS, for 0.4 km/0.25 mile.*
Time: 0:30	**2nd run of the day:** Easy Zone 1–2 jog
SUN Time: 1:30	**Envelope run:** Start easy in Zone 1–2 for the first 10–15 min, then work to a moderate pace on the edge of comfort/discomfort. Look at the power zone you are in, likely Zone 3–4. Stay in that zone, but find a way to go faster. Push that envelope, trying to be quicker without raising your watts. It's a balance of trying to hold or increase speed with technique. Focus on your rhythm, cadence, forward lean, soft foot strike, relaxation, eyes and head position. Last 10 min should be easy Zone 1–2 running.

Total time: 7:50

WEEK 10 Sub-18-Min 5K Plan, 14 Weeks Specific Phase	
MON Time: 0	**Day off:** Actively focus on recovery today: (1) stay off legs all you can; (2) watch nutrition closely (healthy carbs, lean protein, good fats); (3) stretch; (4) drink when thirsty. Other common recovery aids include massage, napping, elevating legs, floating in water, and listening to music.
TUES Time: 1:00	**Fartlek:** Run of surges. Warm up well for about 15 min, building from Zone 1–2 to Zone 3–5. On rolling course, run 1-2-min pickups at faster than 5K pace (Zone 6-7), with recoveries at Zone 1-2 as long as you feel you need between the surges. Form! Cadence! Use the last 10 min to cool down with easy Zone 1 running/walking.
Time: 0:30	**2nd run of the day:** Easy Zone 1–2 jog
WED Time: 0:40	**Easy run/walk:** Zone 1–2 power run. Run 40 min as 4 min run at Zone 2, 1 min walk at Zone 1. Repeat for the duration of the run.
THURS Time: 1:10	**Goal-pace run:** Warm up well for about 15 min, building from Zone 1–2 to Zone 3–5. Then on a track or flat road, run 2 × 2 km at 5K goal pace, with 2 min recovery. Your watts should line up in Zone 6, perhaps some in Zone 7. After the second interval and 2 min rest, do 1 km at 5K goal pace. Cool down for 15 min with easy Zone 2 jogging and Zone 1 walking.
Time: 0:30	**2nd run of the day:** Easy Zone 1–2 jog
FRI Time: 0:40	**Easy run/walk:** Zone 1–2 power run. Run 40 min as 4 min run at Zone 2, 1 min walk at Zone 1. Repeat for the duration of the run.
SAT Time: 1:20	**16 × 400:** Warm up well for about 15 min, building from Zone 1–2 to Zone 3–5. Then, on track, run 16 × 400 at 5K goal pace, with 1 min recovery between. Monitor the power zone in which you run these. They should be in Zone 6, some Zone 7. You might see more Zone 7 later in the workout as you begin to break down. If you are in Zone 7 the whole time, review how realistic your goal pace is or whether your rFTPw is too low. Cool down for 15 min, easy Zone 1–2 jogging and walking. *If you don't have a track, do the intervals on the road, using a GPS, for 0.4 km/0.25 mile.*
Time: 0:30	**2nd run of the day:** Easy Zone 1–2 jog
SUN Time: 1:30	**Envelope run:** Start easy in Zone 1–2 for the first 10–15 min, then work to a moderate pace on the edge of comfort/discomfort. Look at the power zone you are in, likely Zone 3–4. Stay in that zone, but find a way to go faster. Push that envelope, trying to be quicker without raising your watts. It's a balance of trying to hold or increase speed with technique. Focus on your rhythm, cadence, forward lean, soft foot strike, relaxation, eyes and head position. Last 10 min should be easy Zone 1–2 running.

Total time: 7:50

WEEK 11 Sub-18-Min 5K Plan, 14 Weeks Specific Phase	
MON Time: 0	**Day off:** Actively focus on recovery today: (1) stay off legs all you can; (2) watch nutrition closely (healthy carbs, lean protein, good fats); (3) stretch; (4) drink when thirsty. Other common recovery aids include massage, napping, elevating legs, floating in water, and listening to music.
TUES Time: 1:00	**Fartlek:** Run of surges. Warm up well for about 15 min, building from Zone 1–2 to Zone 3–5. On rolling course, run 1-2-min pickups at faster than 5K pace (Zone 6–7), with recoveries at Zone 1–2 as long as you feel you need between the surges. Form! Cadence! Use the last 10 min to cool down with easy Zone 1 running/walking.
Time: 0:30	**2nd run of the day:** Easy Zone 1–2 jog
WED Time: 0:40	**Easy run/walk:** Zone 1–2 power run. Run 40 min as 4 min run at Zone 2, 1 min walk at Zone 1. Repeat for the duration of the run.
THURS Time: 1:10	**Goal-pace run:** Warm-up well for 15 min building from Zone 1–2 to Zone 3–5. Then on a track or flat road, run 2 × 2 km at 5K goal pace, with 2 min recovery. Your watts should line up in Zone 6, perhaps some in Zone 7. After the second interval and 2 min rest, do 1 km at 5K goal pace. Cool down for 15 min with easy Zone 2 jogging and Zone 1 walking.
Time: 0:30	**2nd run of the day:** Easy Zone 1–2 jog
FRI Time: 0:40	**Easy run/walk:** Zone 1–2 power run. Run 40 min as 4 min run at Zone 2, 1 min walk at Zone 1. Repeat for the duration of the run.
SAT Time: 1:20	**16 × 400:** Warm up well for about 15 min, building from Zone 1–2 to Zone 3–5. Then, on track, run 16 × 400 at 5K goal pace, with 1 min recovery between. Monitor the power zone in which you run these. They should be in Zone 6, some Zone 7. You might see more Zone 7 later in the workout as you begin to break down. If you are in Zone 7 the whole time, review how realistic your goal pace is or whether your rFTPw is too low. Cool down for 15 min, easy Zone 1–2 jogging and walking. *If you don't have a track, do the intervals on the road, using a GPS, for 0.4 km/0.25 mile.*
Time: 0:30	**2nd run of the day:** Easy Zone 1–2 jog
SUN Time: 1:30	**Envelope run:** Start easy in Zone 1–2 for the first 10–15 min, then work to a moderate pace on the edge of comfort/discomfort. Look at the power zone you are in, likely Zone 3–4. Stay in that zone, but find a way to go faster. Push that envelope, trying to be quicker without raising your watts. It's a balance of trying to hold or increase speed with technique. Focus on your rhythm, cadence, forward lean, soft foot strike, relaxation, eyes and head position. Last 10 min should be easy Zone 1–2 running.
Time: 0:30	**2nd run of the day:** Easy Zone 1–2 jog

Total time: 8:20

WEEK 12 Sub-18-Min 5K Plan, 14 Weeks Specific Phase

MON Time: 0	**Day off:** Actively focus on recovery today: (1) stay off legs all you can; (2) watch nutrition closely (healthy carbs, lean protein, good fats); (3) stretch; (4) drink when thirsty. Other common recovery aids include massage, napping, elevating legs, floating in water, and listening to music.
TUES Time: 0:40	**Easy run/walk:** Zone 1–2 power run. Run 40 min as 4 min run at Zone 2, 1 min walk at Zone 1. Repeat for the duration of the run.
WED Time: 1:10	**3/9-min Stryd test:** Warm up 15 min, preparing for hard effort at the end; conduct a 3-min interval at maximal effort; recover with 5-min walk, 10 min easy jog, 5 min walk, 5 min easy jog, 5 min walk (30 min total); conduct a 9-min interval at maximal effort; cool down 10–15 min easy. *Follow the protocol for this test and estimating rFTPw and rFTPa per Chapter 4.*
Time: 0:30	**2nd run of the day:** Easy Zone 1–2 jog
THURS Time: 0:40	**Easy run/walk:** Zone 1–2 power run. Run 40 min as 4 min run at Zone 2, 1 min walk at Zone 1. Repeat for the duration of the run.
FRI Time: 1:00	**Envelope run:** Start easy in Zone 1–2 for the first 10–15 min, then work to a moderate pace on the edge of comfort/discomfort. Look at the power zone you are in, likely Zone 3–4. Stay in that zone, but find a way to go faster. Push that envelope, trying to be quicker without raising your watts. It's a balance of trying to hold or increase speed with technique. Focus on your rhythm, cadence, forward lean, soft foot strike, relaxation, eyes and head position. Last 10 min should be easy Zone 1–2 running.
SAT Time: 1:00	**Fartlek:** Run of surges. Warm up well for about 15 min, building from Zone 1–2 to Zone 3–5. On rolling course, run 1–2-min pickups at faster than 5K pace (Zone 6–7), with recoveries at Zone 1–2 as long as you feel you need between the surges. Form! Cadence! Use the last 10 min to cool down with easy Zone 1 running/walking.
Time: 0:30	**2nd run of the day:** Easy Zone 1–2 jog
SUN Time: 0	**Day off:** Actively focus on recovery today: (1) stay off legs all you can; (2) watch nutrition closely (healthy carbs, lean protein, good fats); (3) stretch; (4) drink when thirsty. Other common recovery aids include massage, napping, elevating legs, and compression wear.

Total time: 5:30

WEEK 13 Sub-18-Min 5K Plan, 14 Weeks Specific Phase	
MON Time: 1:10	**Goal-pace run:** Warm up well for 15 min, building from Zone 1–2 to Zone 3–5. Then, on a track or flat road, run 2 × 2 km at 5K goal pace, with 2 min recovery. Your watts should line up in Zone 6, perhaps some in Zone 7. After the second interval and 2 min rest, do 1 km at 5K goal pace. Cool down for 15 min with easy Zone 2 jogging and Zone 1 walking.
TUES Time: 0:40 Time: 0:30	**Easy run/walk:** Zone 1–2 power run. Run 40 min as 4 min run at Zone 2, 1 min walk at Zone 1. Repeat for the duration of the run. **2nd run of the day:** Easy Zone 1–2 jog
WED Time: 1:00	**Fartlek:** Run of surges. Warm up well for about 15 min, building from Zone 1–2 to Zone 3–5. On rolling course, run 1-2-min pickups at faster than 5K pace (Zone 6–7), with recoveries at Zone 1–2 as long as you feel you need between the surges. Form! Cadence! Use the last 10 min to cool down with easy Zone 1 running/walking.
THURS Time: 0:40 Time: 0:30	**Easy run/walk:** Zone 1–2 power run. Run 40 min as 4 min run at Zone 2, 1 min walk at Zone 1. Repeat for the duration of the run. **2nd run of the day:** Easy Zone 1–2 jog
FRI Time: 0	**Day off:** Actively focus on recovery today: (1) stay off legs all you can; (2) watch nutrition closely (healthy carbs, lean protein, good fats); (3) stretch; (4) drink when thirsty. Other common recovery aids include massage, napping, elevating legs, and compression wear.
SAT Time: 1:00 Time: 0:30	**12 × 400:** Warm up well for about 15 min, building from Zone 1–2 to Zone 3–5. Then, on track, run 12 × 400 at 5K goal pace, with 1 min recovery between. Monitor the power zone in which you run these. They should be in Zone 6, some Zone 7. You might see more Zone 7 later in the workout as you begin to break down. If you are in Zone 7 the whole time, review how realistic your goal pace is or whether your rFTPw is too low. Cool down for 15 min, easy Zone 1–2 jogging and walking. *If you don't have a track, do the intervals on the road, using a GPS, for 0.4 km/0.25 mile.* **2nd run of the day:** Easy Zone 1–2 jog
SUN Time: 0:40	**Easy run/walk:** Zone 1–2 power run. Run 40 min as 4 min run at Zone 2, 1 min walk at Zone 1. Repeat for the duration of the run.

Total time: 6:40

WEEK 14 Sub-18-Min 5K Plan, 14 Weeks Specific Phase	
MON Time: 0	**Day off:** Actively focus on recovery today: (1) stay off legs all you can; (2) watch nutrition closely (healthy carbs, lean protein, good fats); (3) stretch; (4) drink when thirsty. Other common recovery aids include massage, napping, elevating legs, and compression wear.
TUES Time: 0:40	**5 × 2 min at Zone 4–6:** 15 min warm-up run, followed by 5 × 2 min, starting at Zone 4 for the first min, then building to Zone 5–6 in the last minute, with 2 min easy recovery jog. Easy cool down in Zone 1–2 to make 40 min
WED Time: 0:40 Time: 0:30	**Easy run/walk:** Zone 1–2 power run. Run 40 min as 4 min run at Zone 2, 1 min walk at Zone 1. Repeat for the duration of the run. **2nd run of the day:** Easy Zone 1–2 jog
THURS Time: 0:30	**Run with surges:** First part of the run is easy, then do 5–7 × 7 sec surges at Zone 6–7 with long recoveries, getting faster over the course of the run. Really focus on forefoot strike, quick cadence, slight forward lean, and fluid motion, not forcing it.
FRI Time: 0:20	**Preview course:** Run start and finish of course. Note landmarks. Include several accelerations to race pace. Otherwise, keep power in Zone 1.
SAT	**5K RACE**

Total time: 2:40

WEEK 1 Sub-32-Min 10K Plan, 14 Weeks Specific Phase	
MON Time: 1:10	**3/9-min Stryd test:** Warm up 15 min, preparing for hard effort at the end; conduct a 3-min interval at maximal effort; recover with 5 min walk, 10 min easy jog, 5 min walk, 5 min easy jog, 5 min walk (30 min total); conduct a 9-min interval at maximal effort; cool down 10–15 min easy. *Follow the protocol for this test and estimating rFTPw and rFTPa per Chapter 4.*
TUES Time: 0:40	**Easy run/walk:** Zone 1–2 power run. Run 40 min as 4 min run at Zone 2, 1 min walk at Zone 1. Repeat for the duration of the run.
WED Time: 0:40	**Easy run/walk:** Zone 1–2 power run. Run 40 min as 4 min run at Zone 2, 1 min walk at Zone 1. Repeat for the duration of the run.
THURS Time: 1:00	**30-min test:** Warm up 15 min, preparing for a hard effort at the end. Start a 30-min time trial (best effort) on a flat road or track, collecting power data (pace and HR data as well if possible). Cool down 10–15 min easy. *Follow the protocol for this test and estimating rFTPw and rFTPa per Chapter 4.*
FRI Time: 0:40 Time: 0:30	**Easy run/walk:** Zone 1–2 power run. Run 40 min as 4 min run at Zone 2, 1 min walk at Zone 1. Repeat for the duration of the run. **2nd run of the day:** Easy Zone 1–2 jog
SAT Time: 0	**Day off:** Actively focus on recovery today: (1) stay off legs all you can; (2) watch nutrition closely (healthy carbs, lean protein, good fats); (3) stretch; (4) drink when thirsty. Other common recovery aids include massage, napping, elevating legs, floating in water, and compression wear.
SUN Time: 1:00 Time: 0:30	**Easy run/walk:** Zone 1–2 power run. Do this as 5 min run at Zone 2, 1 min walk at Zone 1. Repeat for the duration of the run. **2nd run of the day:** Easy Zone 1–2 jog

Total time: 6:10

MON Time: 1:00	**Cruise intervals:** Warm up 15 min, building intensity through the warm-up, starting at Zone 1, then the last min at zones 4–5. Then do 3 × 8 min, build to Zone 5–6 (3-min recoveries). Monitor pace, trying to be faster for the same power output. Cool down to make 1 hour at Zone 1–2.
TUES Time: 0:40	**Easy run/walk:** Zone 1–2 power run. Run 40 min as 4 min run at Zone 2, 1 min walk at Zone 1. Repeat for the duration of the run.
WED Time: 1:00	**Cruise intervals:** Warm up 15 min, building intensity through the warm-up, starting at Zone 1, then the last min at zones 4–5. Then do 3 × 8 min, build to Zone 5–6 (3-min recoveries). Monitor pace, trying to be faster for the same power output. Cool down to make 1 hour at Zone 1–2.
Time: 0:30	**2nd run of the day:** Easy Zone 1–2 jog
THURS Time: 0:40	**Easy run/walk:** Zone 1–2 power run. Run 40 min as 4 min run at Zone 2, 1 min walk at Zone 1. Repeat for the duration of the run.
FRI Time: 1:00	**Envelope run:** Start easy in Zone 1–2 for the first 10–15 min, then work to a moderate pace on the edge of comfort/discomfort. Look at the power zone you are in, likely Zone 3–4. Stay in that zone, but find a way to go faster. Push that envelope, trying to be quicker without raising your watts. It's a balance of trying to hold or increase speed with technique. Focus on your rhythm, cadence, forward lean, soft foot strike, relaxation, eyes and head position. Last 10 min should be easy Zone 1–2 running.
Time: 0:30	**2nd run of the day:** Easy Zone 1–2 jog
SAT Time: 1:00	**Cruise intervals:** Warm up 15 min, building intensity through the warm-up, starting at Zone 1, then the last min at zones 4–5. Then do 4 × 6 min, build to Zone 5–6 (3-min recoveries). Monitor pace, trying to be faster for the same power output. Cool down to make 1 hour at Zone 1–2.
SUN Time: 1:10	**Easy run/walk:** Zone 1–2 power run. Do this as 5 min run at Zone 2, 1 min walk at Zone 1. Repeat for the duration of the run. *The run/walk portion won't divide perfectly, so you will finish with a run. Walk a few minutes after.*
Time: 0:30	**2nd run of the day:** Easy Zone 1–2 jog

Total time: 8:00

WEEK 3 Sub-32-Min 10K Plan, 14 Weeks Specific Phase

MON Time: 0:40	**Easy run/walk:** Zone 1–2 power run. Run 40 min as 4 min run at Zone 2, 1 min walk at Zone 1. Repeat for the duration of the run.
TUES Time: 1:00	**VO$_2$ intervals:** Warm up well for about 15 min, building from Zone 1–2 to Zone 3–5. Then do 5 × 3 min at 5K goal pace. Take note of the power zone you are in at that pace. Try to be more efficient, get more speed per watt while running. Take a 3-min recovery interval as 1 min walk Zone 1, 2 min easy jog Zone 2. Afterward do a 15 min easy Zone 1–2 power cooldown. *You may do this as 5 × 1K on the track if you prefer.*
WED Time: 1:00	**Envelope run:** Start easy in Zone 1–2 for the first 10–15 min, then work to a moderate pace on the edge of comfort/discomfort. Look at the power zone you are in, likely Zone 3–4. Stay in that zone, but find a way to go faster. Push that envelope, trying to be quicker without raising your watts. It's a balance of trying to hold or increase speed with technique. Focus on your rhythm, cadence, forward lean, soft foot strike, relaxation, eyes and head position. Last 10 min should be easy Zone 1–2 running.
Time: 0:30	**2nd run of the day:** Easy Zone 1–2 jog
THURS Time: 0:40	**Easy run/walk:** Zone 1–2 power run. Run 40 min as 4 min run at Zone 2, 1 min walk at Zone 1. Repeat for the duration of the run.
FRI Time: 1:10	**VO$_2$ intervals:** Warm up well for about 15 min, building from Zone 1–2 to Zone 3–5. Then do 5 × 3 min at 5K goal pace. Take note of the power zone you are in at that pace. Try to be more efficient, get more speed per watt while running. Take a 3-min recovery interval as 1 min walk Zone 1, 2 min easy jog Zone 2. Afterward do a 15 min easy Zone 1–2 power cooldown. *You may do this as 5 × 1K on the track if you prefer.*
Time: 0:30	**2nd run of the day:** Easy Zone 1–2 jog
SAT Time: 1:20	**Easy run/walk:** Zone 1–2 power run. Do this as 7 min run at Zone 2, 1 min walk at Zone 1. Repeat for the duration of the run.
Time: 0:30	**2nd run of the day:** Easy Zone 1–2 jog
SUN Time: 0	**Day off:** Actively focus on recovery today: (1) stay off legs all you can; (2) watch nutrition closely (healthy carbs, lean protein, good fats); (3) stretch; (4) drink when thirsty. Other common recovery aids include massage, napping, elevating legs, and compression wear.

Total time: 7:20

WEEK 4 Sub-32-Min 10K Plan, 14 Weeks Specific Phase	
MON Time: 0:40	**Easy run/walk:** Zone 1–2 power run. Run 40 min as 4 min run at Zone 2, 1 min walk at Zone 1. Repeat for the duration of the run.
TUES Time: 1:10	**3/9-min Stryd test:** Warm up 15 min, preparing for hard effort at the end; conduct a 3-min interval at maximal effort; recover with 5-min walk, 10 min easy jog, 5 min walk, 5 min easy jog, 5 min walk (30 min total); conduct a 9-min interval at maximal effort; cool down 10–15 min easy. *Follow the protocol for this test and estimating rFTPw and rFTPa per Chapter 4.*
WED Time: 0:40	**Easy run/walk:** Zone 1–2 power run. Run 40 min as 4 min run at Zone 2, 1 min walk at Zone 1. Repeat for the duration of the run.
THURS Time: 0:40	**Easy run/walk:** Zone 1–2 power run. Run 40 min as 4 min run at Zone 2, 1 min walk at Zone 1. Repeat for the duration of the run.
FRI Time: 1:00	**30-min test:** Warm up 15 min, preparing for a hard effort at the end. Start a 30-min time trial (best effort) on a flat road or track, collecting power data (pace and HR data as well if possible). Cool down 10–15 min easy. *Follow the protocol for this test and estimating rFTPw and rFTPa in Chapter 4. Now you should begin to see a good relationship between the 3/9 test and the 30-min test. To avoid the 30-min test for the rest of the plan, focus on using the 3-min.*
Time: 0:30	**2nd run of the day:** Easy Zone 1–2 jog
SAT Time: 0	**Day off:** Actively focus on recovery today: (1) stay off legs all you can; (2) watch nutrition closely (healthy carbs, lean protein, good fats); (3) stretch; (4) drink when thirsty. Other common recovery aids include massage, napping, elevating legs, floating in water, and listening to music.
SUN Time: 1:30	**Envelope run:** Start easy in Zone 1–2 for the first 10–15 min, then work to a moderate pace on the edge of comfort/discomfort. Look at the power zone you are in, likely Zone 3–4. Stay in that zone, but find a way to go faster. Push that envelope, trying to be quicker without raising your watts. It's a balance of trying to hold or increase speed with technique. Focus on your rhythm, cadence, forward lean, soft foot strike, relaxation, eyes and head position. Last 10 min should be easy Zone 1–2 running.
Time: 0:30	**2nd run of the day:** Easy Zone 1–2 jog

Total time: 6:40

WEEK 5 Sub-32-Min 10K Plan, 14 Weeks Specific Phase	
MON Time: 0:40	**Easy run/walk:** Zone 1–2 power run. Run 40 min as 6 min run at Zone 2, 1 min walk at Zone 1. Repeat for the duration of the run. *This 7-min sequence won't divide evenly into 40, so you will finish on a run. Walk a few minutes after.*
TUES Time: 1:00	**Fartlek:** Run of surges. Warm up well for about 15 min, building from Zone 1–2 to Zone 3–5. On rolling course, run 1–2-min pickups at faster than 5K pace (Zone 6–7), with recoveries at Zone 1–2 as long as you feel you need between the surges. Form! Cadence! Use the last 10 min to cool down with easy Zone 1 running/walking.
WED Time: 1:00	**Envelope run:** Start easy in Zone 1–2 for the first 10–15 min, then work to a moderate pace on the edge of comfort/discomfort. Look at the power zone you are in, likely Zone 3–4. Stay in that zone, but find a way to go faster. Push that envelope, trying to be quicker without raising your watts. It's a balance of trying to hold or increase speed with technique. Focus on your rhythm, cadence, forward lean, soft foot strike, relaxation, eyes and head position. Last 10 min should be easy Zone 1–2 running.
Time: 0:30	**2nd run of the day:** Easy Zone 1–2 jog
THURS Time: 1:10	**8 × 800:** Warm up well for about 15 min, building from Zone 1–2 to Zone 3–5. Then, on track, run 8 × 800 at 10K goal pace, with 2 min recovery between. Monitor the power zone in which you run these. They should be in Zone 5, some Zone 6. You might see more Zone 6 later in the workout as you begin to break down. If you are in Zone 6–7 the whole time, review how realistic your goal pace is or whether your rFTPw is too low. Cool down for 15 min, easy Zone 1–2 jogging and walking. *If you don't have a track, do the intervals on the road, using a GPS, for 0.8 km/0.5 mile.*
FRI Time: 0:40	**Easy run/walk:** Zone 1–2 power run. Run 40 min as 6 min run at Zone 2, 1 min walk at Zone 1. Repeat for the duration of the run. *This 7-min sequence won't divide evenly into 40, so you will finish on a run. Walk a few minutes after.*
Time: 0:30	**2nd run of the day:** Easy Zone 1–2 jog
SAT Time: 1:30	**6 × 1 mile:** Warm up well for about 15 min, building from Zone 1–2 to Zone 3–5. Find a flat stretch and run 6 × 1 mile (or 1.6 km) at Zone 5. Do *not* go above Zone 5. Stay in Zone 5 with 3-min recovery jog at Zone 1–2 between each. Cool down for 15 min with easy Zone 2 jogging and Zone 1 walking.
Time: 0:30	**2nd run of the day:** Easy Zone 1–2 jog
SUN Time: 1:30	**Easy run/walk:** Zone 1–2 power run. Do this as 9 min run at Zone 2, 1 min walk at Zone 1. Repeat for the duration of the run.

Total time: 9:00

WEEK 6 Sub-32-Min 10K Plan, 14 Weeks Specific Phase

MON Time: 0:40	**Easy run/walk:** Zone 1–2 power run. Run 40 min as 6 min run at Zone 2, 1 min walk at Zone 1. Repeat for the duration of the run. *This 7-min sequence won't divide evenly into 40, so you will finish on a run. Walk a few minutes after.*
TUES Time: 1:10	**4 × 1 mile:** Warm up well for about 15 min, building from Zone 1–2 to Zone 3–5. Find a flat stretch and run 4 × 1 mile (or 1.6 km) at Zone 4. Do *not* go above Zone 4. Stay in Zone 4 with 3-min recovery jog at Zone 1–2 between each. Cool down to make 70 min with easy Zone 2 jogging and Zone 1 walking.
WED Time: 1:00	**Envelope run:** Start easy in Zone 1–2 for the first 10–15 min, then work to a moderate pace on the edge of comfort/discomfort. Look at the power zone you are in, likely Zone 3–4. Stay in that zone, but find a way to go faster. Push that envelope, trying to be quicker without raising your watts. It's a balance of trying to hold or increase speed with technique. Focus on your rhythm, cadence, forward lean, soft foot strike, relaxation, eyes and head position. Last 10 min should be easy Zone 1–2 running.
Time: 0:30	**2nd run of the day:** Easy Zone 1–2 jog
THURS Time: 1:10	**VO$_2$ intervals:** Warm up well for about 15 min, building from Zone 1–2 to Zone 3–5. Then do 6 × 3 min at 5K goal pace. Take note of the power zone you are in at that pace. Try to be more efficient, get more speed per watt while running. Take a 3-min recovery interval as 1 min walk Zone 1, 2 min easy jog Zone 2. Afterward do a 15 min easy Zone 1–2 power cooldown. *You may do this as 6 × 800 on the track if you prefer.*
Time: 0:30	**2nd run of the day:** Easy Zone 1–2 jog
FRI Time: 0	**Day off:** Actively focus on recovery today: (1) stay off legs all you can; (2) watch nutrition closely (healthy carbs, lean protein, good fats); (3) stretch; (4) drink when thirsty. Other common recovery aids include massage, napping, elevating legs, floating in water, and listening to music.
SAT Time: 1:20	**Goal-pace run:** Warm up well for about 15 min, building from Zone 1–2 to Zone 3–5. Then, on a track or flat road, run 10 × 800 at 10K goal pace, with 2 min recovery. Your watts should line up in Zone 5, perhaps some in Zone 6. You might see more Zone 6 later in the workout, as you begin to break down. If you are Zone 7 the whole time, you want to review how realistic your goal pace is, or if your rFTPw is too low. After the second interval and 2-min rest, do 1 km at 5K goal pace. Cool down for 15 min with easy Zone 2 jogging and Zone 1 walking. *If you don't have a track, do the intervals on the road, using a GPS, for 0.8 km/0.5 mile.*
Time: 0:30	**2nd run of the day:** Easy Zone 1–2 jog
SUN Time: 1:45	**Easy run/walk:** Zone 1–2 power run. Do this as 9 min run at Zone 2, 1 min walk at Zone 1. Repeat for the duration of the run. *The run/walk portion won't divide perfectly, so you will finish with a run. Walk a few minutes after.*
Time: 0:30	**2nd run of the day:** Easy Zone 1–2 jog

Total time: 9:05

WEEK 7 Sub-32-Min 10K Plan, 14 Weeks Specific Phase	
MON Time: 0:40	**Easy run/walk:** Zone 1–2 power run. Run 40 min as 4 min run at Zone 2, 1 min walk at Zone 1. Repeat for the duration of the run.
TUES Time: 1:10	**4 × 1 mile:** Warm up well for about 15 min, building from Zone 1–2 to Zone 3–5. Find a flat stretch and run 4 × 1 mile (or 1.6 km) at Zone 5. Do *not* go above Zone 5. Stay in Zone 5 with 3-min recovery jog at Zone 1–2 between each. Cool down for 15 min with easy Zone 2 jogging and Zone 1 walking.
WED Time: 0:40	**Easy run/walk:** Zone 1–2 power run. Run 40 min as 4 min run at Zone 2, 1 min walk at Zone 1. Repeat for the duration of the run.
THURS Time: 1:10	**Goal-pace run:** Warm up well for about 15 min, building from Zone 1–2 to Zone 3–5. Then, on a track or flat road, run 5 × 2 km at 10K goal pace, with 3 min recovery. Your watts should line up in Zone 6, perhaps some in Zone 7. Cool down for 15 min with easy Zone 2 jogging and Zone 1 walking. *After this run, assess your EI at your goal pace/intensity.*
Time: 0:30	**2nd run of the day:** Easy Zone 1–2 jog
FRI Time: 0:40	**Easy run/walk:** Zone 1–2 power run. Run 40 min as 4 min run at Zone 2, 1 min walk at Zone 1. Repeat for the duration of the run.
SAT Time: 1:00	**12 × 400:** Warm up well for about 15 min, building from Zone 1–2 to Zone 3–5. Then, on track, run 12 × 400 at 10K goal pace, on a 2 min interval. This means every 2 min you will do a 400, and you have 2 min to conduct the 400 at your goal pace, *and* get your rest, before starting the next 400. So if you run the 400 in 90 sec, you have 30 sec of rest. Monitor the power zone in which you run these. They should be in Zone 5, some Zone 6. You might see more Zone 6 later in the workout as you begin to break down. If you are in Zone 6–7 the whole time, review how realistic your goal pace is or whether your rFTPw is too low. Cool down for 15 min, easy Zone 1–2 jogging and walking. *If you don't have a track, do the intervals on the road, using a GPS, for 0.4 km/0.25 mile.*
Time: 0:30	**2nd run of the day:** Easy Zone 1–2 jog
SUN Time: 1:45	**Easy run/walk:** Zone 1–2 power run. Do this as 9 min run at Zone 2, 1 min walk at Zone 1. Repeat for the duration of the run. *The run/walk portion won't divide perfectly, so you will finish with a run. Walk a few minutes after.*
Time: 0:30	**2nd run of the day:** Easy Zone 1–2 jog

Total time: 8:35

WEEK 8 Sub-32-Min 10K Plan, 14 Weeks Specific Phase	
MON Time: 0	**Day off:** Actively focus on recovery today: (1) stay off legs all you can; (2) watch nutrition closely (healthy carbs, lean protein, good fats); (3) stretch; (4) drink when thirsty. Other common recovery aids include massage, napping, elevating legs, floating in water, and listening to music.
TUES Time: 0:40	**Easy run/walk:** Zone 1–2 power run. Run 40 min as 4 min run at Zone 2, 1 min walk at Zone 1. Repeat for the duration of the run.
WED Time: 1:10	**3/9-min Stryd test:** Warm up 15 min, preparing for hard effort at the end; conduct a 3-min interval at maximal effort; recover with 5-min walk, 10 min easy jog, 5 min walk, 5 min easy jog, 5 min walk (30 min total); conduct a 9-min interval at maximal effort; cool down 10–15 min easy. *Follow the protocol for this test and estimating rFTPw and rFTPa per Chapter 4.*
Time: 0:30	**2nd run of the day:** Easy Zone 1–2 jog
THURS Time: 0:40	**Easy run/walk:** Zone 1–2 power run. Run 40 min as 4 min run at Zone 2, 1 min walk at Zone 1. Repeat for the duration of the run.
FRI Time: 1:00	**Envelope run:** Start easy in Zone 1–2 for the first 10–15 min, then work to a moderate pace on the edge of comfort/discomfort. Look at the power zone you are in, likely Zone 3–4. Stay in that zone, but find a way to go faster. Push that envelope, trying to be quicker without raising your watts. It's a balance of trying to hold or increase speed with technique. Focus on your rhythm, cadence, forward lean, soft foot strike, relaxation, eyes and head position. Last 10 min should be easy Zone 1–2 running.
Time: 0:30	**2nd run of the day:** Easy Zone 1–2 jog
SAT Time: 1:20	**Fartlek:** Run of surges. Warm up well for about 15 min, building from Zone 1–2 to Zone 3–5. On rolling course, run 1–2-min pickups at faster than 5K pace (Zone 6–7), with recoveries at Zone 1–2 as long as you feel you need between the surges. Form! Cadence! Use the last 10 min to cool down with easy Zone 1 running/walking.
Time: 0:30	**2nd run of the day:** Easy Zone 1–2 jog
SUN Time: 1:45	**Envelope run:** Start easy in Zone 1–2 for the first 10–15 min, then work to a moderate pace on the edge of comfort/discomfort. Look at the power zone you are in, likely Zone 3–4. Stay in that zone, but find a way to go faster. Push that envelope, trying to be quicker without raising your watts. It's a balance of trying to hold or increase speed with technique. Focus on your rhythm, cadence, forward lean, soft foot strike, relaxation, eyes and head position. Last 10 min should be easy Zone 1–2 running.
Time: 0:30	**2nd run of the day:** Easy Zone 1–2 jog

Total time: 8:35

WEEK 9 Sub-32-Min 10K Plan, 14 Weeks Specific Phase

MON Time: 0	**Day off:** Actively focus on recovery today: (1) stay off legs all you can; (2) watch nutrition closely (healthy carbs, lean protein, good fats); (3) stretch; (4) drink when thirsty. Other common recovery aids include massage, napping, elevating legs, floating in water, and listening to music.
TUES Time: 1:00	**Fartlek:** Run of surges. Warm up well for about 15 min, building from Zone 1–2 to Zone 3–5. On rolling course, run 1-2-min pickups at faster than 5K pace (Zone 6–7), with recoveries at Zone 1–2 as long as you feel you need between the surges. Form! Cadence! Use the last 10 min to cool down with easy Zone 1 running/walking.
Time: 0:30	**2nd run of the day:** Easy Zone 1–2 jog
WED Time: 0:40	**Easy run/walk:** Zone 1–2 power run. Run 40 min as 4 min run at Zone 2, 1 min walk at Zone 1. Repeat for the duration of the run.
THURS Time: 1:10	**Goal-pace run:** Warm up well for about 15 min, building from Zone 1–2 to Zone 3–5. Then, on a track or flat road, run 5 × 2 km at 10K goal pace, with 3 min recovery. Your watts should line up in Zone 5, perhaps some in Zone 6. Cool down for 15 min with easy Zone 2 jogging and Zone 1 walking. *After this run, assess your EI at your goal pace/intensity.*
Time: 0:30	**2nd run of the day:** Easy Zone 1–2 jog
FRI Time: 0:40	**Easy run/walk:** Zone 1–2 power run. Run 40 min as 4 min run at Zone 2, 1 min walk at Zone 1. Repeat for the duration of the run.
SAT Time: 1:20	**16 × 400:** Warm up well for about 15 min, building from Zone 1–2 to Zone 3–5. Then, on track, run 16 × 400 at 10K goal pace, on a 2 min interval. This means every 2 min you will do a 400, and you have 2 min to conduct the 400 at your goal pace, *and* get your rest, before starting the next 400. So if you run the 400 in 90 sec, you have 30 sec of rest. Monitor the power zone in which you run these. They should be in Zone 5, some Zone 6. You might see more Zone 6 later in the workout as you begin to break down. If you are in Zone 6–7 the whole time, review how realistic your goal pace is or whether your rFTPw is too low. Cool down for 15 min, easy Zone 1–2 jogging and walking. *If you don't have a track, do the intervals on the road, using a GPS, for 0.4 km/0.25 mile.*
Time: 0:30	**2nd run of the day:** Easy Zone 1–2 jog
SUN Time: 1:45	**Envelope run:** Start easy in Zone 1–2 for the first 10–15 min, then work to a moderate pace on the edge of comfort/discomfort. Look at the power zone you are in, likely Zone 3–4. Stay in that zone, but find a way to go faster. Push that envelope, trying to be quicker without raising your watts. It's a balance of trying to hold or increase speed with technique. Focus on your rhythm, cadence, forward lean, soft foot strike, relaxation, eyes and head position. Last 10 min should be easy Zone 1–2 running.
Time: 0:30	**2nd run of the day:** Easy Zone 1–2 jog

Total time: 8:35

	WEEK 10 Sub-32-Min 10K Plan, 14 Weeks Specific Phase
MON Time: 0	**Day off:** Actively focus on recovery today: (1) stay off legs all you can; (2) watch nutrition closely (healthy carbs, lean protein, good fats); (3) stretch; (4) drink when thirsty. Other common recovery aids include massage, napping, elevating legs, floating in water, and listening to music.
TUES Time: 1:00	**Fartlek:** Run of surges. Warm up well for about 15 min, building from Zone 1–2 to Zone 3–5. On rolling course, run 1–2-min pickups at faster than 5K pace (Zone 6–7), with recoveries at Zone 1–2 as long as you feel you need between the surges. Form! Cadence! Use the last 10 min to cool down with easy Zone 1 running/walking.
Time: 0:30	**2nd run of the day:** Easy Zone 1–2 jog
WED Time: 0:40	**Easy run/walk:** Zone 1–2 power run. Run 40 min as 4 min run at Zone 2, 1 min walk at Zone 1. Repeat for the duration of the run.
THURS Time: 1:10	**Goal-pace run:** Warm up well for about 15 min, building from Zone 1–2 to Zone 3–5. Then, on a track or flat road, run 5 × 2 km at 10K goal pace, with 2 min recovery. Your watts should line up in Zone 5, perhaps some in Zone 6. Cool down for 15 min with easy Zone 2 jogging and Zone 1 walking. *After this run, assess your EI at your goal pace/intensity.*
Time: 0:30	**2nd run of the day:** Easy Zone 1–2 jog
FRI Time: 0:40	**Easy run/walk:** Zone 1–2 power run. Run 40 min as 4 min run at Zone 2, 1 min walk at Zone 1. Repeat for the duration of the run.
SAT Time: 1:20	**18 × 400:** Warm up well for about 15 min, building from Zone 1–2 to Zone 3–5. Then, on track, run 18 × 400 at 10K goal pace, on a 2 min interval. This means every 2 min you will do a 400, and you have 2 min to conduct the 400 at your goal pace, *and* get your rest, before starting the next 400. So if you run the 400 in 90 sec, you have 30 sec of rest. Monitor the power zone in which you run these. They should be in Zone 5, some Zone 6. You might see more Zone 6 later in the workout as you begin to break down. If you are in Zone 6–7 the whole time, review how realistic your goal pace is or whether your rFTPw is too low. Cool down for 15 min, easy Zone 1–2 jogging and walking. *If you don't have a track, do the intervals on the road, using a GPS, for 0.4 km/0.25 mile.*
Time: 0:30	**2nd run of the day:** Easy Zone 1–2 jog
SUN Time: 2:00	**Envelope run:** Start easy in Zone 1–2 for the first 10–15 min, then work to a moderate pace on the edge of comfort/discomfort. Look at the power zone you are in, likely Zone 3–4. Stay in that zone, but find a way to go faster. Push that envelope, trying to be quicker without raising your watts. It's a balance of trying to hold or increase speed with technique. Focus on your rhythm, cadence, forward lean, soft foot strike, relaxation, eyes and head position. Last 10 min should be easy Zone 1–2 running.
Time: 0:30	**2nd run of the day:** Easy Zone 1–2 jog

Total time: 8:50

MON Time: 0	**Day off:** Actively focus on recovery today: (1) stay off legs all you can; (2) watch nutrition closely (healthy carbs, lean protein, good fats); (3) stretch; (4) drink when thirsty. Other common recovery aids include massage, napping, elevating legs, floating in water, and listening to music.
TUES Time: 1:00	**Fartlek:** Run of surges. Warm up well for about 15 min, building from Zone 1–2 to Zone 3–5. On rolling course, run 1–2-min pickups at faster than 5K pace (Zone 6–7), with recoveries at Zone 1–2 as long as you feel you need between the surges. Form! Cadence! Use the last 10 min to cool down with easy Zone 1 running/walking.
Time: 0:30	**2nd run of the day:** Easy Zone 1–2 jog
WED Time: 0:40	**Easy run/walk:** Zone 1–2 power run. Run 40 min as 4 min run at Zone 2, 1 min walk at Zone 1. Repeat for the duration of the run.
THURS Time: 1:10	**Goal-pace run:** Warm-up well for 15 min building from Zone 1–2 to Zone 3–5. Then, on a track or flat road, run 3 × 2 km at 10K goal pace, with 3 min recovery. Then do 3 × 1 km, with 2 min recovery. Your watts should line up in Zone 5, perhaps some in Zone 6. Cool down for 15 min with easy Zone 2 jogging and Zone 1 walking. *After this run, assess your EI at your goal pace/intensity.*
Time: 0:30	**2nd run of the day:** Easy Zone 1–2 jog
FRI Time: 0:40	**Easy run/walk:** Zone 1–2 power run. Run 40 min as 4 min run at Zone 2, 1 min walk at Zone 1. Repeat for the duration of the run.
SAT Time: 1:30	**20 × 400:** Warm up well for about 15 min, building from Zone 1–2 to Zone 3–5. Then, on track, run 20 × 400 at 10K goal pace, on a 2 min interval. This means every 2 min you will do a 400, and you have 2 min to conduct the 400 at your goal pace, *and* get your rest, before starting the next 400. So if you run the 400 in 90 sec, you have 30 sec of rest. Monitor the power zone in which you run these. They should be in Zone 5, some Zone 6. You might see more Zone 6 later in the workout as you begin to break down. If you are in Zone 6–7 the whole time, review how realistic your goal pace is or whether your rFTPw is too low. Cool down for 15 min, easy Zone 1–2 jogging and walking. *If you don't have a track, do the intervals on the road, using a GPS, for 0.4 km/0.25 mile.*
Time: 0:30	**2nd run of the day:** Easy Zone 1–2 jog
SUN Time: 2:00	**Envelope run:** Start easy in Zone 1–2 for the first 10–15 min, then work to a moderate pace on the edge of comfort/discomfort. Look at the power zone you are in, likely Zone 3–4. Stay in that zone, but find a way to go faster. Push that envelope, trying to be quicker without raising your watts. It's a balance of trying to hold or increase speed with technique. Focus on your rhythm, cadence, forward lean, soft foot strike, relaxation, eyes and head position. Last 10 min should be easy Zone 1–2 running.
Time: 0:30	**2nd run of the day:** Easy Zone 1–2 jog

Total time: 9:00

MON Time: 0	**Day off:** Actively focus on recovery today: (1) stay off legs all you can; (2) watch nutrition closely (healthy carbs, lean protein, good fats); (3) stretch; (4) drink when thirsty. Other common recovery aids include massage, napping, elevating legs, floating in water, and listening to music.
TUES Time: 0:40	**Easy run/walk:** Zone 1–2 power run. Run 40 min as 4 min run at Zone 2, 1 min walk at Zone 1. Repeat for the duration of the run.
WED Time: 1:10	**3/9-min Stryd test:** Warm up 15 min, preparing for hard effort at the end; conduct a 3-min interval at maximal effort; recover with 5-min walk, 10 min easy jog, 5 min walk, 5 min easy jog, 5 min walk (30 min total); conduct a 9-min interval at maximal effort; cool down 10–15 min easy. *Follow the protocol for this test and estimating rFTPw and rFTPa per Chapter 4.*
Time: 0:30	**2nd run of the day:** Easy Zone 1–2 jog
THURS Time: 0:40	**Easy run/walk:** Zone 1–2 power run. Run 40 min as 4 min run at Zone 2, 1 min walk at Zone 1. Repeat for the duration of the run.
FRI Time: 1:00	**Envelope run:** Start easy in Zone 1–2 for the first 10–15 min, then work to a moderate pace on the edge of comfort/discomfort. Look at the power zone you are in, likely Zone 3–4. Stay in that zone, but find a way to go faster. Push that envelope, trying to be quicker without raising your watts. It's a balance of trying to hold or increase speed with technique. Focus on your rhythm, cadence, forward lean, soft foot strike, relaxation, eyes and head position. Last 10 min should be easy Zone 1–2 running.
SAT Time: 1:00	**Fartlek:** Run of surges. Warm up well for about 15 min, building from Zone 1–2 to Zone 3–5. On rolling course, run 1–2-min pickups at faster than 5K pace (Zone 6–7), with recoveries at Zone 1–2 as long as you feel you need between the surges. Form! Cadence! Use the last 10 min to cool down with easy Zone 1 running/walking.
Time: 0:30	**2nd run of the day:** Easy Zone 1–2 jog
SUN Time: 0	**Day off:** Actively focus on recovery today: (1) stay off legs all you can; (2) watch nutrition closely (healthy carbs, lean protein, good fats); (3) stretch; (4) drink when thirsty. Other common recovery aids include massage, napping, elevating legs, and compression wear.

Total time: 5:30

WEEK 13 Sub-32-Min 10K Plan, 14 Weeks Specific Phase

MON Time: 0:45	**Goal-pace run:** Warm up well for 15 min, building from Zone 1–2 to Zone 3–5. Then, on a track or flat road, run 3 × 2 km at 10K goal pace, with 3 min recovery. Then do 3 × 1 km, with 2 min recovery. Your watts should line up in Zone 5, perhaps some in Zone 6. Cool down for 15 min with easy Zone 2 jogging and Zone 1 walking. *After this run, assess your EI at your goal pace/intensity.*
TUES Time: 0:40	**Easy run/walk:** Zone 1–2 power run. Run 40 min as 4 min run at Zone 2, 1 min walk at Zone 1. Repeat for the duration of the run.
Time: 0:30	**2nd run of the day:** Easy Zone 1–2 jog
WED Time: 1:00	**Fartlek:** Run of surges. Warm up well for about 15 min, building from Zone 1–2 to Zone 3–5. On rolling course, run 1–2-min pickups at faster than 5K pace (Zone 6–7), with recoveries at Zone 1–2 as long as you feel you need between the surges. Form! Cadence! Use the last 10 min to cool down with easy Zone 1 running/walking.
THURS Time: 0:40	**Easy run/walk:** Zone 1–2 power run. Run 40 min as 4 min run at Zone 2, 1 min walk at Zone 1. Repeat for the duration of the run.
Time: 0:30	**2nd run of the day:** Easy Zone 1–2 jog
FRI Time: 0	**Day off:** Actively focus on recovery today: (1) stay off legs all you can; (2) watch nutrition closely (healthy carbs, lean protein, good fats); (3) stretch; (4) drink when thirsty. Other common recovery aids include massage, napping, elevating legs, and compression wear.
SAT Time: 1:00	**12 × 400:** Warm up well for about 15 min, building from Zone 1–2 to Zone 3–5. Then, on track, run 12 × 400 at 10K goal pace, on a 2 min interval. This means every 2 min you will do a 400, and you have 2 min to conduct the 400 at your goal pace, *and* get your rest, before starting the next 400. So if you run the 400 in 90 sec, you have 30 sec of rest. Monitor the power zone in which you run these. They should be in Zone 5, some Zone 6. You might see more Zone 6 later in the workout as you begin to break down. If you are in Zone 6–7 the whole time, review how realistic your goal pace is or whether your rFTPw is too low. Cool down for 15 min, easy Zone 1–2 jogging and walking. *If you don't have a track, do the intervals on the road, using a GPS, for 0.4 km/0.25 mile.*
Time: 0:30	**2nd run of the day:** Easy Zone 1–2 jog
SUN Time: 0:40	**Easy run/walk:** Zone 1–2 power run. Run 40 min as 4 min run at Zone 2, 1 min walk at Zone 1. Repeat for the duration of the run.

Total time: 6:15

WEEK 14 Sub-32-Min 10K Plan, 14 Weeks Specific Phase

MON Time: 0	**Day off:** Actively focus on recovery today: (1) stay off legs all you can; (2) watch nutrition closely (healthy carbs, lean protein, good fats); (3) stretch; (4) drink when thirsty. Other common recovery aids include massage, napping, elevating legs, and compression wear.
TUES Time: 0:40	**5 × 2 min at Zone 4–6:** 15 min warm-up run, followed by 5 × 2 min, starting at Zone 4 for the first min, then building to Zone 5–6 in the last min, with 2 min easy recovery jog. Easy cool down in Zone 1–2 to make 40 min.
WED Time: 0:40 Time: 0:30	**Easy run/walk:** Zone 1–2 power run. Run 40 min as 4 min run at Zone 2, 1 min walk at Zone 1. Repeat for the duration of the run. **2nd run of the day:** Easy Zone 1–2 jog
THURS Time: 0:30	**Run with surges:** First part of the run is easy, then do 5–7 × 7 sec surges at Zone 6–7 with long recoveries, getting faster over the course of the run. Really focus on forefoot strike, quick cadence, slight forward lean, and fluid motion, not forcing it.
FRI Time: 0:20	**Preview course:** Run start and finish of course. Note landmarks. Include several accelerations to race pace. Otherwise, keep power in Zone 1.
SAT	**10K RACE**

Total time: 2:40

WEEK 1	Sub-40-Min 10K Plan, 14 Weeks Specific Phase
MON Time: 1:10	**3/9-min Stryd test:** Warm up 15 min, preparing for hard effort at the end; conduct a 3-min interval at maximal effort; recover with 5-min walk, 10 min easy jog, 5 min walk, 5 min easy jog, 5 min walk (30 min total); conduct a 9-min interval at maximal effort; cool down 10–15 min easy. *Follow the protocol for this test and estimating rFTPw and rFTPa per Chapter 4.*
TUES Time: 0:40	**Easy run/walk:** Zone 1–2 power run. Run 40 min as 4 min run at Zone 2, 1 min walk at Zone 1. Repeat for the duration of the run.
WED Time: 0:40	**Easy run/walk:** Zone 1–2 power run. Run 40 min as 4 min run at Zone 2, 1 min walk at Zone 1. Repeat for the duration of the run.
THURS Time: 1:00	**30-min test:** Warm up 15 min, preparing for a hard effort at the end. Start a 30-min time trial (best effort) on a flat road or track, collecting power data (pace and HR data as well if possible). Cool down 10–15 min easy. *Follow the protocol for this test and estimating rFTPw and rFTPa per Chapter 4.*
FRI Time: 0:40 Time: 0:30	**Easy run/walk:** Zone 1–2 power run. Run 40 min as 4 min run at Zone 2, 1 min walk at Zone 1. Repeat for the duration of the run. **2nd run of the day:** Easy Zone 1–2 jog
SAT Time: 0	**Day off:** Actively focus on recovery today: (1) stay off legs all you can; (2) watch nutrition closely (healthy carbs, lean protein, good fats); (3) stretch; (4) drink when thirsty. Other common recovery aids include massage, napping, elevating legs, floating in water, and compression wear.
SUN Time: 1:00 Time: 0:30	**Easy run/walk:** Zone 1–2 power run. Do this as 5 min run at Zone 2, 1 min walk at Zone 1. Repeat for the duration of the run. **2nd run of the day:** Easy Zone 1–2 jog

Total time: 6:10

WEEK 2 Sub-40-Min 10K Plan, 14 Weeks Specific Phase

MON Time: 1:00	**Cruise intervals:** Warm up 15 min, building intensity through the warm-up, starting at Zone 1, then the last min at zones 4–5. Then do 3 × 8 min, build to Zone 5–6 (3-min recoveries). Monitor pace, trying to be faster for the same power output. Cool down 15 min, at Zone 1–2.
TUES Time: 0:40	**Easy run/walk:** Zone 1–2 power run. Run 40 min as 4 min run at Zone 2, 1 min walk at Zone 1. Repeat for the duration of the run.
WED Time: 1:00	**Cruise intervals:** Warm up 15 min, building intensity through the warm-up, starting at Zone 1, then the last min at zones 4–5. Then do 3 × 8 min, build to Zone 5–6 (3-min recoveries). Monitor pace, trying to be faster for the same power output. Cool down 15 min, at Zone 1–2.
Time: 0:30	**2nd run of the day:** Easy Zone 1–2 jog
THURS Time: 0:40	**Easy run/walk:** Zone 1–2 power run. Run 40 min as 4 min run at Zone 2, 1 min walk at Zone 1. Repeat for the duration of the run.
FRI Time: 1:00	**Envelope run:** Start easy in Zone 1–2 for the first 10–15 min, then work to a moderate pace on the edge of comfort/discomfort. Look at the power zone you are in, likely Zone 3–4. Stay in that zone, but find a way to go faster. Push that envelope, trying to be quicker without raising your watts. It's a balance of trying to hold or increase speed with technique. Focus on your rhythm, cadence, forward lean, soft foot strike, relaxation, eyes and head position. Last 10 min should be easy Zone 1–2 running.
Time: 0:30	**2nd run of the day:** Easy Zone 1–2 jog
SAT Time: 1:00	**Cruise intervals:** Warm up 15 min, building intensity through the warm-up, starting at Zone 1, then the last min at zones 4–5. Then do 3 × 8 min, build to Zone 5–6 (3-min recoveries). Monitor pace, trying to be faster for the same power output. Cool down 15 min, at Zone 1–2.
SUN Time: 1:10	**Easy run/walk:** Zone 1–2 power run. Do this as 5 min run at Zone 2, 1 min walk at Zone 1. Repeat for the duration of the run. *The run/walk portion won't divide perfectly, so you will finish with a run. Walk a few minutes after.*
Time: 0:30	**2nd run of the day:** Easy Zone 1–2 jog

Total time: 8:00

WEEK 3 Sub-40-Min 10K Plan, 14 Weeks Specific Phase	
MON Time: 0:40	**Easy run/walk:** Zone 1–2 power run. Run 40 min as 4 min run at Zone 2, 1 min walk at Zone 1. Repeat for the duration of the run.
TUES Time: 1:00	**VO$_2$ intervals:** Warm up well for about 15 min, building from Zone 1–2 to Zone 3–5. Then do 5 × 3 min at 5K goal pace. Take note of the power zone you are in at that pace. Try to be more efficient, get more speed per watt while running. Take a 3-min recovery interval as 1 min walk Zone 1, 2 min easy jog Zone 2. Afterward do a 15 min easy Zone 1–2 power cooldown. *You may do this as 6 × 800 on the track if you prefer.*
WED Time: 1:00 Time: 0:30	**Envelope run:** Start easy in Zone 1–2 for the first 10–15 min, then work to a moderate pace on the edge of comfort/discomfort. Look at the power zone you are in, likely Zone 3–4. Stay in that zone, but find a way to go faster. Push that envelope, trying to be quicker without raising your watts. It's a balance of trying to hold or increase speed with technique. Focus on your rhythm, cadence, forward lean, soft foot strike, relaxation, eyes and head position. Last 10 min should be easy Zone 1–2 running. **2nd run of the day:** Easy Zone 1–2 jog
THURS Time: 0:40	**Easy run/walk:** Zone 1–2 power run. Run 40 min as 4 min run at Zone 2, 1 min walk at Zone 1. Repeat for the duration of the run.
FRI Time: 1:00 Time: 0:30	**VO$_2$ intervals:** Warm up well for about 15 min, building from Zone 1–2 to Zone 3–5. Then do 5 × 3 min at 5K goal pace. Take note of the power zone you are in at that pace. Try to be more efficient, get more speed per watt while running. Take a 3-min recovery interval as 1 min walk Zone 1, 2 min easy jog Zone 2. Afterward do a 15 min easy Zone 1–2 power cooldown. *You may do this as 6 × 800 on the track if you prefer.* **2nd run of the day:** Easy Zone 1–2 jog
SAT Time: 1:20 Time: 0:30	**Easy run/walk:** Zone 1–2 power run. Do this as 7 min run at Zone 2, 1 min walk at Zone 1. Repeat for the duration of the run. **2nd run of the day:** Easy Zone 1–2 jog
SUN Time: 0	**Day off:** Actively focus on recovery today: (1) stay off legs all you can; (2) watch nutrition closely (healthy carbs, lean protein, good fats); (3) stretch; (4) drink when thirsty. Other common recovery aids include massage, napping, elevating legs, and compression wear.

Total time: 7:10

WEEK 4 Sub-40-Min 10K Plan, 14 Weeks Specific Phase	
MON Time: 0:40	**Easy run/walk:** Zone 1–2 power run. Run 40 min as 4 min run at Zone 2, 1 min walk at Zone 1. Repeat for the duration of the run.
TUES Time: 1:10	**3/9-min Stryd test:** Warm up 15 min, preparing for hard effort at the end; conduct a 3-min interval at maximal effort; recover with 5-min walk, 10 min easy jog, 5 min walk, 5 min easy jog, 5 min walk (30 min total); conduct a 9-min interval at maximal effort; cool down 10–15 min easy. *Follow the protocol for this test and estimating rFTPw and rFTPa per Chapter 4.*
WED Time: 0:40	**Easy run/walk:** Zone 1–2 power run. Run 40 min as 4 min run at Zone 2, 1 min walk at Zone 1. Repeat for the duration of the run.
THURS Time: 0:40	**Easy run/walk:** Zone 1–2 power run. Run 40 min as 4 min run at Zone 2, 1 min walk at Zone 1. Repeat for the duration of the run.
FRI Time: 1:00	**30-min test:** Warm up 15 min, preparing for a hard effort at the end. Start a 30-min time trial (best effort) on a flat road or track, collecting power data (pace and HR data as well if possible). Cool down 10–15 min easy. *Follow the protocol for this test and estimating rFTPw and rFTPa in Chapter 4. Now you should begin to see a good relationship between the 3/9 test and the 30-min test. To avoid the 30-min test for the rest of the plan, focus on using the 3-min.*
Time: 0:30	**2nd run of the day:** Easy Zone 1–2 jog
SAT Time: 0	**Day off:** Actively focus on recovery today: (1) stay off legs all you can; (2) watch nutrition closely (healthy carbs, lean protein, good fats); (3) stretch; (4) drink when thirsty. Other common recovery aids include massage, napping, elevating legs, floating in water, and listening to music.
SUN Time: 1:30	**Envelope run:** Start easy in Zone 1–2 for the first 10–15 min, then work to a moderate pace on the edge of comfort/discomfort. Look at the power zone you are in, likely Zone 3–4. Stay in that zone, but find a way to go faster. Push that envelope, trying to be quicker without raising your watts. It's a balance of trying to hold or increase speed with technique. Focus on your rhythm, cadence, forward lean, soft foot strike, relaxation, eyes and head position. Last 10 min should be easy Zone 1–2 running.
Time: 0:30	**2nd run of the day:** Easy Zone 1–2 jog

Total time: 6:40

WEEK 5 Sub-40-Min 10K Plan, 14 Weeks Specific Phase

MON Time: 0:40	**Easy run/walk:** Zone 1–2 power run. Run 40 min as 6 min run at Zone 2, 1 min walk at Zone 1. Repeat for the duration of the run. *This 7-min sequence won't divide evenly into 40, so you will finish on a run. Walk a few minutes after.*
TUES Time: 1:00	**Fartlek:** Run of surges. Warm up well for about 15 min, building from Zone 1–2 to Zone 3–5. On rolling course, run 1–2-min pickups at faster than 5K pace (Zone 6–7), with recoveries at Zone 1–2 as long as you feel you need between the surges. Form! Cadence! Use the last 10 min to cool down with easy Zone 1 running/walking.
WED Time: 1:00	**Envelope run:** Start easy in Zone 1–2 for the first 10–15 min, then work to a moderate pace on the edge of comfort/discomfort. Look at the power zone you are in, likely Zone 3–4. Stay in that zone, but find a way to go faster. Push that envelope, trying to be quicker without raising your watts. It's a balance of trying to hold or increase speed with technique. Focus on your rhythm, cadence, forward lean, soft foot strike, relaxation, eyes and head position. Last 10 min should be easy Zone 1–2 running.
Time: 0:30	**2nd run of the day:** Easy Zone 1–2 jog
THURS Time: 0:40	**Easy run/walk:** Zone 1–2 power run. Run 40 min as 6 min run at Zone 2, 1 min walk at Zone 1. Repeat for the duration of the run. *This 7-min sequence won't divide evenly into 40, so you will finish on a run. Walk a few minutes after.*
FRI Time: 1:10	**8 × 800:** Warm up well for about 15 min, building from Zone 1–2 to Zone 3–5. Then, on track, run 8 × 800 at 10K goal pace, with 2 min recovery between. Monitor the power zone in which you run these. They should be in Zone 5, some Zone 6. You might see more Zone 6 later in the workout as you begin to break down. If you are in Zone 6–7 the whole time, review how realistic your goal pace is or whether your rFTPw is too low. Cool down for 15 min, easy Zone 1–2 jogging and walking. *If you don't have a track, do the intervals on the road, using a GPS, for 0.8 km/0.5 mile.*
Time: 0:30	**2nd run of the day:** Easy Zone 1–2 jog
SAT Time: 1:30	**6 × 1 mile:** Warm up well for about 15 min, building from Zone 1–2 to Zone 3–5. Find a flat stretch and run 6 × 1 mile (or 1.6 km) at Zone 4. Do *not* go above Zone 4. Stay in Zone 4 with 3-min recovery jog at Zone 1–2 between each. Cool down for 15 min with easy Zone 2 jogging and Zone 1 walking.
Time: 0:30	**2nd run of the day:** Easy Zone 1–2 jog
SUN Time: 1:30	**Easy run/walk:** Zone 1–2 power run. Do this as 9 min run at Zone 2, 1 min walk at Zone 1. Repeat for the duration of the run.

Total time: 9:00

WEEK 6 Sub-40-Min 10K Plan, 14 Weeks Specific Phase	
MON Time: 0:40	**Easy run/walk:** Zone 1–2 power run. Run 40 min as 6 min run at Zone 2, 1 min walk at Zone 1. Repeat for the duration of the run. *This 7-min sequence won't divide evenly into 40, so you will finish on a run. Walk a few minutes after.*
TUES Time: 1:10	**4 × 1 mile:** Warm up well for about 15 min, building from Zone 1–2 to Zone 3–5. Find a flat stretch and run 4 × 1 mile (or 1.6 km) at Zone 4. Do *not* go above Zone 4. Stay in Zone 4 with 3-min recovery jog at Zone 1–2 between each. Cool down for 15 min with easy Zone 2 jogging and Zone 1 walking.
WED Time: 1:00 Time: 0:30	**Envelope run:** Start easy in Zone 1–2 for the first 10–15 min, then work to a moderate pace on the edge of comfort/discomfort. Look at the power zone you are in, likely Zone 3–4. Stay in that zone, but find a way to go faster. Push that envelope, trying to be quicker without raising your watts. It's a balance of trying to hold or increase speed with technique. Focus on your rhythm, cadence, forward lean, soft foot strike, relaxation, eyes and head position. Last 10 min should be easy Zone 1–2 running. **2nd run of the day:** Easy Zone 1–2 jog
THURS Time: 1:10 Time: 0:30	**VO₂ intervals:** Warm up well for about 15 min, building from Zone 1–2 to Zone 3–5. Then do 6 × 3 min at 5K goal pace. Take note of the power zone you are in at that pace. Try to be more efficient, get more speed per watt while running. Take a 3-min recovery interval as 1 min walk Zone 1, 2 min easy jog Zone 2. Afterward do a 15 min easy Zone 1–2 power cooldown. *You may do this as 6 × 800 on the track if you prefer.* **2nd run of the day:** Easy Zone 1–2 jog
FRI Time: 0	**Day off:** Actively focus on recovery today: (1) stay off legs all you can; (2) watch nutrition closely (healthy carbs, lean protein, good fats); (3) stretch; (4) drink when thirsty. Other common recovery aids include massage, napping, elevating legs, floating in water, and listening to music.
SAT Time: 1:20 Time: 0:30	**10 × 800:** Warm up well for about 15 min, building from Zone 1–2 to Zone 3–5. Then, on track, run 10 × 800 at 10K goal pace, with 2 min recovery between. Monitor the power zone in which you run these. They should be in Zone 5, some Zone 6. You might see more Zone 6 later in the workout as you begin to break down. If you are in Zone 7 the whole time, review how realistic your goal pace is or whether your rFTPw is too low. Cool down for 15 min, easy Zone 1–2 jogging and walking. *If you don't have a track, do the intervals on the road, using a GPS, for 0.8 km/0.5 mile.* **2nd run of the day:** Easy Zone 1–2 jog
SUN Time: 1:45 Time: 0:30	**Easy run/walk:** Zone 1–2 power run. Do this as 9 min run at Zone 2, 1 min walk at Zone 1. Repeat for the duration of the run. *The run/walk portion won't divide perfectly, so you will finish with a run. Walk a few minutes after.* **2nd run of the day:** Easy Zone 1–2 jog

Total time: 9:05

WEEK 7 Sub-40-Min 10K Plan, 14 Weeks Specific Phase

MON Time: 0:40	**Easy run/walk:** Zone 1–2 power run. Run 40 min as 4 min run at Zone 2, 1 min walk at Zone 1. Repeat for the duration of the run.
TUES Time: 1:10	**4 × 1 mile:** Warm up well for about 15 min, building from Zone 1–2 to Zone 3–5. Find a flat stretch and run 4 × 1 mile (or 1.6 km) at Zone 5. Do *not* go above Zone 5. Stay in Zone 5 with 3-min recovery jog at Zone 1–2 between each. Cool down for 15 min with easy Zone 2 jogging and Zone 1 walking.
WED Time: 0:40	**Easy run/walk:** Zone 1–2 power run. Run 40 min as 4 min run at Zone 2, 1 min walk at Zone 1. Repeat for the duration of the run.
THURS Time: 1:20	**Goal-pace run:** Warm up well for about 15 min, building from Zone 1–2 to Zone 3–5. Then, on a track or flat road, run 4 × 2 km at 10K goal pace, with 3 min recovery. Your watts should line up in Zone 5, perhaps some in Zone 6. Cool down for 15 min with easy Zone 2 jogging and Zone 1 walking. *After this run, assess your EI at your goal pace/intensity.*
Time: 0:30	**2nd run of the day:** Easy Zone 1–2 jog
FRI Time: 0:40	**Easy run/walk:** Zone 1–2 power run. Run 40 min as 4 min run at Zone 2, 1 min walk at Zone 1. Repeat for the duration of the run.
SAT Time: 1:00	**12 × 400:** Warm up well for about 15 min, building from Zone 1–2 to Zone 3–5. Then, on track, run 12 × 400 at 10K goal pace, on a 2 min interval. This means every 2 min you will do a 400, and you have 2 min to conduct the 400 at your goal pace, *and* get your rest, before starting the next 400. So if you run the 400 in 90 sec, you have 30 sec of rest. Monitor the power zone in which you run these. They should be in Zone 5, some Zone 6. You might see more Zone 6 later in the workout as you begin to break down. If you are in Zone 6–7 the whole time, review how realistic your goal pace is or whether your rFTPw is too low. Cool down for 15 min, easy Zone 1–2 jogging and walking. *If you don't have a track, do the intervals on the road, using a GPS, for 0.4 km/0.25 mile.*
Time: 0:30	**2nd run of the day:** Easy Zone 1–2 jog
SUN Time: 1:45	**Easy run/walk:** Zone 1–2 power run. Do this as 9 min run at Zone 2, 1 min walk at Zone 1. Repeat for the duration of the run. *The run/walk portion won't divide perfectly, so you will finish with a run. Walk a few minutes after.*
Time: 0:30	**2nd run of the day:** Easy Zone 1–2 jog

Total time: 8:45

WEEK 8 Sub-40-Min 10K Plan, 14 Weeks Specific Phase

MON Time: 0	**Day off:** Actively focus on recovery today: (1) stay off legs all you can; (2) watch nutrition closely (healthy carbs, lean protein, good fats); (3) stretch; (4) drink when thirsty. Other common recovery aids include massage, napping, elevating legs, and compression wear.
TUES Time: 0:40	**Easy run/walk:** Zone 1–2 power run. Run 40 min as 4 min run at Zone 2, 1 min walk at Zone 1. Repeat for the duration of the run.
WED Time: 1:10	**3/9-min Stryd test:** Warm up 15 min, preparing for hard effort at the end; conduct a 3-min interval at maximal effort; recover with 5-min walk, 10 min easy jog, 5 min walk, 5 min easy jog, 5 min walk (30 min total); conduct a 9-min interval at maximal effort; cool down 10–15 min easy. *Follow the protocol for this test and estimating rFTPw and rFTPa per Chapter 4.*
Time: 0:30	**2nd run of the day:** Easy Zone 1–2 jog
THURS Time: 0:40	**Easy run/walk:** Zone 1–2 power run. Run 40 min as 4 min run at Zone 2, 1 min walk at Zone 1. Repeat for the duration of the run.
FRI Time: 1:00	**Envelope run:** Start easy in Zone 1–2 for the first 10–15 min, then work to a moderate pace on the edge of comfort/discomfort. Look at the power zone you are in, likely Zone 3–4. Stay in that zone, but find a way to go faster. Push that envelope, trying to be quicker without raising your watts. It's a balance of trying to hold or increase speed with technique. Focus on your rhythm, cadence, forward lean, soft foot strike, relaxation, eyes and head position. Last 10 min should be easy Zone 1–2 running.
Time: 0:30	**2nd run of the day:** Easy Zone 1–2 jog
SAT Time: 1:20	**Fartlek:** Run of surges. Warm up well for about 15 min, building from Zone 1–2 to Zone 3–5. On rolling course, run 1–2-min pickups at faster than 5K pace (Zone 6–7), with recoveries at Zone 1–2 as long as you feel you need between the surges. Form! Cadence! Use the last 10 min to cool down with easy Zone 1 running/walking.
Time: 0:30	**2nd run of the day:** Easy Zone 1–2 jog
SUN Time: 1:45	**Envelope run:** Start easy in Zone 1–2 for the first 10–15 min, then work to a moderate pace on the edge of comfort/discomfort. Look at the power zone you are in, likely Zone 3–4. Stay in that zone, but find a way to go faster. Push that envelope, trying to be quicker without raising your watts. It's a balance of trying to hold or increase speed with technique. Focus on your rhythm, cadence, forward lean, soft foot strike, relaxation, eyes and head position. Last 10 min should be easy Zone 1–2 running.
Time: 0:30	**2nd run of the day:** Easy Zone 1–2 jog

Total time: 8:35

MON Time: 0	**Day off:** Actively focus on recovery today: (1) stay off legs all you can; (2) watch nutrition closely (healthy carbs, lean protein, good fats); (3) stretch; (4) drink when thirsty. Other common recovery aids include massage, napping, elevating legs, floating in water, and listening to music.
TUES Time: 1:00	**Fartlek:** Run of surges. Warm up well for about 15 min, building from Zone 1–2 to Zone 3–5. On rolling course, run 1–2-min pickups at faster than 5K pace (Zone 6–7), with recoveries at Zone 1–2 as long as you feel you need between the surges. Form! Cadence! Use the last 10 min to cool down with easy Zone 1 running/walking.
Time: 0:30	**2nd run of the day:** Easy Zone 1–2 jog
WED Time: 0:40	**Easy run/walk:** Zone 1–2 power run. Run 40 min as 4 min run at Zone 2, 1 min walk at Zone 1. Repeat for the duration of the run.
THURS Time: 1:20	**Goal-pace run:** Warm up well for about 15 min, building from Zone 1–2 to Zone 3–5. Then, on a track or flat road, run 4 × 2 km at 10K goal pace, with 3 min recovery. Your watts should line up in Zone 5, perhaps some in Zone 6. Cool down for 15 min with easy Zone 2 jogging and Zone 1 walking. *After this run, assess your EI at your goal pace/intensity.*
Time: 0:30	**2nd run of the day:** Easy Zone 1–2 jog
FRI Time: 0:40	**Easy run/walk:** Zone 1–2 power run. Run 40 min as 4 min run at Zone 2, 1 min walk at Zone 1. Repeat for the duration of the run.
SAT Time: 1:20	**16 × 400:** Warm up well for about 15 min, building from Zone 1–2 to Zone 3–5. Then, on track, run 16 × 400 at 10K goal pace, on a 2 min interval. This means every 2 min you will do a 400, and you have 2 min to conduct the 400 at your goal pace, *and* get your rest, before starting the next 400. So if you run the 400 in 90 sec, you have 30 sec of rest. Monitor the power zone in which you run these. They should be in Zone 5, some Zone 6. You might see more Zone 6 later in the workout as you begin to break down. If you are in Zone 6–7 the whole time, review how realistic your goal pace is or whether your rFTPw is too low. Cool down for 15 min, easy Zone 1–2 jogging and walking. *If you don't have a track, do the intervals on the road, using a GPS, for 0.4 km/0.25 mile.*
Time: 0:30	**2nd run of the day:** Easy Zone 1–2 jog
SUN Time: 1:45	**Envelope run:** Start easy in Zone 1–2 for the first 10–15 min, then work to a moderate pace on the edge of comfort/discomfort. Look at the power zone you are in, likely Zone 3–4. Stay in that zone, but find a way to go faster. Push that envelope, trying to be quicker without raising your watts. It's a balance of trying to hold or increase speed with technique. Focus on your rhythm, cadence, forward lean, soft foot strike, relaxation, eyes and head position. Last 10 min should be easy Zone 1–2 running.
Time: 0:30	**2nd run of the day:** Easy Zone 1–2 jog

Total time: 8:45

MON Time: 0	**Day off:** Actively focus on recovery today: (1) stay off legs all you can; (2) watch nutrition closely (healthy carbs, lean protein, good fats); (3) stretch; (4) drink when thirsty. Other common recovery aids include massage, napping, elevating legs, floating in water, and listening to music.
TUES Time: 1:00	**Fartlek:** Run of surges. Warm up well for about 15 min, building from Zone 1–2 to Zone 3–5. On rolling course, run 1-2-min pickups at faster than 5K pace (Zone 6–7), with recoveries at Zone 1–2 as long as you feel you need between the surges. Form! Cadence! Use the last 10 min to cool down with easy Zone 1 running/walking.
Time: 0:30	**2nd run of the day:** Easy Zone 1–2 jog
WED Time: 0:40	**Easy run/walk:** Zone 1–2 power run. Run 40 min as 4 min run at Zone 2, 1 min walk at Zone 1. Repeat for the duration of the run.
THURS Time: 1:10	**Goal-pace run:** Warm up well for about 15 min, building from Zone 1–2 to Zone 3–5. Then, on a track or flat road, run 4 × 2 km at 10K goal pace, with 3 min recovery. Your watts should line up in Zone 5, perhaps some in Zone 6. Cool down for 15 min with easy Zone 2 jogging and Zone 1 walking. *After this run, assess your EI at your goal pace/intensity.*
Time: 0:30	**2nd run of the day:** Easy Zone 1–2 jog
FRI Time: 0:40	**Easy run/walk:** Zone 1–2 power run. Run 40 min as 4 min run at Zone 2, 1 min walk at Zone 1. Repeat for the duration of the run.
SAT Time: 1:20	**18 × 400:** Warm up well for about 15 min, building from Zone 1–2 to Zone 3–5. Then, on track, run 18 × 400 at 10K goal pace, on a 2 min interval. This means every 2 min you will do a 400, and you have 2 min to conduct the 400 at your goal pace, *and* get your rest, before starting the next 400. So if you run the 400 in 90 sec, you have 30 sec of rest. Monitor the power zone in which you run these. They should be in Zone 5, some Zone 6. You might see more Zone 6 later in the workout as you begin to break down. If you are in Zone 6–7 the whole time, review how realistic your goal pace is or whether your rFTPw is too low. Cool down for 15 min, easy Zone 1–2 jogging and walking. *If you don't have a track, do the intervals on the road, using a GPS, for 0.4 km/0.25 mile.*
Time: 0:30	**2nd run of the day:** Easy Zone 1–2 jog
SUN Time: 2:00	**Envelope run:** Start easy in Zone 1–2 for the first 10–15 min, then work to a moderate pace on the edge of comfort/discomfort. Look at the power zone you are in, likely Zone 3–4. Stay in that zone, but find a way to go faster. Push that envelope, trying to be quicker without raising your watts. It's a balance of trying to hold or increase speed with technique. Focus on your rhythm, cadence, forward lean, soft foot strike, relaxation, eyes and head position. Last 10 min should be easy Zone 1–2 running.
Time: 0:30	**2nd run of the day:** Easy Zone 1–2 jog

Total time: 8:50

WEEK 11	Sub-40-Min 10K Plan, 14 Weeks Specific Phase
MON Time: 0	**Day off:** Actively focus on recovery today: (1) stay off legs all you can; (2) watch nutrition closely (healthy carbs, lean protein, good fats); (3) stretch; (4) drink when thirsty. Other common recovery aids include massage, napping, elevating legs, floating in water, and listening to music.
TUES Time: 1:00	**Fartlek:** Run of surges. Warm up well for about 15 min, building from Zone 1–2 to Zone 3–5. On rolling course, run 1-2-min pickups at faster than 5K pace (Zone 6–7), with recoveries at Zone 1–2 as long as you feel you need between the surges. Form! Cadence! Use the last 10 min to cool down with easy Zone 1 running/walking.
Time: 0:30	**2nd run of the day:** Easy Zone 1–2 jog
WED Time: 0:40	**Easy run/walk:** Zone 1–2 power run. Run 40 min as 4 min run at Zone 2, 1 min walk at Zone 1. Repeat for the duration of the run.
THURS Time: 1:20	**Goal-pace run:** Warm-up well for 15 min building from Zone 1–2 to Zone 3–5. Then, on a track or flat road, run 4 × 2 km at 10K goal pace, with 3 min recovery. Your watts should line up in Zone 5, perhaps some in Zone 6. Cool down for 15 min with easy Zone 2 jogging and Zone 1 walking. *After this run, assess your EI at your goal pace/intensity.*
Time: 0:30	**2nd run of the day:** Easy Zone 1–2 jog
FRI Time: 0:40	**Easy run/walk:** Zone 1–2 power run. Run 40 min as 4 min run at Zone 2, 1 min walk at Zone 1. Repeat for the duration of the run.
SAT Time: 1:30	**20 × 400:** Warm up well for about 15 min, building from Zone 1–2 to Zone 3–5. Then, on track, run 20 × 400 at 10K goal pace, on a 2 min interval. This means every 2 min you will do a 400, and you have 2 min to conduct the 400 at your goal pace, *and* get your rest, before starting the next 400. So if you run the 400 in 90 sec, you have 30 sec of rest. Monitor the power zone in which you run these. They should be in Zone 5, some Zone 6. You might see more Zone 6 later in the workout as you begin to break down. If you are in Zone 6–7 the whole time, review how realistic your goal pace is or whether your rFTPw is too low. Cool down for 15 min, easy Zone 1–2 jogging and walking. *If you don't have a track, do the intervals on the road, using a GPS, for 0.4 km/0.25 mile.*
Time: 0:30	**2nd run of the day:** Easy Zone 1–2 jog
SUN Time: 2:00	**Envelope run:** Start easy in Zone 1–2 for the first 10–15 min, then work to a moderate pace on the edge of comfort/discomfort. Look at the power zone you are in, likely Zone 3–4. Stay in that zone, but find a way to go faster. Push that envelope, trying to be quicker without raising your watts. It's a balance of trying to hold or increase speed with technique. Focus on your rhythm, cadence, forward lean, soft foot strike, relaxation, eyes and head position. Last 10 min should be easy Zone 1–2 running.
Time: 0:30	**2nd run of the day:** Easy Zone 1–2 jog

Total time: 9:10

WEEK 12 Sub-40-Min 10K Plan, 14 Weeks Specific Phase

MON Time: 0	**Day off:** Actively focus on recovery today: (1) stay off legs all you can; (2) watch nutrition closely (healthy carbs, lean protein, good fats); (3) stretch; (4) drink when thirsty. Other common recovery aids include massage, napping, elevating legs, floating in water, and listening to music.
TUES Time: 0:40	**Easy run/walk:** Zone 1–2 power run. Run 40 min as 4 min run at Zone 2, 1 min walk at Zone 1. Repeat for the duration of the run.
WED Time: 1:10	**3/9-min Stryd test:** Warm up 15 min, preparing for hard effort at the end; conduct a 3-min interval at maximal effort; recover with 5-min walk, 10 min easy jog, 5 min walk, 5 min easy jog, 5 min walk (30 min total); conduct a 9-min interval at maximal effort; cool down 10–15 min easy. *Follow the protocol for this test and estimating rFTPw and rFTPa per Chapter 4.*
Time: 0:30	**2nd run of the day:** Easy Zone 1–2 jog
THURS Time: 0:40	**Easy run/walk:** Zone 1–2 power run. Run 40 min as 4 min run at Zone 2, 1 min walk at Zone 1. Repeat for the duration of the run.
FRI Time: 1:00	**Envelope run:** Start easy in Zone 1–2 for the first 10–15 min, then work to a moderate pace on the edge of comfort/discomfort. Look at the power zone you are in, likely Zone 3–4. Stay in that zone, but find a way to go faster. Push that envelope, trying to be quicker without raising your watts. It's a balance of trying to hold or increase speed with technique. Focus on your rhythm, cadence, forward lean, soft foot strike, relaxation, eyes and head position. Last 10 min should be easy Zone 1–2 running.
SAT Time: 1:00	**Fartlek:** Run of surges. Warm up well for about 15 min, building from Zone 1–2 to Zone 3–5. On rolling course, run 1–2-min pickups at faster than 5K pace (Zone 6–7), with recoveries at Zone 1–2 as long as you feel you need between the surges. Form! Cadence! Use the last 10 min to cool down with easy Zone 1 running/walking.
Time: 0:30	**2nd run of the day:** Easy Zone 1–2 jog
SUN Time: 0	**Day off:** Actively focus on recovery today: (1) stay off legs all you can; (2) watch nutrition closely (healthy carbs, lean protein, good fats); (3) stretch; (4) drink when thirsty. Other common recovery aids include massage, napping, elevating legs, and compression wear.

Total time: 5:30

WEEK 13 Sub-40-Min 10K Plan, 14 Weeks Specific Phase	
MON Time: 1:20	**Goal-pace run:** Warm up well for 15 min, building from Zone 1–2 to Zone 3–5. Then, on a track or flat road, run 4 × 2 km at 10K goal pace, with 3 min recovery. Your watts should line up in Zone 5, perhaps some in Zone 6. Cool down for 15 min with easy Zone 2 jogging and Zone 1 walking. *After this run, assess your EI at your goal pace/intensity.*
TUES Time: 0:40	**Easy run/walk:** Zone 1–2 power run. Run 40 min as 4 min run at Zone 2, 1 min walk at Zone 1. Repeat for the duration of the run.
Time: 0:30	**2nd run of the day:** Easy Zone 1–2 jog
WED Time: 1:00	**Fartlek:** Run of surges. Warm up well for about 15 min, building from Zone 1–2 to Zone 3–5. On rolling course, run 1-2-min pickups at faster than 5K pace (Zone 6–7), with recoveries at Zone 1–2 as long as you feel you need between the surges. Form! Cadence! Use the last 10 min to cool down with easy Zone 1 running/walking.
THURS Time: 0:40	**Easy run/walk:** Zone 1–2 power run. Run 40 min as 4 min run at Zone 2, 1 min walk at Zone 1. Repeat for the duration of the run.
Time: 0:30	**2nd run of the day:** Easy Zone 1–2 jog
FRI Time: 0	**Day off:** Actively focus on recovery today: (1) stay off legs all you can; (2) watch nutrition closely (healthy carbs, lean protein, good fats); (3) stretch; (4) drink when thirsty. Other common recovery aids include massage, napping, elevating legs, and compression wear.
SAT Time: 1:00	**12 × 400:** Warm up well for about 15 min, building from Zone 1–2 to Zone 3–5. Then, on track, run 12 × 400 at 10K goal pace, on a 2 min interval. This means every 2 min you will do a 400, and you have 2 min to conduct the 400 at your goal pace, *and* get your rest, before starting the next 400. So if you run the 400 in 90 sec, you have 30 sec of rest. Monitor the power zone in which you run these. They should be in Zone 5, some Zone 6. You might see more Zone 6 later in the workout as you begin to break down. If you are in Zone 6–7 the whole time, review how realistic your goal pace is or whether your rFTPw is too low. Cool down for 15 min, easy Zone 1–2 jogging and walking. *If you don't have a track, do the intervals on the road, using a GPS, for 0.4 km/0.25 mile.*
Time: 0:30	**2nd run of the day:** Easy Zone 1–2 jog
SUN Time: 0:40	**Easy run/walk:** Zone 1–2 power run. Run 40 min as 4 min run at Zone 2, 1 min walk at Zone 1. Repeat for the duration of the run.

Total time: 6:50

WEEK 14 Sub-40-Min 10K Plan, 14 Weeks Specific Phase

MON Time: 0	**Day off:** Actively focus on recovery today: (1) stay off legs all you can; (2) watch nutrition closely (healthy carbs, lean protein, good fats); (3) stretch; (4) drink when thirsty. Other common recovery aids include massage, napping, elevating legs, and compression wear.
TUES Time: 0:40	**5 × 2 min at Zone 4–6:** 15 min warm-up run, followed by 5 × 2 min, starting at Zone 4 for the first min, then building to Zone 5–6 in the last min, with 2 min easy recovery jog. Easy cool down in Zone 1–2 to make 40 min.
WED Time: 0:40 Time: 0:30	**Easy run/walk:** Zone 1–2 power run. Run 40 min as 4 min run at Zone 2, 1 min walk at Zone 1. Repeat for the duration of the run. **2nd run of the day:** Easy Zone 1–2 jog
THURS Time: 0:30	**Run with surges:** First part of the run is easy, then do 5–7 × 7 sec surges at Zone 6–7 with long recoveries, getting faster over the course of the run. Really focus on forefoot strike, quick cadence, slight forward lean, and fluid motion, not forcing it.
FRI Time: 0:20	**Preview course:** Run start and finish of course. Note landmarks. Include several accelerations to race pace. Otherwise, keep power in Zone 1.
SAT	**10K RACE**

Total time: 2:40

WEEK 1 Sub-1:20 Half-Marathon Plan, 14 Weeks Specific Phase	
MON Time: 1:10	**3/9-min Stryd test:** Warm up 15 min, preparing for hard effort at the end; conduct a 3-min interval at maximal effort; recover with 5-min walk, 10 min easy jog, 5 min walk, 5 min easy jog, 5 min walk (30 min total); conduct a 9-min interval at maximal effort; cool down 10–15 min easy. *Follow the protocol for this test and estimating rFTPw and rFTPa per Chapter 4.*
TUES Time: 0:40	**Easy run/walk:** Zone 1–2 power run. Run 40 min as 4 min run at Zone 2, 1 min walk at Zone 1. Repeat for the duration of the run.
WED Time: 0:40	**Easy run/walk:** Zone 1–2 power run. Run 40 min as 4 min run at Zone 2, 1 min walk at Zone 1. Repeat for the duration of the run.
THURS Time: 1:00	**30-min test:** Warm up 15 min, preparing for a hard effort at the end. Start a 30-min time trial (best effort) on a flat road or track, collecting power data (pace and HR data as well if possible). Cool down 10–15 min easy. *Follow the protocol for this test and estimating rFTPw and rFTPa per Chapter 4.*
FRI Time: 0:40 Time: 0:30	**Easy run/walk:** Zone 1–2 power run. Run 40 min as 4 min run at Zone 2, 1 min walk at Zone 1. Repeat for the duration of the run. **2nd run of the day:** Easy Zone 1–2 jog
SAT Time: 0	**Day off:** Actively focus on recovery today: (1) stay off legs all you can; (2) watch nutrition closely (healthy carbs, lean protein, good fats); (3) stretch; (4) drink when thirsty. Other common recovery aids include massage, napping, elevating legs, floating in water, and compression wear.
SUN Time: 1:00 Time: 0:30	**Easy run/walk:** Zone 1–2 power run. Do this as 5 min run at Zone 2, 1 min walk at Zone 1. Repeat for the duration of the run. **2nd run of the day:** Easy Zone 1–2 jog

Total time: 6:10

WEEK 2 Sub-1:20 Half-Marathon Plan, 14 Weeks Specific Phase

MON Time: 1:10	**Cruise intervals:** Warm up 15 min, building intensity through the warm-up, starting at Zone 1, then the last min at zones 4–5. Then do 4 × 8 min, build to Zone 3–4 (2-min recoveries). Monitor pace, trying to be faster for the same power output. Cool down 15 min, at Zone 1–2.
TUES Time: 0:40	**Easy run/walk:** Zone 1–2 power run. Run 40 min as 4 min run at Zone 2, 1 min walk at Zone 1. Repeat for the duration of the run.
WED Time: 1:00	**Cruise intervals:** Warm up 15 min, building intensity through the warm-up, starting at Zone 1, then the last min at zones 4–5. Then do 3 × 8 min, build to Zone 5–6 (3-min recoveries). Monitor pace, trying to be faster for the same power output. Cool down 15 min, at Zone 1–2.
Time: 0:30	**2nd run of the day:** Easy Zone 1–2 jog
THURS Time: 0:40	**Easy run/walk:** Zone 1–2 power run. Run 40 min as 4 min run at Zone 2, 1 min walk at Zone 1. Repeat for the duration of the run.
FRI Time: 1:00	**Envelope run:** Start easy in Zone 1–2 for the first 10–15 min, then work to a moderate pace on the edge of comfort/discomfort. Look at the power zone you are in, likely Zone 3–4. Stay in that zone, but find a way to go faster. Push that envelope, trying to be quicker without raising your watts. It's a balance of trying to hold or increase speed with technique. Focus on your rhythm, cadence, forward lean, soft foot strike, relaxation, eyes and head position. Last 10 min should be easy Zone 1–2 running.
Time: 0:30	**2nd run of the day:** Easy Zone 1–2 jog
SAT Time: 1:10	**Cruise intervals:** Warm up 15 min, building intensity through the warm-up, starting at Zone 1, then the last min at zones 4–5. Then do 5 × 6 min, build to Zone 5 (2-min recoveries). Monitor pace, trying to be faster for the same power output. Cool down 15 min, at Zone 1–2.
SUN Time: 1:15	**Easy run/walk:** Zone 1–2 power run. Do this as 5 min run at Zone 2, 1 min walk at Zone 1. Repeat for the duration of the run. *The run/walk portion won't divide perfectly, so you will finish with a run. Walk a few minutes after.*
Time: 0:30	**2nd run of the day:** Easy Zone 1–2 jog

Total time: 8:25

WEEK 3 Sub-1:20 Half-Marathon Plan, 14 Weeks Specific Phase

MON Time: 0:40	**Easy run/walk:** Zone 1–2 power run. Run 40 min as 4 min run at Zone 2, 1 min walk at Zone 1. Repeat for the duration of the run.
TUES Time: 1:00	**Goal-pace tempo run:** Warm up well for about 15 min, building to Zone 4 for the last min. As you build, do a few surges at Zone 5, lasting about 10–15 sec each. Rest for a few min. Then do a 30-min tempo run at your half-marathon goal pace, at Zone 4–5, on a course similar to the race. Cool down for 15 min, easy Zone 1–2 jogging and walking.
WED Time: 0:40 Time: 0:30	**Easy run/walk:** Zone 1–2 power run. Run 40 min as 4 min run at Zone 2, 1 min walk at Zone 1. Repeat for the duration of the run. **2nd run of the day:** Easy Zone 1–2 jog
THURS Time: 1:00 Time: 0:30	**Fartlek:** Run of surges. Warm up well for about 15 min, building from Zone 1–2 to Zone 3–5. On rolling course, run 1–2-min pickups at faster than 10K pace (Zone 5–6), with recoveries at Zone 1–2 as long as you feel you need between the surges. Form! Cadence! Use the last 10 min to cool down with easy Zone 1 running/walking. **2nd run of the day:** Easy Zone 1–2 jog
FRI Time: 1:00	**Envelope run:** Start easy in Zone 1–2 for the first 10–15 min, then work to a moderate pace on the edge of comfort/discomfort. Look at the power zone you are in, likely Zone 3–4. Stay in that zone, but find a way to go faster. Push that envelope, trying to be quicker without raising your watts. It's a balance of trying to hold or increase speed with technique. Focus on your rhythm, cadence, forward lean, soft foot strike, relaxation, eyes and head position. Last 10 min should be easy Zone 1–2 running.
SAT Time: 1:30 Time: 0:30	**Easy run/walk:** Zone 1–2 power run. Do this as 9 min run at Zone 2, 1 min walk at Zone 1. Repeat for the duration of the run. **2nd run of the day:** Easy Zone 1–2 jog
SUN Time: 0	**Day off:** Actively focus on recovery today: (1) stay off legs all you can; (2) watch nutrition closely (healthy carbs, lean protein, good fats); (3) stretch; (4) drink when thirsty. Other common recovery aids include massage, napping, elevating legs, and compression wear.

Total time: 7:20

WEEK 4 Sub-1:20 Half-Marathon Plan, 14 Weeks Specific Phase	
MON Time: 0:40	**Easy run/walk:** Zone 1–2 power run. Run 40 min as 4 min run at Zone 2, 1 min walk at Zone 1. Repeat for the duration of the run.
TUES Time: 1:10	**3/9-min Stryd test:** Warm up 15 min, preparing for hard effort at the end; conduct a 3-min interval at maximal effort; recover with 5-min walk, 10 min easy jog, 5 min walk, 5 min easy jog, 5 min walk (30 min total); conduct a 9-min interval at maximal effort; cool down 10–15 min easy. *Follow the protocol for this test and estimating rFTPw and rFTPa per Chapter 4.*
WED Time: 0:40	**Easy run/walk:** Zone 1–2 power run. Run 40 min as 4 min run at Zone 2, 1 min walk at Zone 1. Repeat for the duration of the run.
THURS Time: 0:40	**Easy run/walk:** Zone 1–2 power run. Run 40 min as 4 min run at Zone 2, 1 min walk at Zone 1. Repeat for the duration of the run.
FRI Time: 1:00	**30-min test:** Warm up 15 min, preparing for a hard effort at the end. Start a 30-min time trial (best effort) on a flat road or track, collecting power data (pace and HR data as well if possible). Cool down 10–15 min easy. *Follow the protocol for this test and estimating rFTPw and rFTPa in Chapter 4. Now you should begin to see a good relationship between the 3/9 test and the 30-min test. To avoid the 30-min test for the rest of the plan, focus on using the 3-min.*
Time: 0:30	**2nd run of the day:** Easy Zone 1–2 jog
SAT Time: 0	**Day off:** Actively focus on recovery today: (1) stay off legs all you can; (2) watch nutrition closely (healthy carbs, lean protein, good fats); (3) stretch; (4) drink when thirsty. Other common recovery aids include massage, napping, elevating legs, floating in water, and listening to music.
SUN Time: 1:30	**Envelope run:** Start easy in Zone 1–2 for the first 10–15 min, then work to a moderate pace on the edge of comfort/discomfort. Look at the power zone you are in, likely Zone 3–4. Stay in that zone, but find a way to go faster. Push that envelope, trying to be quicker without raising your watts. It's a balance of trying to hold or increase speed with technique. Focus on your rhythm, cadence, forward lean, soft foot strike, relaxation, eyes and head position. Last 10 min should be easy Zone 1–2 running.
Time: 0:30	**2nd run of the day:** Easy Zone 1–2 jog

Total time: 6:40

WEEK 5 Sub-1:20 Half-Marathon Plan, 14 Weeks Specific Phase	
MON Time: 0:40	**Easy run/walk:** Zone 1–2 power run. Run 40 min as 6 min run at Zone 2, 1 min walk at Zone 1. Repeat for the duration of the run. *This 7-min sequence won't divide evenly into 40, so you will finish on a run. Walk a few minutes after.*
TUES Time: 1:00	**Fartlek:** Run of surges. Warm up well for about 15 min, building from Zone 1–2 to Zone 3–5. On rolling course, run 1–2-min pickups at faster than 10K pace (Zone 6–7), with recoveries at Zone 1–2 as long as you feel you need between the surges. Form! Cadence! Use the last 10 min to cool down with easy Zone 1 running/walking.
WED Time: 1:00	**Envelope run:** Start easy in Zone 1–2 for the first 10–15 min, then work to a moderate pace on the edge of comfort/discomfort. Look at the power zone you are in, likely Zone 3–4. Stay in that zone, but find a way to go faster. Push that envelope, trying to be quicker without raising your watts. It's a balance of trying to hold or increase speed with technique. Focus on your rhythm, cadence, forward lean, soft foot strike, relaxation, eyes and head position. Last 10 min should be easy Zone 1–2 running.
Time: 0:30	**2nd run of the day:** Easy Zone 1–2 jog
THURS Time: 1:10	**6 × 1 mile:** Warm up well for about 15 min, building from Zone 1–2 to Zone 3–5. Find a flat stretch and run 6 × 1 mile (or 1.6 km) at your half-marathon goal pace, Zone 4–5. Do *not* go above Zone 5. Recover with 2-min jog/walk at Zone 1–2 between each mile. Cool down for 15 min with easy Zone 2 jogging and Zone 1 walking.
Time: 0:30	**2nd run of the day:** Easy Zone 1–2 jog
FRI Time: 0:40	**Easy run/walk:** Zone 1–2 power run. Run 40 min as 6 min run at Zone 2, 1 min walk at Zone 1. Repeat for the duration of the run. *This 7-min sequence won't divide evenly into 40, so you will finish on a run. Walk a few minutes after.*
SAT Time: 1:20	**Goal-pace tempo run:** Warm up well for about 15 min, building to Zone 4 for the last min. As you build, do a few surges in Zone 5, lasting about 10–15 sec each. Rest for a few min. Then do a 4 × 10-min tempo run at your half-marathon goal pace, in Zone 4–5, on a course similar to the race, with 2-min recoveries between. Cool down for 15 min, easy Zone 1–2 jogging and walking.
Time: 0:30	**2nd run of the day:** Easy Zone 1–2 jog
SUN Time: 1:30	**Easy run/walk:** Zone 1–2 power run. Do this as 9 min run at Zone 2, 1 min walk at Zone 1. Repeat for the duration of the run.
Time: 0:30	**2nd run of the day:** Easy Zone 1–2 jog

Total time: 9:20

WEEK 6 Sub-1:20 Half-Marathon Plan, 14 Weeks Specific Phase	
MON Time: 0:40	**Easy run/walk:** Zone 1–2 power run. Run 40 min as 6 min run at Zone 2, 1 min walk at Zone 1. Repeat for the duration of the run. *This 7-min sequence won't divide evenly into 40, so you will finish on a run. Walk a few minutes after.*
TUES Time: 1:10	**4 × 1 mile:** Warm up well for about 15 min, building from Zone 1–2 to Zone 3–5. Find a flat stretch and run 4 × 1 mile (or 1.6 km) at Zone 4. Do *not* go above Zone 4. Recover with 3-min jog/walk at Zone 1–2 between each mile. Cool down for 15 min with easy Zone 2 jogging and Zone 1 walking.
WED Time: 1:00	**Fartlek:** Run of surges. Warm up well for about 15 min, building from Zone 1–2 to Zone 3–5. On rolling course, run 1-2-min pickups at faster than 5K pace (Zone 6–7), with recoveries at Zone 1–2 as long as you feel you need between the surges. Form! Cadence! Use the last 10 min to cool down with easy Zone 1 running/walking.
Time: 0:30	**2nd run of the day:** Easy Zone 1–2 jog
THURS Time: 1:00	**Envelope run:** Start easy in Zone 1–2 for the first 10–15 min, then work to a moderate pace on the edge of comfort/discomfort. Look at the power zone you are in, likely Zone 3–4. Stay in that zone, but find a way to go faster. Push that envelope, trying to be quicker without raising your watts. It's a balance of trying to hold or increase speed with technique. Focus on your rhythm, cadence, forward lean, soft foot strike, relaxation, eyes and head position. Last 10 min should be easy Zone 1–2 running.
Time: 0:30	**2nd run of the day:** Easy Zone 1–2 jog
FRI Time: 0	**Day off:** Actively focus on recovery today: (1) stay off legs all you can; (2) watch nutrition closely (healthy carbs, lean protein, good fats); (3) stretch; (4) drink when thirsty. Other common recovery aids include massage, napping, elevating legs, and compression wear.
SAT Time: 1:20	**Goal-pace tempo run:** Warm up well for about 15 min, building to Zone 4 for the last min. As you build, do a few surges at Zone 5, lasting about 10–15 sec each. Rest for a few min. Then do a 4 × 10-min tempo run at your half-marathon goal pace, at Zone 4–5, on a course similar to the race, with 2-min recoveries between. Cool down for 15 min, easy Zone 1–2 jogging and walking.
Time: 0:30	**2nd run of the day:** Easy Zone 1–2 jog
SUN Time: 2:00	**Easy run/walk:** Zone 1–2 power run. Do this as 9 min run at Zone 2, 1 min walk at Zone 1. Repeat for the duration of the run.
Time: 0:30	**2nd run of the day:** Easy Zone 1–2 jog

Total time: 9:10

WEEK 7 Sub-1:20 Half-Marathon Plan, 14 Weeks Specific Phase	
MON Time: 0:40	**Easy run/walk:** Zone 1–2 power run. Run 40 min as 4 min run at Zone 2, 1 min walk at Zone 1. Repeat for the duration of the run.
TUES Time: 1:10	**4 × 1 mile:** Warm up well for about 15 min, building from Zone 1–2 to Zone 3–5. Find a flat stretch and run 4 × 1 mile (or 1.6 km) at Zone 4. Do *not* go above Zone 4. Recover with 3-min jog/walk at Zone 1–2 between each mile. Cool down for 15 min with easy Zone 2 jogging and Zone 1 walking.
Time: 0:30	**2nd run of the day:** Easy Zone 1–2 jog
WED Time: 0:40	**Easy run/walk:** Zone 1–2 power run. Run 40 min as 4 min run at Zone 2, 1 min walk at Zone 1. Repeat for the duration of the run.
THURS Time: 1:00	**Fartlek:** Run of surges. Warm up well for about 15 min, building from Zone 1–2 to Zone 3–5. On rolling course, run 1–2-min pickups at faster than 10K pace (Zone 6–7), with recoveries at Zone 1–2 as long as you feel you need between the surges. Form! Cadence! Use the last 10 min to cool down with easy Zone 1 running/walking.
Time: 0:30	**2nd run of the day:** Easy Zone 1–2 jog
FRI Time: 0:40	**Easy run/walk:** Zone 1–2 power run. Run 40 min as 4 min run at Zone 2, 1 min walk at Zone 1. Repeat for the duration of the run.
SAT Time: 1:30	**Goal-pace tempo run:** Warm up well for about 15 min, building to Zone 4 for the last min. As you build, do a few surges at Zone 5, lasting about 10–15 sec each. Rest for a few min. Then do a 4 × 12-min tempo run at your half-marathon goal pace, at Zone 4–5, on a course similar to the race, with 2-min recoveries between. Cool down for 15 min, easy Zone 1–2 jogging and walking.
Time: 0:30	**2nd run of the day:** Easy Zone 1–2 jog
SUN Time: 2:00	**Easy run/walk:** Zone 1–2 power run. Do this as 9 min run at Zone 2, 1 min walk at Zone 1. Repeat for the duration of the run.
Time: 0:30	**2nd run of the day:** Easy Zone 1–2 jog

Total time: 9:40

WEEK 8 Sub-1:20 Half-Marathon Plan, 14 Weeks Specific Phase

MON Time: 0	**Day off:** Actively focus on recovery today: (1) stay off legs all you can; (2) watch nutrition closely (healthy carbs, lean protein, good fats); (3) stretch; (4) drink when thirsty. Other common recovery aids include massage, napping, elevating legs, and compression wear.
TUES Time: 0:40	**Easy run/walk:** Zone 1–2 power run. Run 40 min as 4 min run at Zone 2, 1 min walk at Zone 1. Repeat for the duration of the run.
WED Time: 1:10	**3/9-min Stryd test:** Warm up 15 min, preparing for hard effort at the end; conduct a 3-min interval at maximal effort; recover with 5-min walk, 10 min easy jog, 5 min walk, 5 min easy jog, 5 min walk (30 min total); conduct a 9-min interval at maximal effort; cool down 10–15 min easy. *Follow the protocol for this test and estimating rFTPw and rFTPa per Chapter 4.*
Time: 0:30	**2nd run of the day:** Easy Zone 1–2 jog
THURS Time: 0:40	**Easy run/walk:** Zone 1–2 power run. Run 40 min as 4 min run at Zone 2, 1 min walk at Zone 1. Repeat for the duration of the run.
FRI Time: 1:00	**Envelope run:** Start easy in Zone 1–2 for the first 10–15 min, then work to a moderate pace on the edge of comfort/discomfort. Look at the power zone you are in, likely Zone 3–4. Stay in that zone, but find a way to go faster. Push that envelope, trying to be quicker without raising your watts. It's a balance of trying to hold or increase speed with technique. Focus on your rhythm, cadence, forward lean, soft foot strike, relaxation, eyes and head position. Last 10 min should be easy Zone 1–2 running.
Time: 0:30	**2nd run of the day:** Easy Zone 1–2 jog
SAT Time: 1:00	**Fartlek:** Run of surges. Warm up well for about 15 min, building from Zone 1–2 to Zone 3–5. On rolling course, run 1–2-min pickups at faster than 10K pace (Zone 6–7), with recoveries at Zone 1–2 as long as you feel you need between the surges. Form! Cadence! Use the last 10 min to cool down with easy Zone 1 running/walking.
Time: 0:30	**2nd run of the day:** Easy Zone 1–2 jog
SUN Time: 1:45	**Envelope run:** Start easy in Zone 1–2 for the first 10–15 min, then work to a moderate pace on the edge of comfort/discomfort. Look at the power zone you are in, likely Zone 3–4. Stay in that zone, but find a way to go faster. Push that envelope, trying to be quicker without raising your watts. It's a balance of trying to hold or increase speed with technique. Focus on your rhythm, cadence, forward lean, soft foot strike, relaxation, eyes and head position. Last 10 min should be easy Zone 1–2 running.
Time: 0:30	**2nd run of the day:** Easy Zone 1–2 jog

Total time: 8:15

WEEK 9 Sub-1:20 Half-Marathon Plan, 14 Weeks Specific Phase	
MON Time: 0	**Day off:** Actively focus on recovery today: (1) stay off legs all you can; (2) watch nutrition closely (healthy carbs, lean protein, good fats); (3) stretch; (4) drink when thirsty. Other common recovery aids include massage, napping, elevating legs, and compression wear.
TUES Time: 1:00	**Fartlek:** Run of surges. Warm up well for about 15 min, building from Zone 1–2 to Zone 3–5. On rolling course, run 1–2-min pickups at faster than 10K pace (Zone 6–7), with recoveries at Zone 1–2 as long as you feel you need between the surges. Form! Cadence! Use the last 10 min to cool down with easy Zone 1 running/walking.
Time: 0:30	**2nd run of the day:** Easy Zone 1–2 jog
WED Time: 0:40	**Easy run/walk:** Zone 1–2 power run. Run 40 min as 4 min run at Zone 2, 1 min walk at Zone 1. Repeat for the duration of the run.
THURS Time: 1:10	**4 × 1 mile:** Warm up well for about 15 min, building from Zone 1–2 to Zone 3–5. Find a flat stretch and run 4 × 1 mile (or 1.6 km) at Zone 4. Do *not* go above Zone 4. Recover with 3-min jog/walk at Zone 1–2 between each mile. Cool down for 15 min with easy Zone 2 jogging and Zone 1 walking.
Time: 0:30	**2nd run of the day:** Easy Zone 1–2 jog
FRI Time: 0:40	**Easy run/walk:** Zone 1–2 power run. Run 40 min as 4 min run at Zone 2, 1 min walk at Zone 1. Repeat for the duration of the run.
SAT Time: 1:30	**Goal-pace tempo run:** Warm up well for about 15 min, building to Zone 4 for the last min. As you build, do a few surges at Zone 5, lasting about 10–15 sec each. Rest for a few min. Then do a 4 × 12-min tempo run at your half-marathon goal pace, at Zone 4–5, on a course similar to the race, with 2-min recoveries between. Cool down for 15 min, easy Zone 1–2 jogging and walking.
Time: 0:30	**2nd run of the day:** Easy Zone 1–2 jog
SUN Time: 1:45	**Envelope run:** Start easy in Zone 1–2 for the first 10–15 min, then work to a moderate pace on the edge of comfort/discomfort. Look at the power zone you are in, likely Zone 3–4. Stay in that zone, but find a way to go faster. Push that envelope, trying to be quicker without raising your watts. It's a balance of trying to hold or increase speed with technique. Focus on your rhythm, cadence, forward lean, soft foot strike, relaxation, eyes and head position. Last 10 min should be easy Zone 1–2 running.
Time: 0:30	**2nd run of the day:** Easy Zone 1–2 jog

Total time: 8:45

MON Time: 0	**Day off:** Actively focus on recovery today: (1) stay off legs all you can; (2) watch nutrition closely (healthy carbs, lean protein, good fats); (3) stretch; (4) drink when thirsty. Other common recovery aids include massage, napping, elevating legs, floating in water, and listening to music.
TUES Time: 1:00	**Fartlek:** Run of surges. Warm up well for about 15 min, building from Zone 1–2 to Zone 3–5. On rolling course, run 1–2-min pickups at faster than 10K pace (Zone 6–7), with recoveries at Zone 1–2 as long as you feel you need between the surges. Form! Cadence! Use the last 10 min to cool down with easy Zone 1 running/walking.
Time: 0:30	**2nd run of the day:** Easy Zone 1–2 jog
WED Time: 0:40	**Easy run/walk:** Zone 1–2 power run. Run 40 min as 4 min run at Zone 2, 1 min walk at Zone 1. Repeat for the duration of the run.
THURS Time: 1:00	**Goal-pace tempo run:** Warm up well for about 15 min, building to Zone 4 for the last min. As you build, do a few surges at Zone 5, lasting about 10–15 sec each. Rest for a few min. Then do a 30-min tempo run at your half-marathon goal pace, at Zone 4–5, on a course similar to the race. Cool down for 15 min, easy Zone 1–2 jogging and walking.
Time: 0:30	**2nd run of the day:** Easy Zone 1–2 jog
FRI Time: 0:40	**Easy run/walk:** Zone 1–2 power run. Run 40 min as 4 min run at Zone 2, 1 min walk at Zone 1. Repeat for the duration of the run.
SAT Time: 1:45	**Goal-pace tempo run:** Warm up well for about 15 min, building to Zone 4 for the last min. As you build, do a few surges at Zone 5, lasting about 10–15 sec each. Rest for a few min. Then do a 4 × 15-min tempo run at your half-marathon goal pace, at Zone 4–5, on a course similar to the race, with 2-min recoveries between. Cool down for 15 min, easy Zone 1–2 jogging and walking.
Time: 0:30	**2nd run of the day:** Easy Zone 1–2 jog
SUN Time: 2:00	**Easy run/walk:** Zone 1–2 power run. Do this as 9 min run at Zone 2, 1 min walk at Zone 1. Repeat for the duration of the run.
Time: 0:30	**2nd run of the day:** Easy Zone 1–2 jog

Total time: 9:05

WEEK 11 Sub-1:20 Half-Marathon Plan, 14 Weeks Specific Phase

MON Time: 0	**Day off:** Actively focus on recovery today: (1) stay off legs all you can; (2) watch nutrition closely (healthy carbs, lean protein, good fats); (3) stretch; (4) drink when thirsty. Other common recovery aids include massage, napping, elevating legs, and compression wear.
TUES Time: 1:00	**Fartlek:** Run of surges. Warm up well for about 15 min, building from Zone 1–2 to Zone 3–5. On rolling course, run 1–2-min pickups at faster than 10K pace (Zone 6–7), with recoveries at Zone 1–2 as long as you feel you need between the surges. Form! Cadence! Use the last 10 min to cool down with easy Zone 1 running/walking.
Time: 0:30	**2nd run of the day:** Easy Zone 1–2 jog
WED Time: 0:40	**Easy run/walk:** Zone 1–2 power run. Run 40 min as 4 min run at Zone 2, 1 min walk at Zone 1. Repeat for the duration of the run.
THURS Time: 1:10	**4 × 1 mile:** Warm up well for about 15 min, building from Zone 1–2 to Zone 3–5. Find a flat stretch and run 4 × 1 mile (or 1.6 km) at Zone 4. Do *not* go above Zone 4. Recover with 3-min jog/walk at Zone 1–2 between each mile. Cool down for 15 min with easy Zone 2 jogging and Zone 1 walking.
Time: 0:30	**2nd run of the day:** Easy Zone 1–2 jog
FRI Time: 0:40	**Easy run/walk:** Zone 1–2 power run. Run 40 min as 4 min run at Zone 2, 1 min walk at Zone 1. Repeat for the duration of the run.
SAT Time: 1:45	**Goal-pace tempo run:** Warm up well for about 15 min, building to Zone 4 for the last min. As you build, do a few surges at Zone 5, lasting about 10–15 sec each. Rest for a few min. Then do a 4 × 15-min tempo run at your half-marathon goal pace, at Zone 4–5, on a course similar to the race, with 2-min recoveries between. Cool down for 15 min, easy Zone 1–2 jogging and walking.
Time: 0:30	**2nd run of the day:** Easy Zone 1–2 jog
SUN Time: 2:00	**Envelope run:** Start easy in Zone 1–2 for the first 10–15 min, then work to a moderate pace on the edge of comfort/discomfort. Look at the power zone you are in, likely Zone 3–4. Stay in that zone, but find a way to go faster. Push that envelope, trying to be quicker without raising your watts. It's a balance of trying to hold or increase speed with technique. Focus on your rhythm, cadence, forward lean, soft foot strike, relaxation, eyes and head position. Last 10 min should be easy Zone 1–2 running.
Time: 0:30	**2nd run of the day:** Easy Zone 1–2 jog

Total time: 9:15

WEEK 12 Sub-1:20 Half-Marathon Plan, 14 Weeks Specific Phase

MON Time: 0	**Day off:** Actively focus on recovery today: (1) stay off legs all you can; (2) watch nutrition closely (healthy carbs, lean protein, good fats); (3) stretch; (4) drink when thirsty. Other common recovery aids include massage, napping, elevating legs, and compression wear.
TUES Time: 0:40	**Easy run/walk:** Zone 1–2 power run. Run 40 min as 4 min run at Zone 2, 1 min walk at Zone 1. Repeat for the duration of the run.
WED Time: 1:10	**3/9-min Stryd test:** Warm up 15 min, preparing for hard effort at the end; conduct a 3-min interval at maximal effort; recover with 5-min walk, 10 min easy jog, 5 min walk, 5 min easy jog, 5 min walk (30 min total); conduct a 9-min interval at maximal effort; cool down 10–15 min easy. *Follow the protocol for this test and estimating rFTPw and rFTPa per Chapter 4.*
Time: 0:30	**2nd run of the day:** Easy Zone 1–2 jog
THURS Time: 1:00	**Envelope run:** Start easy in Zone 1–2 for the first 10–15 min, then work to a moderate pace on the edge of comfort/discomfort. Look at the power zone you are in, likely Zone 3–4. Stay in that zone, but find a way to go faster. Push that envelope, trying to be quicker without raising your watts. It's a balance of trying to hold or increase speed with technique. Focus on your rhythm, cadence, forward lean, soft foot strike, relaxation, eyes and head position. Last 10 min should be easy Zone 1–2 running.
FRI Time: 0:40	**Easy run/walk:** Zone 1–2 power run. Run 40 min as 4 min run at Zone 2, 1 min walk at Zone 1. Repeat for the duration of the run.
SAT Time: 1:45	**Goal-pace tempo run:** Warm up well for about 15 min, building to Zone 4 for the last min. As you build, do a few surges at Zone 5, lasting about 10–15 sec each. Rest for a few min. Then do a 4 × 15-min tempo run at your half-marathon goal pace, at Zone 4–5, on a course similar to the race, with 2-min recoveries between. Cool down for 15 min, easy Zone 1–2 jogging and walking.
Time: 0:30	**2nd run of the day:** Easy Zone 1–2 jog
SUN Time: 0	**Day off:** Actively focus on recovery today: (1) stay off legs all you can; (2) watch nutrition closely (healthy carbs, lean protein, good fats); (3) stretch; (4) drink when thirsty. Other common recovery aids include massage, napping, elevating legs, floating in water, and listening to music.

Total time: 6:15

WEEK 13 Sub-1:20 Half-Marathon Plan, 14 Weeks Specific Phase	
MON Time: 0:40	**Easy run/walk:** Zone 1–2 power run. Run 40 min as 4 min run at Zone 2, 1 min walk at Zone 1. Repeat for the duration of the run.
TUES Time: 1:10	**4 × 1 mile:** Warm up well for about 15 min, building from Zone 1–2 to Zone 3–5. Find a flat stretch and run 4 × 1 mile (or 1.6 km) at Zone 4. Do *not* go above Zone 4. Recover with 3-min jog/walk at Zone 1–2 between each mile. Cool down for 15 min with easy Zone 2 jogging and Zone 1 walking.
Time: 0:30	**2nd run of the day:** Easy Zone 1–2 jog
WED Time: 0:40	**Easy run/walk:** Zone 1–2 power run. Run 40 min as 4 min run at Zone 2, 1 min walk at Zone 1. Repeat for the duration of the run.
Time: 0:30	**2nd run of the day:** Easy Zone 1–2 jog
THURS Time: 0:40	**Fartlek:** Run of surges. Warm up well for about 15 min, building from Zone 1–2 to Zone 3–5. On rolling course, run 1–2-min pickups at faster than 10K pace (Zone 6–7), with recoveries at Zone 1–2 as long as you feel you need between the surges. Form! Cadence! Use the last 10 min to cool down with easy Zone 1 running/walking.
FRI Time: 0	**Day off:** Actively focus on recovery today: (1) stay off legs all you can; (2) watch nutrition closely (healthy carbs, lean protein, good fats); (3) stretch; (4) drink when thirsty. Other common recovery aids include massage, napping, elevating legs, and compression wear.
SAT Time: 1:10	**Goal-pace tempo run:** Warm up well for about 15 min, building to Zone 4 for the last min. As you build, do a few surges at Zone 5, lasting about 10–15 sec each. Rest for a few min. Then do a 3 × 10-min tempo run at your half-marathon goal pace, at Zone 4–5, on a course similar to the race, with 2-min recoveries between. Cool down for 15 min, easy Zone 1–2 jogging and walking.
Time: 0:30	**2nd run of the day:** Easy Zone 1–2 jog
SUN Time: 0:40	**Easy run/walk:** Zone 1–2 power run. Run 40 min as 4 min run at Zone 2, 1 min walk at Zone 1. Repeat for the duration of the run.

Total time: 6:30

WEEK 14 Sub-1:20 Half-Marathon Plan, 14 Weeks Specific Phase

MON Time: 0	**Day off:** Actively focus on recovery today: (1) stay off legs all you can; (2) watch nutrition closely (healthy carbs, lean protein, good fats); (3) stretch; (4) drink when thirsty. Other common recovery aids include massage, napping, elevating legs, and compression wear.
TUES Time: 0:40	**5 × 2 min at Zone 4–6:** 15 min warm-up run, followed by 5 × 2 min, starting at Zone 4 for the first min, then building to Zone 5–6 in the last min, with 2 min easy recovery jog. Easy cool down in Zone 1–2 to make 40 min
WED Time: 0:40 Time: 0:30	**Easy run/walk:** Zone 1–2 power run. Run 40 min as 4 min run at Zone 2, 1 min walk at Zone 1. Repeat for the duration of the run. **2nd run of the day:** Easy Zone 1–2 jog
THURS Time: 0:30	**Run with surges:** First part of the run is easy, then do 5–7 × 7 sec surges at Zone 6–7 with long recoveries, getting faster over the course of the run. Really focus on forefoot strike, quick cadence, slight forward lean, and fluid motion, not forcing it.
FRI Time: 0:20	**Preview course:** Run start and finish of course. Note landmarks. Include several accelerations to race pace. Otherwise, keep power in Zone 1.
SAT	**HALF-MARATHON RACE**

Total time: 2:40

WEEK 1 Sub-1:40 Half-Marathon Plan, 14 Weeks Specific Phase	
MON Time: 1:10	**3/9-min Stryd test:** Warm up 15 min, preparing for hard effort at the end; conduct a 3-min interval at maximal effort; recover with 5-min walk, 10 min easy jog, 5 min walk, 5 min easy jog, 5 min walk (30 min total); conduct a 9-min interval at maximal effort; cool down 10–15 min easy. *Follow the protocol for this test and estimating rFTPw and rFTPa per Chapter 4.*
TUES Time: 0:40	**Easy run/walk:** Zone 1–2 power run. Run 40 min as 4 min run at Zone 2, 1 min walk at Zone 1. Repeat for the duration of the run.
WED Time: 0:40	**Easy run/walk:** Zone 1–2 power run. Run 40 min as 4 min run at Zone 2, 1 min walk at Zone 1. Repeat for the duration of the run.
THURS Time: 1:00	**30-min test:** Warm up 15 min, preparing for a hard effort at the end. Start a 30-min time trial (best effort) on a flat road or track, collecting power data (pace and HR data as well if possible). Cool down 10–15 min easy. *Follow the protocol for this test and estimating rFTPw and rFTPa per Chapter 4.*
FRI Time: 0:40 Time: 0:30	**Easy run/walk:** Zone 1–2 power run. Run 40 min as 4 min run at Zone 2, 1 min walk at Zone 1. Repeat for the duration of the run. **2nd run of the day:** Easy Zone 1–2 jog
SAT Time: 0	**Day off:** Actively focus on recovery today: (1) stay off legs all you can; (2) watch nutrition closely (healthy carbs, lean protein, good fats); (3) stretch; (4) drink when thirsty. Other common recovery aids include massage, napping, elevating legs, floating in water, and compression wear.
SUN Time: 1:00 Time: 0:30	**Easy run/walk:** Zone 1–2 power run. Do this as 5 min run at Zone 2, 1 min walk at Zone 1. Repeat for the duration of the run. **2nd run of the day:** Easy Zone 1–2 jog

Total time: 6:10

WEEK 2 Sub-1:40 Half-Marathon Plan, 14 Weeks Specific Phase

MON Time: 1:10	**Cruise intervals:** Warm up 15 min, building intensity through the warm-up, starting at Zone 1, then the last min at zones 4–5. Then do 4 × 8 min, build to Zone 3–4 (2-min recoveries). Monitor pace, trying to be faster for the same power output. Cool down 15 min, at Zone 1–2.
TUES Time: 0:40	**Easy run/walk:** Zone 1–2 power run. Run 40 min as 4 min run at Zone 2, 1 min walk at Zone 1. Repeat for the duration of the run.
WED Time: 1:15	**Cruise intervals:** Warm up 15 min, building intensity through the warm-up, starting at Zone 1, then the last min at Zone 4–5. Then do 4 × 8 min, build to Zone 5–6 (3-min recoveries). Monitor pace, trying to be faster for the same power output. Cool down 15 min, at Zone 1–2.
Time: 0:30	**2nd run of the day:** Easy Zone 1–2 jog
THURS Time: 0:40	**Easy run/walk:** Zone 1–2 power run. Run 40 min as 4 min run at Zone 2, 1 min walk at Zone 1. Repeat for the duration of the run.
FRI Time: 1:00	**Envelope run:** Start easy in Zone 1–2 for the first 10–15 min, then work to a moderate pace on the edge of comfort/discomfort. Look at the power zone you are in, likely Zone 3–4. Stay in that zone, but find a way to go faster. Push that envelope, trying to be quicker without raising your watts. It's a balance of trying to hold or increase speed with technique. Focus on your rhythm, cadence, forward lean, soft foot strike, relaxation, eyes and head position. Last 10 min should be easy Zone 1–2 running.
Time: 0:30	**2nd run of the day:** Easy Zone 1–2 jog
SAT Time: 1:10	**Cruise intervals:** Warm up 15 min, building intensity through the warm-up, starting at Zone 1, then the last min at Zone 4–5. Then do 5 × 6 min, build to Zone 5 (2-min recoveries). Monitor pace, trying to be faster for the same power output. Cool down 15 min, at Zone 1–2.
SUN Time: 1:15	**Easy run/walk:** Zone 1–2 power run. Do this as 5 min run at Zone 2, 1 min walk at Zone 1. Repeat for the duration of the run. *The run/walk portion won't divide perfectly, so you will finish with a run. Walk a few minutes after.*
Time: 0:30	**2nd run of the day:** Easy Zone 1–2 jog

Total time: 8:40

WEEK 3 Sub-1:40 Half-Marathon Plan, 14 Weeks Specific Phase

MON Time: 0:40	**Easy run/walk:** Zone 1–2 power run. Run 40 min as 4 min run at Zone 2, 1 min walk at Zone 1. Repeat for the duration of the run.
TUES Time: 1:00	**Goal-pace tempo run:** Warm up well for about 15 min, building to Zone 4 for the last min. As you build, do a few surges at Zone 5, lasting about 10–15 sec each. Rest for a few min. Then do a 30-min tempo run at your half-marathon goal pace, at Zone 3–4, on a course similar to the race. Cool down for 15 min, easy Zone 1–2 jogging and walking.
WED Time: 0:40	**Easy run/walk:** Zone 1–2 power run. Run 40 min as 4 min run at Zone 2, 1 min walk at Zone 1. Repeat for the duration of the run.
Time: 0:30	**2nd run of the day:** Easy Zone 1–2 jog
THURS Time: 1:00	**Fartlek:** Run of surges. Warm up well for about 15 min, building from Zone 1–2 to Zone 3–5. On rolling course, run 1–2-min pickups at faster than 10K pace (Zone 5–6), with recoveries at Zone 1–2 as long as you feel you need between the surges. Form! Cadence! Use the last 10 min to cool down with easy Zone 1 running/walking.
Time: 0:30	**2nd run of the day:** Easy Zone 1–2 jog
FRI Time: 1:00	**Envelope run:** Start easy in Zone 1–2 for the first 10–15 min, then work to a moderate pace on the edge of comfort/discomfort. Look at the power zone you are in, likely Zone 3–4. Stay in that zone, but find a way to go faster. Push that envelope, trying to be quicker without raising your watts. It's a balance of trying to hold or increase speed with technique. Focus on your rhythm, cadence, forward lean, soft foot strike, relaxation, eyes and head position. Last 10 min should be easy Zone 1–2 running.
SAT Time: 1:30	**Easy run/walk:** Zone 1–2 power run. Do this as 9 min run at Zone 2, 1 min walk at Zone 1. Repeat for the duration of the run.
Time: 0:30	**2nd run of the day:** Easy Zone 1–2 jog
SUN Time: 0	**Day off:** Actively focus on recovery today: (1) stay off legs all you can; (2) watch nutrition closely (healthy carbs, lean protein, good fats); (3) stretch; (4) drink when thirsty. Other common recovery aids include massage, napping, elevating legs, and compression wear.

Total time: 7:20

WEEK 4 Sub-1:40 Half-Marathon Plan, 14 Weeks Specific Phase

MON Time: 0:40	**Easy run/walk:** Zone 1–2 power run. Run 40 min as 4 min run at Zone 2, 1 min walk at Zone 1. Repeat for the duration of the run.
TUES Time: 1:10	**3/9-min Stryd test:** Warm up 15 min, preparing for hard effort at the end; conduct a 3-min interval at maximal effort; recover with 5-min walk, 10 min easy jog, 5 min walk, 5 min easy jog, 5 min walk (30 min total); conduct a 9-min interval at maximal effort; cool down 10–15 min easy. *Follow the protocol for this test and estimating rFTPw and rFTPa per Chapter 4.*
WED Time: 0:40	**Easy run/walk:** Zone 1–2 power run. Run 40 min as 4 min run at Zone 2, 1 min walk at Zone 1. Repeat for the duration of the run.
THURS Time: 0:40	**Easy run/walk:** Zone 1–2 power run. Run 40 min as 4 min run at Zone 2, 1 min walk at Zone 1. Repeat for the duration of the run.
FRI Time: 1:00	**30-min test:** Warm up 15 min, preparing for a hard effort at the end. Start a 30-min time trial (best effort) on a flat road or track, collecting power data (pace and HR data as well if possible). Cool down 10–15 min easy. *Follow the protocol for this test and estimating rFTPw and rFTPa in Chapter 4. Now you should begin to see a good relationship between the 3/9 test and the 30-min test. To avoid the 30-min test for the rest of the plan, focus on using the 3-min.*
Time: 0:30	**2nd run of the day:** Easy Zone 1–2 jog
SAT Time: 0	**Day off:** Actively focus on recovery today: (1) stay off legs all you can; (2) watch nutrition closely (healthy carbs, lean protein, good fats); (3) stretch; (4) drink when thirsty. Other common recovery aids include massage, napping, elevating legs, floating in water, and listening to music.
SUN Time: 1:30	**Envelope run:** Start easy in Zone 1–2 for the first 10–15 min, then work to a moderate pace on the edge of comfort/discomfort. Look at the power zone you are in, likely Zone 3–4. Stay in that zone, but find a way to go faster. Push that envelope, trying to be quicker without raising your watts. It's a balance of trying to hold or increase speed with technique. Focus on your rhythm, cadence, forward lean, soft foot strike, relaxation, eyes and head position. Last 10 min should be easy Zone 1–2 running.
Time: 0:30	**2nd run of the day:** Easy Zone 1–2 jog

Total time: 6:40

WEEK 5 Sub-1:40 Half-Marathon Plan, 14 Weeks Specific Phase

MON Time: 0:40	**Easy run/walk:** Zone 1–2 power run. Run 40 min as 6 min run at Zone 2, 1 min walk at Zone 1. Repeat for the duration of the run. *This 7-min sequence won't divide evenly into 40, so you will finish on a run. Walk a few minutes after.*
TUES Time: 1:00	**Fartlek:** Run of surges. Warm up well for about 15 min, building from Zone 1–2 to Zone 3–5. On rolling course, run 1–2-min pickups at faster than 10K pace (Zone 5–6), with recoveries at Zone 1–2 as long as you feel you need between the surges. Form! Cadence! Use the last 10 min to cool down with easy Zone 1 running/walking.
WED Time: 1:00	**Envelope run:** Start easy in Zone 1–2 for the first 10–15 min, then work to a moderate pace on the edge of comfort/discomfort. Look at the power zone you are in, likely Zone 3–4. Stay in that zone, but find a way to go faster. Push that envelope, trying to be quicker without raising your watts. It's a balance of trying to hold or increase speed with technique. Focus on your rhythm, cadence, forward lean, soft foot strike, relaxation, eyes and head position. Last 10 min should be easy Zone 1–2 running.
Time: 0:30	**2nd run of the day:** Easy Zone 1–2 jog
THURS Time: 1:00	**5 × 1 mile:** Warm up well for about 15 min, building from Zone 1–2 to Zone 3–5. Find a flat stretch and run 5 × 1 mile (or 1.6 km) at your half-marathon goal pace, Zone 3–4. Do *not* go above Zone 4. Recover with 2-min jog/walk at Zone 1–2 between each mile. Cool down for 15 min with easy Zone 2 jogging and Zone 1 walking.
Time: 0:30	**2nd run of the day:** Easy Zone 1–2 jog
FRI Time: 0:40	**Easy run/walk:** Zone 1–2 power run. Run 40 min as 6 min run at Zone 2, 1 min walk at Zone 1. Repeat for the duration of the run. *This 7-min sequence won't divide evenly into 40, so you will finish on a run. Walk a few minutes after.*
SAT Time: 1:20	**Goal-pace tempo run:** Warm up well for about 15 min, building to Zone 4 for the last min. As you build, do a few surges at Zone 5, lasting about 10–15 sec each. Rest for a few min. Then do a 4 × 10-min tempo run at your half-marathon goal pace, at Zone 3–4, on a course similar to the race, with 2-min recoveries between. Cool down for 15 min, easy Zone 1–2 jogging and walking.
Time: 0:30	**2nd run of the day:** Easy Zone 1–2 jog
SUN Time: 1:30	**Easy run/walk:** Zone 1–2 power run. Do this as 9 min run at Zone 2, 1 min walk at Zone 1. Repeat for the duration of the run.
Time: 0:30	**2nd run of the day:** Easy Zone 1–2 jog

Total time: 9:10

WEEK 6 Sub-1:40 Half-Marathon Plan, 14 Weeks Specific Phase

MON Time: 0:40	**Easy run/walk:** Zone 1–2 power run. Run 40 min as 6 min run at Zone 2, 1 min walk at Zone 1. Repeat for the duration of the run. *This 7-min sequence won't divide evenly into 40, so you will finish on a run. Walk a few minutes after.*
TUES Time: 1:10	**4 × 1 mile:** Warm up well for about 15 min, building from Zone 1–2 to Zone 3–5. Find a flat stretch and run 4 × 1 mile (or 1.6 km) at Zone 4. Do *not* go above Zone 4. Recover with 3-min jog/walk at Zone 1–2 between each mile. Cool down for 15 min with easy Zone 2 jogging and Zone 1 walking.
WED Time: 1:00	**Fartlek:** Run of surges. Warm up well for about 15 min, building from Zone 1–2 to Zone 3–5. On rolling course, run 1–2-min pickups at faster than 10K pace (Zone 6–7), with recoveries at Zone 1–2 as long as you feel you need between the surges. Form! Cadence! Use the last 10 min to cool down with easy Zone 1 running/walking.
Time: 0:30	**2nd run of the day:** Easy Zone 1–2 jog
THURS Time: 1:00	**Envelope run:** Start easy in Zone 1–2 for the first 10–15 min, then work to a moderate pace on the edge of comfort/discomfort. Look at the power zone you are in, likely Zone 3–4. Stay in that zone, but find a way to go faster. Push that envelope, trying to be quicker without raising your watts. It's a balance of trying to hold or increase speed with technique. Focus on your rhythm, cadence, forward lean, soft foot strike, relaxation, eyes and head position. Last 10 min should be easy Zone 1–2 running.
Time: 0:30	**2nd run of the day:** Easy Zone 1–2 jog
FRI Time: 0	**Day off:** Actively focus on recovery today: (1) stay off legs all you can; (2) watch nutrition closely (healthy carbs, lean protein, good fats); (3) stretch; (4) drink when thirsty. Other common recovery aids include massage, napping, elevating legs, and compression wear.
SAT Time: 1:20	**Goal-pace tempo run:** Warm up well for about 15 min, building to Zone 4 for the last min. As you build, do a few surges in Zone 5, lasting about 10–15 sec each. Rest for a few min. Then do a 4 × 10-min tempo run at your half-marathon goal pace, in Zone 3–4, on a course similar to the race, with 2-min recoveries between. Cool down for 15 min, easy Zone 1–2 jogging and walking.
Time: 0:30	**2nd run of the day:** Easy Zone 1–2 jog
SUN Time: 2:00	**Easy run/walk:** Zone 1–2 power run. Do this as 9 min run at Zone 2, 1 min walk at Zone 1. Repeat for the duration of the run.
Time: 0:30	**2nd run of the day:** Easy Zone 1–2 jog

Total time: 9:10

WEEK 7 Sub-1:40 Half-Marathon Plan, 14 Weeks Specific Phase	
MON Time: 0:40	**Easy run/walk:** Zone 1–2 power run. Run 40 min as 4 min run at Zone 2, 1 min walk at Zone 1. Repeat for the duration of the run.
TUES Time: 1:10	**4 × 1 mile:** Warm up well for about 15 min, building from Zone 1–2 to Zone 3–5. Find a flat stretch and run 4 × 1 mile (or 1.6 km) at Zone 4. Do *not* go above Zone 4. Recover with 3-min jog/walk at Zone 1–2 between each mile. Cool down for 15 min with easy Zone 2 jogging and Zone 1 walking.
Time: 0:30	**2nd run of the day:** Easy Zone 1–2 jog
WED Time: 0:40	**Easy run/walk:** Zone 1–2 power run. Run 40 min as 4 min run at Zone 2, 1 min walk at Zone 1. Repeat for the duration of the run.
THURS Time: 1:00	**Fartlek:** Run of surges. Warm up well for about 15 min, building from Zone 1–2 to Zone 3–5. On rolling course, run 1–2-min pickups at faster than 10K pace (Zone 6–7), with recoveries at Zone 1–2 as long as you feel you need between the surges. Form! Cadence! Use the last 10 min to cool down with easy Zone 1 running/walking.
Time: 0:30	**2nd run of the day:** Easy Zone 1–2 jog
FRI Time: 0:40	**Easy run/walk:** Zone 1–2 power run. Run 40 min as 4 min run at Zone 2, 1 min walk at Zone 1. Repeat for the duration of the run.
SAT Time: 1:30	**Goal-pace tempo run:** Warm up well for about 15 min, building to Zone 4 for the last min. As you build, do a few surges at Zone 5, lasting about 10–15 sec each. Rest for a few min. Then do a 4 × 12-min tempo run at your half-marathon goal pace, at Zone 3–4, on a course similar to the race, with 2-min recoveries between. Cool down for 15 min, easy Zone 1–2 jogging and walking.
Time: 0:30	**2nd run of the day:** Easy Zone 1–2 jog
SUN Time: 2:00	**Easy run/walk:** Zone 1–2 power run. Do this as 9 min run at Zone 2, 1 min walk at Zone 1. Repeat for the duration of the run.
Time: 0:30	**2nd run of the day:** Easy Zone 1–2 jog

Total time: 9:40

WEEK 8 Sub-1:40 Half-Marathon Plan, 14 Weeks Specific Phase

MON Time: 0	**Day off:** Actively focus on recovery today: (1) stay off legs all you can; (2) watch nutrition closely (healthy carbs, lean protein, good fats); (3) stretch; (4) drink when thirsty. Other common recovery aids include massage, napping, elevating legs, and compression wear.
TUES Time: 0:40	**Easy run/walk:** Zone 1–2 power run. Run 40 min as 4 min. run at Zone 2, 1 min walk at Zone 1. Repeat for the duration of the run.
WED Time: 1:10	**3/9-min Stryd test:** Warm up 15 min, preparing for hard effort at the end; conduct a 3-min interval at maximal effort; recover with 5-min walk, 10 min easy jog, 5 min walk, 5 min easy jog, 5 min walk (30 min total); conduct a 9-min interval at maximal effort; cool down 10–15 min easy. *Follow the protocol for this test and estimating rFTPw and rFTPa per Chapter 4.*
Time: 0:30	**2nd run of the day:** Easy Zone 1–2 jog
THURS Time: 0:40	**Easy run/walk:** Zone 1–2 power run. Run 40 min as 4 min run at Zone 2, 1 min walk at Zone 1. Repeat for the duration of the run.
FRI Time: 1:00	**Envelope run:** Start easy in Zone 1–2 for the first 10–15 min, then work to a moderate pace on the edge of comfort/discomfort. Look at the power zone you are in, likely Zone 3–4. Stay in that zone, but find a way to go faster. Push that envelope, trying to be quicker without raising your watts. It's a balance of trying to hold or increase speed with technique. Focus on your rhythm, cadence, forward lean, soft foot strike, relaxation, eyes and head position. Last 10 min should be easy Zone 1–2 running.
Time: 0:30	**2nd run of the day:** Easy Zone 1–2 jog
SAT Time: 1:00	**Fartlek:** Run of surges. Warm up well for about 15 min, building from Zone 1–2 to Zone 3–5. On rolling course, run 1–2-min pickups at faster than 10K pace (Zone 6–7), with recoveries at Zone 1–2 as long as you feel you need between the surges. Form! Cadence! Use the last 10 min to cool down with easy Zone 1 running/walking.
Time: 0:30	**2nd run of the day:** Easy Zone 1–2 jog
SUN Time: 1:45	**Envelope run:** Start easy in Zone 1–2 for the first 10–15 min, then work to a moderate pace on the edge of comfort/discomfort. Look at the power zone you are in, likely Zone 3–4. Stay in that zone, but find a way to go faster. Push that envelope, trying to be quicker without raising your watts. It's a balance of trying to hold or increase speed with technique. Focus on your rhythm, cadence, forward lean, soft foot strike, relaxation, eyes and head position. Last 10 min should be easy Zone 1–2 running.
Time: 0:30	**2nd run of the day:** Easy Zone 1–2 jog

Total time: 8:15

WEEK 9 Sub-1:40 Half-Marathon Plan, 14 Weeks Specific Phase

MON Time: 0	**Day off:** Actively focus on recovery today: (1) stay off legs all you can; (2) watch nutrition closely (healthy carbs, lean protein, good fats); (3) stretch; (4) drink when thirsty. Other common recovery aids include massage, napping, elevating legs, and compression wear.
TUES Time: 1:00	**Fartlek:** Run of surges. Warm up well for about 15 min, building from Zone 1–2 to Zone 3–5. On rolling course, run 1–2-min pickups at faster than 10K pace (Zone 6–7), with recoveries at Zone 1–2 as long as you feel you need between the surges. Form! Cadence! Use the last 10 min to cool down with easy Zone 1 running/walking.
Time: 0:30	**2nd run of the day:** Easy Zone 1–2 jog
WED Time: 0:40	**Easy run/walk:** Zone 1–2 power run. Run 40 min as 4 min run at Zone 2, 1 min walk at Zone 1. Repeat for the duration of the run.
THURS Time: 1:10	**4 × 1 mile:** Warm up well for about 15 min, building from Zone 1–2 to Zone 3–5. Find a flat stretch and run 4 × 1 mile (or 1.6 km) at Zone 4. Do *not* go above Zone 4. Recover with 3-min jog/walk at Zone 1–2 between each mile. Cool down for 15 min with easy Zone 2 jogging and Zone 1 walking.
Time: 0:30	**2nd run of the day:** Easy Zone 1–2 jog
FRI Time: 0:40	**Easy run/walk:** Zone 1–2 power run. Run 40 min as 4 min run at Zone 2, 1 min walk at Zone 1. Repeat for the duration of the run.
SAT Time: 1:30	**Goal-pace tempo run:** Warm up well for about 15 min, building to Zone 4 for the last min. As you build, do a few surges at Zone 5, lasting about 10–15 sec each. Rest for a few min. Then do a 4 × 12-min tempo run at your half-marathon goal pace, at Zone 3–4, on a course similar to the race, with 2-min recoveries between. Cool down for 15 min, easy Zone 1–2 jogging and walking.
Time: 0:30	**2nd run of the day:** Easy Zone 1–2 jog
SUN Time: 1:45	**Envelope run:** Start easy in Zone 1–2 for the first 10–15 min, then work to a moderate pace on the edge of comfort/discomfort. Look at the power zone you are in, likely Zone 3–4. Stay in that zone, but find a way to go faster. Push that envelope, trying to be quicker without raising your watts. It's a balance of trying to hold or increase speed with technique. Focus on your rhythm, cadence, forward lean, soft foot strike, relaxation, eyes and head position. Last 10 min should be easy Zone 1–2 running.
Time: 0:30	**2nd run of the day:** Easy Zone 1–2 jog

Total time: 8:45

MON Time: 0	**Day off:** Actively focus on recovery today: (1) stay off legs all you can; (2) watch nutrition closely (healthy carbs, lean protein, good fats); (3) stretch; (4) drink when thirsty. Other common recovery aids include massage, napping, elevating legs, floating in water, and listening to music.
TUES Time: 1:00	**Fartlek:** Run of surges. Warm up well for about 15 min, building from Zone 1–2 to Zone 3–5. On rolling course, run 1–2-min pickups at faster than 10K pace (Zone 6–7), with recoveries at Zone 1–2 as long as you feel you need between the surges. Form! Cadence! Use the last 10 min to cool down with easy Zone 1 running/walking.
Time: 0:30	**2nd run of the day:** Easy Zone 1–2 jog
WED Time: 0:40	**Easy run/walk:** Zone 1–2 power run. Run 40 min as 4 min run at Zone 2, 1 min walk at Zone 1. Repeat for the duration of the run.
THURS Time: 1:00	**Goal-pace tempo run:** Warm up well for about 15 min, building to Zone 4 for the last min. As you build, do a few surges at Zone 5, lasting about 10–15 sec each. Rest for a few min. Then do a 30-min tempo run at your half-marathon goal pace, at Zone 3–4, on a course similar to the race. Cool down for 15 min, easy Zone 1–2 jogging and walking.
Time: 0:30	**2nd run of the day:** Easy Zone 1–2 jog
FRI Time: 0:40	**Easy run/walk:** Zone 1–2 power run. Run 40 min as 4 min run at Zone 2, 1 min walk at Zone 1. Repeat for the duration of the run.
SAT Time: 1:45	**Goal-pace tempo run:** Warm up well for about 15 min, building to Zone 4 for the last min. As you build, do a few surges at Zone 5, lasting about 10–15 sec each. Rest for a few min. Then do a 4 × 15-min tempo run at your half-marathon goal pace, at Zone 3–4, on a course similar to the race, with 2-min recoveries between. Cool down for 15 min, easy Zone 1–2 jogging and walking.
Time: 0:30	**2nd run of the day:** Easy Zone 1–2 jog
SUN Time: 2:00	**Easy run/walk:** Zone 1–2 power run. Do this as 9 min run at Zone 2, 1 min walk at Zone 1. Repeat for the duration of the run.
Time: 0:30	**2nd run of the day:** Easy Zone 1–2 jog

Total time: 9:05

WEEK 11 Sub-1:40 Half-Marathon Plan, 14 Weeks Specific Phase	
MON Time: 0	**Day off:** Actively focus on recovery today: (1) stay off legs all you can; (2) watch nutrition closely (healthy carbs, lean protein, good fats); (3) stretch; (4) drink when thirsty. Other common recovery aids include massage, napping, elevating legs, and compression wear.
TUES Time: 1:00	**Fartlek:** Run of surges. Warm up well for about 15 min, building from Zone 1-2 to Zone 3-5. On rolling course, run 1-2-min pickups at faster than 10K pace (Zone 6-7), with recoveries at Zone 1-2 as long as you feel you need between the surges. Form! Cadence! Use the last 10 min to cool down with easy Zone 1 running/walking.
Time: 0:30	**2nd run of the day:** Easy Zone 1-2 jog
WED Time: 0:40	**Easy run/walk:** Zone 1-2 power run. Run 40 min as 4 min run at Zone 2, 1 min walk at Zone 1. Repeat for the duration of the run.
THURS Time: 1:10	**4 × 1 mile:** Warm up well for about 15 min, building from Zone 1-2 to Zone 3-5. Find a flat stretch and run 4 × 1 mile (or 1.6 km) at Zone 4. Do *not* go above Zone 4. Recover with 3-min jog/walk at Zone 1-2 between each mile. Cool down for 15 min with easy Zone 2 jogging and Zone 1 walking.
Time: 0:30	**2nd run of the day:** Easy Zone 1-2 jog
FRI Time: 0:40	**Easy run/walk:** Zone 1-2 power run. Run 40 min as 4 min run at Zone 2, 1 min walk at Zone 1. Repeat for the duration of the run.
SAT Time: 1:45	**Goal-pace tempo run:** Warm up well for about 15 min, building to Zone 4 for the last min. As you build, do a few surges at Zone 5, lasting about 10-15 sec each. Rest for a few min. Then do a 4 × 15-min tempo run at your half-marathon goal pace, at Zone 3-4, on a course similar to the race, with 3-min recoveries between. Cool down for 15 min, easy Zone 1-2 jogging and walking.
Time: 0:30	**2nd run of the day:** Easy Zone 1-2 jog
SUN Time: 2:00	**Envelope run:** Start easy in Zone 1-2 for the first 10-15 min, then work to a moderate pace on the edge of comfort/discomfort. Look at the power zone you are in, likely Zone 3-4. Stay in that zone, but find a way to go faster. Push that envelope, trying to be quicker without raising your watts. It's a balance of trying to hold or increase speed with technique. Focus on your rhythm, cadence, forward lean, soft foot strike, relaxation, eyes and head position. Last 10 min should be easy Zone 1-2 running.
Time: 0:30	**2nd run of the day:** Easy Zone 1-2 jog

Total time: 9:15

MON Time: 0	**Day off:** Actively focus on recovery today: (1) stay off legs all you can; (2) watch nutrition closely (healthy carbs, lean protein, good fats); (3) stretch; (4) drink when thirsty. Other common recovery aids include massage, napping, elevating legs, and compression wear.
TUES Time: 0:40	**Easy run/walk:** Zone 1–2 power run. Run 40 min as 4 min run at Zone 2, 1 min walk at Zone 1. Repeat for the duration of the run.
WED Time: 1:10	**3/9-min Stryd test:** Warm up 15 min, preparing for hard effort at the end; conduct a 3-min interval at maximal effort; recover with 5-min walk, 10 min easy jog, 5 min walk, 5 min easy jog, 5 min walk (30 min total); conduct a 9-min interval at maximal effort; cool down 10–15 min easy. *Follow the protocol for this test and estimating rFTPw and rFTPa per Chapter 4.*
Time: 0:30	**2nd run of the day:** Easy Zone 1–2 jog
THURS Time: 1:00	**Envelope run:** Start easy in Zone 1–2 for the first 10–15 min, then work to a moderate pace on the edge of comfort/discomfort. Look at the power zone you are in, likely Zone 3–4. Stay in that zone, but find a way to go faster. Push that envelope, trying to be quicker without raising your watts. It's a balance of trying to hold or increase speed with technique. Focus on your rhythm, cadence, forward lean, soft foot strike, relaxation, eyes and head position. Last 10 min should be easy Zone 1–2 running.
FRI Time: 0:40	**Easy run/walk:** Zone 1–2 power run. Run 40 min as 4 min run at Zone 2, 1 min walk at Zone 1. Repeat for the duration of the run.
SAT Time: 1:45	**Goal-pace tempo run:** Warm up well for about 15 min, building to Zone 4 for the last min. As you build, do a few surges at Zone 5, lasting about 10–15 sec each. Rest for a few min. Then do a 4 × 15-min tempo run at your half-marathon goal pace, at Zone 3–4, on a course similar to the race, with 3-min recoveries between. Cool down for 15 min, easy Zone 1–2 jogging and walking.
Time: 0:30	**2nd run of the day:** Easy Zone 1–2 jog
SUN Time: 0	**Day off:** Actively focus on recovery today: (1) stay off legs all you can; (2) watch nutrition closely (healthy carbs, lean protein, good fats); (3) stretch; (4) drink when thirsty. Other common recovery aids include massage, napping, elevating legs, floating in water, and listening to music.

Total time: 6:15

WEEK 13 Sub-1:40 Half-Marathon Plan, 14 Weeks Specific Phase	
MON Time: 0:40	**Easy run/walk:** Zone 1–2 power run. Run 40 min as 4 min run at Zone 2, 1 min walk at Zone 1. Repeat for the duration of the run.
TUES Time: 1:10	**4 × 1 mile:** Warm up well for about 15 min, building from Zone 1–2 to Zone 3–5. Find a flat stretch and run 4 × 1 mile (or 1.6 km) at Zone 4. Do *not* go above Zone 4. Recover with 3-min jog/walk at Zone 1–2 between each mile. Cool down for 15 min with easy Zone 2 jogging and Zone 1 walking.
Time: 0:30	**2nd run of the day:** Easy Zone 1–2 jog
WED Time: 0:40	**Easy run/walk:** Zone 1–2 power run. Run 40 min as 4 min run at Zone 2, 1 min walk at Zone 1. Repeat for the duration of the run.
Time: 0:30	**2nd run of the day:** Easy Zone 1–2 jog
THURS Time: 0:40	**Fartlek:** Run of surges. Warm up well for about 15 min, building from Zone 1–2 to Zone 3–5. On rolling course, run 1–2-min pickups at faster than 10K pace (Zone 6–7), with recoveries at Zone 1–2 as long as you feel you need between the surges. Form! Cadence! Use the last 10 min to cool down with easy Zone 1 running/walking.
FRI Time: 0	**Day off:** Actively focus on recovery today: (1) stay off legs all you can; (2) watch nutrition closely (healthy carbs, lean protein, good fats); (3) stretch; (4) drink when thirsty. Other common recovery aids include massage, napping, elevating legs, and compression wear.
SAT Time: 1:10	**Goal-pace tempo run:** Warm up well for about 15 min, building to Zone 4 for the last min. As you build, do a few surges at Zone 5, lasting about 10–15 sec each. Rest for a few min. Then do a 3 × 10-min tempo run at your half-marathon goal pace, at Zone 3–4, on a course similar to the race, with 2-min recoveries between. Cool down for 15 min, easy Zone 1–2 jogging and walking.
Time: 0:30	**2nd run of the day:** Easy Zone 1–2 jog
SUN Time: 0:40	**Easy run/walk:** Zone 1–2 power run. Run 40 min as 4 min run at Zone 2, 1 min walk at Zone 1. Repeat for the duration of the run.

Total time: 6:30

WEEK 14 Sub-1:40 Half-Marathon Plan, 14 Weeks Specific Phase

MON Time: 0	**Day off:** Actively focus on recovery today: (1) stay off legs all you can; (2) watch nutrition closely (healthy carbs, lean protein, good fats); (3) stretch; (4) drink when thirsty. Other common recovery aids include massage, napping, elevating legs, and compression wear.
TUES Time: 0:40	**5 × 2 min at Zone 3–4:** 15 min warm-up run, followed by 5 × 2 min, starting at Zone 3 for the first min, then building to Zone 4 in the last min, with 2 min easy recovery jog. Easy cool down in Zone 1–2 to make 40 min.
WED Time: 0:40 Time: 0:30	**Easy run/walk:** Zone 1–2 power run. Run 40 min as 4 min run at Zone 2, 1 min walk at Zone 1. Repeat for the duration of the run. **2nd run of the day:** Easy Zone 1–2 jog
THURS Time: 0:30	**Run with surges:** First part of the run is easy, then do 5–7 × 7 sec surges at Zone 6–7 with long recoveries, getting faster over the course of the run. Really focus on forefoot strike, quick cadence, slight forward lean, and fluid motion, not forcing it.
FRI Time: 0:20	**Preview course:** Run start and finish of course. Note landmarks. Include several accelerations to race pace. Otherwise, keep power in Zone 1.
SAT	**HALF-MARATHON RACE**

Total time: 2:40

WEEK 1 Sub-2:30 Marathon Plan, 14 Weeks Specific Phase	
MON Time: 1:10	**3/9-min Stryd test:** Warm up 15 min, preparing for hard effort at the end; conduct a 3-min interval at maximal effort; recover with 5-min walk, 10 min easy jog, 5 min walk, 5 min easy jog, 5 min walk (30 min total); conduct a 9-min interval at maximal effort; cool down 10–15 min easy. *Follow the protocol for this test and estimating rFTPw and rFTPa per Chapter 4.*
TUES Time: 0:40	**Easy run/walk:** Zone 1–2 power run. Run 40 min as 4 min run at Zone 2, 1 min walk at Zone 1. Repeat for the duration of the run.
WED Time: 0:40	**Easy run/walk:** Zone 1–2 power run. Run 40 min as 4 min run at Zone 2, 1 min walk at Zone 1. Repeat for the duration of the run.
THURS Time: 1:00	**30-min test:** Warm up 15 min, preparing for a hard effort at the end. Start a 30-min time trial (best effort) on a flat road or track, collecting power data (pace and HR data as well if possible). Cool down 10–15 min easy. *Follow the protocol for this test and estimating rFTPw and rFTPa per Chapter 4.*
FRI Time: 0:40 Time: 0:30	**Easy run/walk:** Zone 1–2 power run. Run 40 min as 4 min run at Zone 2, 1 min walk at Zone 1. Repeat for the duration of the run. **2nd run of the day:** Easy Zone 1–2 jog
SAT Time: 0	**Day off:** Actively focus on recovery today: (1) stay off legs all you can; (2) watch nutrition closely (healthy carbs, lean protein, good fats); (3) stretch; (4) drink when thirsty. Other common recovery aids include massage, napping, elevating legs, floating in water, and compression wear.
SUN Time: 1:30 Time: 0:30	**Easy run/walk:** Zone 1–2 power run. Run 40 min as 4 min run at Zone 2, 1 min walk at Zone 1. Repeat for the duration of the run. **2nd run of the day:** Easy Zone 1–2 jog

Total time: 6:40

WEEK 2 Sub-2:30 Marathon Plan, 14 Weeks Specific Phase

MON Time: 1:00	**Cruise intervals:** Warm up 15 min, building intensity through the warm-up, starting at Zone 1, then the last min at Zone 4–5. Then do 3 × 8 min, build to Zone 3–4 (3-min recoveries). Monitor pace, trying to be faster for the same power output. Cool down 15 min, at Zone 1–2.
TUES Time: 1:00	**Goal-pace tempo run:** Warm up well for about 15 min, building to Zone 4 for the last min. As you build, do a few surges at Zone 5, lasting about 10–15 sec each. Rest for a few min. Then do a 30-min tempo run at your marathon goal pace on a course similar to the race. Cool down for 15 min, easy Zone 1–2 jogging and walking.
Time: 0:40	**2nd run of the day:** Easy Zone 1–2 jog
WED Time: 1:00	**Envelope run:** Start easy in Zone 1–2 for the first 10–15 min, then work to a moderate pace on the edge of comfort/discomfort. Look at the power zone you are in, likely Zone 3–4. Stay in that zone, but find a way to go faster. Push that envelope, trying to be quicker without raising your watts. It's a balance of trying to hold or increase speed with technique. Focus on your rhythm, cadence, forward lean, soft foot strike, relaxation, eyes and head position. Last 10 min should be easy Zone 1–2 running.
Time: 0:30	**2nd run of the day:** Easy Zone 1–2 jog
THURS Time: 0:40	**Easy run/walk:** Zone 1–2 power run. Run 40 min as 4 min run at Zone 2, 1 min walk at Zone 1. Repeat for the duration of the run.
FRI Time: 1:00	**Envelope run:** Start easy in Zone 1–2 for the first 10–15 min, then work to a moderate pace on the edge of comfort/discomfort. Look at the power zone you are in, likely Zone 3–4. Stay in that zone, but find a way to go faster. Push that envelope, trying to be quicker without raising your watts. It's a balance of trying to hold or increase speed with technique. Focus on your rhythm, cadence, forward lean, soft foot strike, relaxation, eyes and head position. Last 10 min should be easy Zone 1–2 running.
Time: 0:30	**2nd run of the day:** Easy Zone 1–2 jog
SAT Time: 1:20	**Goal-pace tempo run:** Warm up well for about 15 min, building to Zone 4 for the last min. As you build, do a few surges in Zone 5, lasting about 10–15 sec each. Rest for a few min. Then do a 4 × 10-min tempo run at your marathon goal pace on a course similar to the race, with 2-min recoveries between. Cool down for 15 min, easy Zone 1–2 jogging and walking.
Time: 0:30	**2nd run of the day:** Easy Zone 1–2 jog
SUN Time: 1:30	**Envelope run:** Start easy in Zone 1–2 for the first 10–15 min, then work to a moderate pace on the edge of comfort/discomfort. Look at the power zone you are in, likely Zone 3–4. Stay in that zone, but find a way to go faster. Push that envelope, trying to be quicker without raising your watts. It's a balance of trying to hold or increase speed with technique. Focus on your rhythm, cadence, forward lean, soft foot strike, relaxation, eyes and head position. Last 10 min should be easy Zone 1–2 running.
Time: 0:30	**2nd run of the day:** Easy Zone 1–2 jog

Total time: 10:10

WEEK 3 Sub-2:30 Marathon Plan, 14 Weeks Specific Phase	
MON Time: 0:40	**Easy run/walk:** Zone 1–2 power run. Run 40 min as 4 min run at Zone 2, 1 min walk at Zone 1. Repeat for the duration of the run.
TUES Time: 1:15	**Goal-pace tempo run:** Warm up well for about 15 min, building to Zone 4 for the last min. As you build, do a few surges at Zone 5, lasting about 10–15 sec each. Rest for a few min. Then do a 45-min tempo run at your marathon goal pace on a course similar to the race. Cool down for 15 min, easy Zone 1–2 jogging and walking.
Time: 0:30	**2nd run of the day:** Easy Zone 1–2 jog
WED Time: 0:40	**Easy run/walk:** Zone 1–2 power run. Run 40 min as 4 min run at Zone 2, 1 min walk at Zone 1. Repeat for the duration of the run.
Time: 0:30	**2nd run of the day:** Easy Zone 1–2 jog
THURS Time: 1:20	**Goal-pace tempo run:** Warm up well for about 15 min, building to Zone 4 for the last min. As you build, do a few surges at Zone 5, lasting about 10–15 sec each. Rest for a few min. Then do a 4 × 10-min tempo run at your marathon goal pace on a course similar to the race, with 2-min recoveries between. Cool down for 15 min, easy Zone 1–2 jogging and walking.
FRI Time: 1:00	**Envelope run:** Start easy in Zone 1–2 for the first 10–15 min, then work to a moderate pace on the edge of comfort/discomfort. Look at the power zone you are in, likely Zone 3–4. Stay in that zone, but find a way to go faster. Push that envelope, trying to be quicker without raising your watts. It's a balance of trying to hold or increase speed with technique. Focus on your rhythm, cadence, forward lean, soft foot strike, relaxation, eyes and head position. Last 10 min should be easy Zone 1–2 running.
Time: 0:30	**2nd run of the day:** Easy Zone 1–2 jog
SAT Time: 1:45	**Easy run/walk:** Zone 1–2 power run. Do this as 5 min run at Zone 2, 1 min walk at Zone 1. Repeat for the duration of the run. *The run/walk portion won't divide perfectly, so you will finish with a run. Walk a few minutes after.*
Time: 0:30	**2nd run of the day:** Easy Zone 1–2 jog
SUN Time: 0	**Day off:** Actively focus on recovery today: (1) stay off legs all you can; (2) watch nutrition closely (healthy carbs, lean protein, good fats); (3) stretch; (4) drink when thirsty. Other common recovery aids include massage, napping, elevating legs, and compression wear.

Total time: 8:40

WEEK 4 Sub-2:30 Marathon Plan, 14 Weeks Specific Phase

MON Time: 0:40	**Easy run/walk:** Zone 1–2 power run. Run 40 min as 4 min run at Zone 2, 1 min walk at Zone 1. Repeat for the duration of the run.
TUES Time: 1:10	**3/9-min Stryd test:** Warm up 15 min, preparing for hard effort at the end; conduct a 3-min interval at maximal effort; recover with 5-min walk, 10 min easy jog, 5 min easy jog, 5 min walk (30 min total); conduct a 9-min interval at maximal effort; cool down 10–15 min easy. *Follow the protocol for this test and estimating rFTPw and rFTPa per Chapter 4.*
WED Time: 0:40	**Easy run/walk:** Zone 1–2 power run. Run 40 min as 4 min run at Zone 2, 1 min walk at Zone 1. Repeat for the duration of the run.
THURS Time: 0:40	**Easy run/walk:** Zone 1–2 power run. Run 40 min as 4 min run at Zone 2, 1 min walk at Zone 1. Repeat for the duration of the run.
FRI Time: 1:00	**30-min test:** Warm up 15 min, preparing for a hard effort at the end. Start a 30-min time trial (best effort) on a flat road or track, collecting power data (pace and HR data as well if possible). Cool down 10–15 min easy. *Follow the protocol for this test and estimating rFTPw and rFTPa in Chapter 4.*
Time: 0:30	**2nd run of the day:** Easy Zone 1–2 jog
SAT Time: 0	**Day off:** Actively focus on recovery today: (1) stay off legs all you can; (2) watch nutrition closely (healthy carbs, lean protein, good fats); (3) stretch; (4) drink when thirsty. Other common recovery aids include massage, napping, elevating legs, and compression wear.
SUN Time: 2:00	**Easy run/walk:** Zone 1–2 power run. Do this as 9 min run at Zone 2, 1 min walk at Zone 1. Repeat for the duration of the run.
Time: 0:30	**2nd run of the day:** Easy Zone 1–2 jog

Total time: 7:10

WEEK 5 Sub-2:30 Marathon Plan, 14 Weeks Specific Phase	
MON Time: 0:40	**Easy run/walk:** Zone 1–2 power run. Run 40 min as 6 min run at Zone 2, 1 min walk at Zone 1. Repeat for the duration of the run. *This 7-min sequence won't divide evenly into 40, so you will finish on a run. Walk a few minutes after.*
TUES Time: 0:40	**Easy run/walk:** Zone 1–2 power run. Run 40 min as 6 min run at Zone 2, 1 min walk at Zone 1. Repeat for the duration of the run. *This 7-min sequence won't divide evenly into 40, so you will finish on a run. Walk a few minutes after.*
Time: 0:30	**2nd run of the day:** Easy Zone 1–2 jog
WED Time: 1:30	**8 × 1 mile:** Warm up well for about 15 min, building from Zone 1–2 to Zone 3–5. Find a flat stretch and run 8 × 1 mile (or 1.6 km) at your marathon goal pace, Zone 3–4. Do *not* go above Zone 4. Recover with 2-min jog/walk at Zone 1–2 between each mile. Cool down for 15 min with easy Zone 2 jogging and Zone 1 walking.
Time: 0:30	**2nd run of the day:** Easy Zone 1–2 jog
THURS Time: 1:30	**Envelope run:** Start easy in Zone 1–2 for the first 10–15 min, then work to a moderate pace on the edge of comfort/discomfort. Look at the power zone you are in, likely Zone 3–4. Stay in that zone, but find a way to go faster. Push that envelope, trying to be quicker without raising your watts. It's a balance of trying to hold or increase speed with technique. Focus on your rhythm, cadence, forward lean, soft foot strike, relaxation, eyes and head position. Last 10 min should be easy Zone 1–2 running.
Time: 0:30	**2nd run of the day:** Easy Zone 1–2 jog
FRI Time: 0:40	**Easy run/walk:** Zone 1–2 power run. Run 40 min as 6 min run at Zone 2, 1 min walk at Zone 1. Repeat for the duration of the run. *This 7-min sequence won't divide evenly into 40, so you will finish on a run. Walk a few minutes after.*
SAT Time: 1:45	**Goal-pace tempo run:** Warm up well for about 15 min, building to Zone 4 for the last min. As you build, do a few surges in Zone 5, lasting about 10–15 sec each. Rest for a few min. Then do a 4 × 15-min tempo run at your marathon goal pace on a course similar to the race, with 3-min recoveries between. Cool down for 15 min, easy Zone 1–2 jogging and walking.
Time: 0:30	**2nd run of the day:** Easy Zone 1–2 jog
SUN Time: 2:30	**Easy run/walk:** Zone 1–2 power run. Do this as 9 min run at Zone 2, 1 min walk at Zone 1. Repeat for the duration of the run.
Time: 0:30	**2nd run of the day:** Easy Zone 1–2 jog

Total time: 11:45

WEEK 6 Sub-2:30 Marathon Plan, 14 Weeks Specific Phase	
MON Time: 0:40	**Easy run/walk:** Zone 1–2 power run. Run 40 min as 6 min run at Zone 2, 1 min walk at Zone 1. Repeat for the duration of the run. *This 7-min sequence won't divide evenly into 40, so you will finish on a run. Walk a few minutes after.*
TUES Time: 0:40	**Easy run/walk:** Zone 1–2 power run. Do this as 7 min run at Zone 2, 1 min walk at Zone 1. Repeat for the duration of the run. *This 8-min sequence won't divide evenly into 40, so you will finish on a run. Walk a few minutes after.*
Time: 0:30	**2nd run of the day:** Easy Zone 1–2 jog
WED Time: 1:30	**5 × 2 mile:** Warm up well for about 15 min, building from Zone 1–2 to Zone 3–5. Find a flat stretch and run 5 × 2 mile (or 1.6 km) at Zone 3–4. Do *not* go above Zone 4. Recover with 3-min jog/walk at Zone 1–2 between each mile. Cool down for 15 min with easy Zone 2 jogging and Zone 1 walking.
Time: 0:30	**2nd run of the day:** Easy Zone 1–2 jog
THURS Time: 1:00	**Envelope run:** Start easy in Zone 1–2 for the first 10–15 min, then work to a moderate pace on the edge of comfort/discomfort. Look at the power zone you are in, likely Zone 3–4. Stay in that zone, but find a way to go faster. Push that envelope, trying to be quicker without raising your watts. It's a balance of trying to hold or increase speed with technique. Focus on your rhythm, cadence, forward lean, soft foot strike, relaxation, eyes and head position. Last 10 min should be easy Zone 1–2 running.
Time: 0:30	**2nd run of the day:** Easy Zone 1–2 jog
FRI Time: 0	**Day off:** Actively focus on recovery today: (1) stay off legs all you can; (2) watch nutrition closely (healthy carbs, lean protein, good fats); (3) stretch; (4) drink when thirsty. Other common recovery aids include massage, napping, elevating legs, and compression wear.
SAT Time: 2:00	**Goal-pace tempo run:** Warm up well for about 15 min, building to Zone 4 for the last min. As you build, do a few surges at Zone 5, lasting about 10–15 sec each. Rest for a few min. Then do a 4 × 20-min tempo run at your marathon goal pace on a course similar to the race, with 3-min recoveries between. Cool down for 15 min, easy Zone 1–2 jogging and walking.
Time: 0:30	**2nd run of the day:** Easy Zone 1–2 jog
SUN Time: 2:30	**Easy run/walk:** Zone 1–2 power run. Do this as 9 min run at Zone 2, 1 min walk at Zone 1. Repeat for the duration of the run.
Time: 0:30	**2nd run of the day:** Easy Zone 1–2 jog

Total time: 10:50

WEEK 7 Sub-2:30 Marathon Plan, 14 Weeks Specific Phase	
MON Time: 0:40	**Easy run/walk:** Zone 1–2 power run. Run 40 min as 4 min run at Zone 2, 1 min walk at Zone 1. Repeat for the duration of the run.
TUES Time: 1:15	**5 × 1 mile:** Warm up well for about 15 min, building from Zone 1–2 to Zone 3–5. Find a flat stretch and run 5 × 1 mile (or 1.6 km) at Zone 3–4. Do *not* go above Zone 4. Recover with 3-min jog/walk at Zone 1–2 between each mile. Cool down for 15 min with easy Zone 2 jogging and Zone 1 walking.
Time: 0:30	**2nd run of the day:** Easy Zone 1–2 jog
WED Time: 0:40	**Easy run/walk:** Zone 1–2 power run. Run 40 min as 4 min run at Zone 2, 1 min walk at Zone 1. Repeat for the duration of the run.
Time: 0:30	**2nd run of the day:** Easy Zone 1–2 jog
THURS Time: 1:30	**5 × 2 mile:** Warm up well for about 15 min, building from Zone 1–2 to Zone 3–5. Find a flat stretch and run 5 × 2 mile (or 1.6 km) at Zone 3–4. Do *not* go above Zone 4. Recover with 3-min jog/walk at Zone 1–2 between each mile. Cool down for 15 min with easy Zone 2 jogging and Zone 1 walking.
Time: 0:30	**2nd run of the day:** Easy Zone 1–2 jog
FRI Time: 0:40	**Easy run/walk:** Zone 1–2 power run. Run 40 min as 4 min run at Zone 2, 1 min walk at Zone 1. Repeat for the duration of the run.
SAT Time: 2:30	**Goal-pace tempo run:** Warm up well for about 15 min, building to Zone 4 for the last min. As you build, do a few surges at Zone 5, lasting about 10–15 sec each. Rest for a few min. Then do a 3 × 30-min tempo run at your marathon goal pace on a course similar to the race, with 3-min recoveries between. Cool down for 15 min, easy Zone 1–2 jogging and walking.
Time: 0:30	**2nd run of the day:** Easy Zone 1–2 jog
SUN Time: 2:30	**Easy run/walk:** Zone 1–2 power run. Do this as 9 min run at Zone 2, 1 min walk at Zone 1. Repeat for the duration of the run.
Time: 0:30	**2nd run of the day:** Easy Zone 1–2 jog

Total time: 12:15

WEEK 8 Sub-2:30 Marathon Plan, 14 Weeks Specific Phase

MON Time: 0	**Day off:** Actively focus on recovery today: (1) stay off legs all you can; (2) watch nutrition closely (healthy carbs, lean protein, good fats); (3) stretch; (4) drink when thirsty. Other common recovery aids include massage, napping, elevating legs, and compression wear.
TUES Time: 0:40	**Easy run/walk:** Zone 1–2 power run. Run 40 min as 4 min run at Zone 2, 1 min walk at Zone 1. Repeat for the duration of the run.
WED Time: 1:10	**3/9-min Stryd test:** Warm up 15 min, preparing for hard effort at the end; conduct a 3-min interval at maximal effort; recover with 5-min walk, 10 min easy jog, 5 min walk, 5 min easy jog, 5 min walk (30 min total); conduct a 9-min interval at maximal effort; cool down 10–15 min easy. *Follow the protocol for this test and estimating rFTPw and rFTPa per Chapter 4.*
Time: 0:30	**2nd run of the day:** Easy Zone 1–2 jog
THURS Time: 0:40	**Easy run/walk:** Zone 1–2 power run. Run 40 min as 4 min run at Zone 2, 1 min walk at Zone 1. Repeat for the duration of the run.
FRI Time: 1:00	**Envelope run:** Start easy in Zone 1–2 for the first 10–15 min, then work to a moderate pace on the edge of comfort/discomfort. Look at the power zone you are in, likely Zone 3–4. Stay in that zone, but find a way to go faster. Push that envelope, trying to be quicker without raising your watts. It's a balance of trying to hold or increase speed with technique. Focus on your rhythm, cadence, forward lean, soft foot strike, relaxation, eyes and head position. Last 10 min should be easy Zone 1–2 running.
Time: 0:30	**2nd run of the day:** Easy Zone 1–2 jog
SAT Time: 2:30	**Goal-pace tempo run:** Warm up well for about 15 min, building to Zone 4 for the last min. As you build, do a few surges at Zone 5, lasting about 10–15 sec each. Rest for a few min. Then do a 3 × 30-min tempo run at your marathon goal pace on a course similar to the race, with 3-min recoveries between. Cool down for 15 min, easy Zone 1–2 jogging and walking.
Time: 0:30	**2nd run of the day:** Easy Zone 1–2 jog
SUN Time: 2:30	**Easy run/walk:** Zone 1–2 power run. Do this as 9 min run at Zone 2, 1 min walk at Zone 1. Repeat for the duration of the run.
Time: 0:30	**2nd run of the day:** Easy Zone 1–2 jog

Total time: 10:30

WEEK 9 Sub-2:30 Marathon Plan, 14 Weeks Specific Phase	
MON Time: 0	**Day off:** Actively focus on recovery today: (1) stay off legs all you can; (2) watch nutrition closely (healthy carbs, lean protein, good fats); (3) stretch; (4) drink when thirsty. Other common recovery aids include massage, napping, elevating legs, and compression wear.
TUES Time: 1:45	**Goal-pace tempo run:** Warm up well for about 15 min, building to Zone 4 for the last min. As you build, do a few surges at Zone 5, lasting about 10–15 sec each. Rest for a few min. Then do a 4 × 15-min tempo run at your marathon goal pace on a course similar to the race, with 3-min recoveries between. Cool down for 15 min, easy Zone 1–2 jogging and walking.
Time: 0:30	**2nd run of the day:** Easy Zone 1–2 jog
WED Time: 0:40	**Easy run/walk:** Zone 1–2 power run. Run 40 min as 4 min run at Zone 2, 1 min walk at Zone 1. Repeat for the duration of the run.
Time: 0:30	**2nd run of the day:** Easy Zone 1–2 jog
THURS Time: 1:10	**4 × 1 mile:** Warm up well for about 15 min, building from Zone 1–2 to Zone 3–5. Find a flat stretch and run 4 × 1 mile (or 1.6 km) at Zone 3–4. Do *not* go above Zone 4. Recover with 3-min jog/walk at Zone 1–2 between each mile. Cool down for 15 min with easy Zone 2 jogging and Zone 1 walking.
Time: 0:30	**2nd run of the day:** Easy Zone 1–2 jog
FRI Time: 0:40	**Easy run/walk:** Zone 1–2 power run. Run 40 min as 4 min run at Zone 2, 1 min walk at Zone 1. Repeat for the duration of the run.
SAT Time: 2:30	**Goal-pace tempo run:** Warm up well for about 15 min, building to Zone 4 for the last min. As you build, do a few surges at Zone 5, lasting about 10–15 sec each. Rest for a few min. Then do a 3 × 30-min tempo run at your marathon goal pace on a course similar to the race, with 5-min recoveries between. Cool down for 15 min, easy Zone 1–2 jogging and walking.
Time: 0:30	**2nd run of the day:** Easy Zone 1–2 jog
SUN Time: 2:30	**Easy run/walk:** Zone 1–2 power run. Do this as 9 min run at Zone 2, 1 min walk at Zone 1. Repeat for the duration of the run.
Time: 0:30	**2nd run of the day:** Easy Zone 1–2 jog

Total time: 11:45

WEEK 10 Sub-2:30 Marathon Plan, 14 Weeks Specific Phase	
MON Time: 0	**Day off:** Actively focus on recovery today: (1) stay off legs all you can; (2) watch nutrition closely (healthy carbs, lean protein, good fats); (3) stretch; (4) drink when thirsty. Other common recovery aids include massage, napping, elevating legs, and compression wear.
TUES Time: 1:30	**5 × 2 mile:** Warm up well for about 15 min, building from Zone 1–2 to Zone 3–5. Find a flat stretch and run 5 × 2 mile (or 1.6 km) at Zone 3–4. Do *not* go above Zone 4. Recover with 3-min jog/walk at Zone 1–2 between each mile. Cool down for 15 min with easy Zone 2 jogging and Zone 1 walking.
Time: 0:30	**2nd run of the day:** Easy Zone 1–2 jog
WED Time: 0:40	**Easy run/walk:** Zone 1–2 power run. Run 40 min as 4 min run at Zone 2, 1 min walk at Zone 1. Repeat for the duration of the run.
Time: 0:30	**2nd run of the day:** Easy Zone 1–2 jog
THURS Time: 1:00	**Goal-pace tempo run:** Warm up well for about 15 min, building to Zone 4 for the last min. As you build, do a few surges at Zone 5, lasting about 10–15 sec each. Rest for a few min. Then do a 30-min tempo run at your marathon goal pace on a course similar to the race. Cool down for 15 min, easy Zone 1–2 jogging and walking.
Time: 0:30	**2nd run of the day:** Easy Zone 1–2 jog
FRI Time: 0:40	**Easy run/walk:** Zone 1–2 power run. Run 40 min as 4 min run at Zone 2, 1 min walk at Zone 1. Repeat for the duration of the run.
SAT Time: 2:00	**Goal-pace tempo run:** Warm up well for about 15 min, building to Zone 4 for the last min. As you build, do a few surges at Zone 5, lasting about 10–15 sec each. Rest for a few min. Then do a 4 × 20-min tempo run at your marathon goal pace on a course similar to the race, with 3-min recoveries between. Cool down for 15 min, easy Zone 1–2 jogging and walking.
Time: 0:30	**2nd run of the day:** Easy Zone 1–2 jog
SUN Time: 2:00	**Easy run/walk:** Zone 1–2 power run. Do this as 9 min run at Zone 2, 1 min walk at Zone 1. Repeat for the duration of the run.
Time: 0:30	**2nd run of the day:** Easy Zone 1–2 jog

Total time: 10:20

WEEK 11 Sub-2:30 Marathon Plan, 14 Weeks Specific Phase	
MON Time: 0	**Day off:** Actively focus on recovery today: (1) stay off legs all you can; (2) watch nutrition closely (healthy carbs, lean protein, good fats); (3) stretch; (4) drink when thirsty. Other common recovery aids include massage, napping, elevating legs, and compression wear.
TUES Time: 1:30	**Goal-pace tempo run:** Warm up well for about 15 min, building to Zone 4 for the last min. As you build, do a few surges at Zone 5, lasting about 10–15 sec each. Rest for a few min. Then do a 60-min tempo run at your marathon goal pace on a course similar to the race. Cool down for 15 min, easy Zone 1–2 jogging and walking.
Time: 0:30	**2nd run of the day:** Easy Zone 1–2 jog
WED Time: 0:40	**Easy run/walk:** Zone 1–2 power run. Run 40 min as 4 min run at Zone 2, 1 min walk at Zone 1. Repeat for the duration of the run.
Time: 0:30	**2nd run of the day:** Easy Zone 1–2 jog
THURS Time: 1:10	**4 × 1 mile:** Warm up well for about 15 min, building from Zone 1–2 to Zone 3–5. Find a flat stretch and run 4 × 1 mile (or 1.6 km) at Zone 3–4. Do *not* go above Zone 4. Recover with 3-min jog/walk at Zone 1–2 between each mile. Cool down for 15 min with easy Zone 2 jogging and Zone 1 walking.
Time: 0:30	**2nd run of the day:** Easy Zone 1–2 jog
FRI Time: 0:40	**Easy run/walk:** Zone 1–2 power run. Run 40 min as 4 min run at Zone 2, 1 min walk at Zone 1. Repeat for the duration of the run.
SAT Time: 2:00	**Goal-pace tempo run:** Warm up well for about 15 min, building to Zone 4 for the last min. As you build, do a few surges at Zone 5, lasting about 10–15 sec each. Rest for a few min. Then do a 4 × 20-min tempo run at your marathon goal pace on a course similar to the race, with 3-min recoveries between. Cool down for 15 min, easy Zone 1–2 jogging and walking.
Time: 0:30	**2nd run of the day:** Easy Zone 1–2 jog
SUN Time: 2:00	**Envelope run:** Start easy in Zone 1–2 for the first 10–15 min, then work to a moderate pace on the edge of comfort/discomfort. Look at the power zone you are in, likely Zone 3–4. Stay in that zone, but find a way to go faster. Push that envelope, trying to be quicker without raising your watts. It's a balance of trying to hold or increase speed with technique. Focus on your rhythm, cadence, forward lean, soft foot strike, relaxation, eyes and head position. Last 10 min should be easy Zone 1–2 running.
Time: 0:30	**2nd run of the day:** Easy Zone 1–2 jog

Total time: 10:30

MON Time: 0	**Day off:** Actively focus on recovery today: (1) stay off legs all you can; (2) watch nutrition closely (healthy carbs, lean protein, good fats); (3) stretch; (4) drink when thirsty. Other common recovery aids include massage, napping, elevating legs, and compression wear.
TUES Time: 0:40	**Easy run/walk:** Zone 1–2 power run. Run 40 min as 4 min run at Zone 2, 1 min walk at Zone 1. Repeat for the duration of the run.
WED Time: 1:10	**3/9-min Stryd test:** Warm up 15 min, preparing for hard effort at the end; conduct a 3-min interval at maximal effort; recover with 5-min walk, 10 min easy jog, 5 min walk, 5 min easy jog, 5 min walk (30 min total); conduct a 9-min interval at maximal effort; cool down 10–15 min easy. *Follow the protocol for this test and estimating rFTPw and rFTPa per Chapter 4.*
Time: 0:30	**2nd run of the day:** Easy Zone 1–2 jog
THURS Time: 1:00	**Envelope run:** Start easy in Zone 1–2 for the first 10–15 min, then work to a moderate pace on the edge of comfort/discomfort. Look at the power zone you are in, likely Zone 3–4. Stay in that zone, but find a way to go faster. Push that envelope, trying to be quicker without raising your watts. It's a balance of trying to hold or increase speed with technique. Focus on your rhythm, cadence, forward lean, soft foot strike, relaxation, eyes and head position. Last 10 min should be easy Zone 1–2 running.
Time: 0:30	**2nd run of the day:** Easy Zone 1–2 jog
FRI Time: 0:40	**Easy run/walk:** Zone 1–2 power run. Run 40 min as 4 min run at Zone 2, 1 min walk at Zone 1. Repeat for the duration of the run.
SAT Time: 2:00	**Goal-pace tempo run:** Warm up well for about 15 min, building to Zone 4 for the last min. As you build, do a few surges at Zone 5, lasting about 10–15 sec each. Rest for a few min. Then do a 5 × 15-min tempo run at your marathon goal pace on a course similar to the race, with 3-min recoveries between. Cool down for 15 min, easy Zone 1–2 jogging and walking.
Time: 0:30	**2nd run of the day:** Easy Zone 1–2 jog
SUN Time: 0	**Day off:** Actively focus on recovery today: (1) stay off legs all you can; (2) watch nutrition closely (healthy carbs, lean protein, good fats); (3) stretch; (4) drink when thirsty. Other common recovery aids include massage, napping, elevating legs, and compression wear.

Total time: 7:00

WEEK 13 Sub-2:30 Marathon Plan, 14 Weeks Specific Phase

MON Time: 0:40	**Easy run/walk:** Zone 1–2 power run. Run 40 min as 4 min run at Zone 2, 1 min walk at Zone 1. Repeat for the duration of the run.
TUES Time: 1:15	**5 × 1 mile:** Warm up well for about 15 min, building from Zone 1–2 to Zone 3–5. Find a flat stretch and run 5 × 1 mile (or 1.6 km) at Zone 3–4. Do *not* go above Zone 4. Recover with 3-min jog/walk at Zone 1–2 between each mile. Cool down for 15 min with easy Zone 2 jogging and Zone 1 walking.
Time: 0:30	**2nd run of the day:** Easy Zone 1–2 jog
WED Time: 0:40	**Easy run/walk:** Zone 1–2 power run. Run 40 min as 4 min run at Zone 2, 1 min walk at Zone 1. Repeat for the duration of the run.
Time: 0:30	**2nd run of the day:** Easy Zone 1–2 jog
THURS Time: 0:40	**Fartlek:** Run of surges. Warm up well for about 15 min, building from Zone 1–2 to Zone 3–5. On rolling course, run 1–2-min pickups at faster than 5K pace (Zone 6–7), with recoveries at Zone 1–2 as long as you feel you need between the surges. Form! Cadence! Use the last 10 min to cool down with easy Zone 1 running/walking.
FRI Time: 0	**Day off:** Actively focus on recovery today: (1) stay off legs all you can; (2) watch nutrition closely (healthy carbs, lean protein, good fats); (3) stretch; (4) drink when thirsty. Other common recovery aids include massage, napping, elevating legs, and compression wear.
SAT Time: 1:20	**Goal-pace tempo run:** Warm up well for about 15 min, building to Zone 4 for the last min. As you build, do a few surges at Zone 5, lasting about 10–15 sec each. Rest for a few min. Then do a 3 × 15-min tempo run at your marathon goal pace on a course similar to the race, with 2-min recoveries between. Cool down for 15 min, easy Zone 1–2 jogging and walking.
Time: 0:30	**2nd run of the day:** Easy Zone 1–2 jog
SUN Time: 0:40	**Easy run/walk:** Zone 1–2 power run. Run 40 min as 4 min run at Zone 2, 1 min walk at Zone 1. Repeat for the duration of the run.

Total time: 6:45

WEEK 14 Sub-2:30 Marathon Plan, 14 Weeks Specific Phase

MON Time: 0	**Day off:** Actively focus on recovery today: (1) stay off legs all you can; (2) watch nutrition closely (healthy carbs, lean protein, good fats); (3) stretch; (4) drink when thirsty. Other common recovery aids include massage, napping, elevating legs, and compression wear.
TUES Time: 0:40	**5 × 2 min at Zone 3–4:** 15 min warm-up run, followed by 5 × 2 min, starting at Zone 3 for the first min, then building to Zone 4 in the last min, with 2 min easy recovery jog. Easy cool down in Zone 1–2 to make 40 min.
WED Time: 0:40 Time: 0:30	**Easy run/walk:** Zone 1–2 power run. Run 40 min as 4 min run at Zone 2, 1 min walk at Zone 1. Repeat for the duration of the run. **2nd run of the day:** Easy Zone 1–2 jog
THURS Time: 0:30	**Run with surges:** First part of the run is easy, then do 5–7 × 7 sec surges at Zone 6–7 with long recoveries, getting faster over the course of the run. Really focus on forefoot strike, quick cadence, slight forward lean, and fluid motion, not forcing it.
FRI Time: 0:20	**Preview course:** Run start and finish of course. Note landmarks. Include several accelerations to race pace. Otherwise, keep power in Zone 1.
SAT	**MARATHON RACE**

Total time: 2:40

WEEK 1 Sub-3:30 Marathon Plan, 14 Weeks Specific Phase	
MON Time: 1:10	**3/9-min Stryd test:** Warm up 15 min, preparing for hard effort at the end; conduct a 3-min interval at maximal effort; recover with 5-min walk, 10 min easy jog, 5 min walk, 5 min easy jog, 5 min walk (30 min total); conduct a 9-min interval at maximal effort; cool down 10–15 min easy. *Follow the protocol for this test and estimating rFTPw and rFTPa per Chapter 4.*
TUES Time: 0:40	**Easy run/walk:** Zone 1–2 power run. Run 40 min as 4 min run at Zone 2, 1 min walk at Zone 1. Repeat for the duration of the run.
WED Time: 0:40	**Easy run/walk:** Zone 1–2 power run. Run 40 min as 4 min run at Zone 2, 1 min walk at Zone 1. Repeat for the duration of the run.
THURS Time: 1:00	**30-min test:** Warm up 15 min, preparing for a hard effort at the end. Start a 30-min time trial (best effort) on a flat road or track, collecting power data (pace and HR data as well if possible). Cool down 10–15 min easy. *Follow the protocol for this test and estimating rFTPw and rFTPa per Chapter 4.*
FRI Time: 0:40 Time: 0:30	**Easy run/walk:** Zone 1–2 power run. Run 40 min as 4 min run at Zone 2, 1 min walk at Zone 1. Repeat for the duration of the run. **2nd run of the day:** Easy Zone 1–2 jog
SAT Time: 0	**Day off:** Actively focus on recovery today: (1) stay off legs all you can; (2) watch nutrition closely (healthy carbs, lean protein, good fats); (3) stretch; (4) drink when thirsty. Other common recovery aids include massage, napping, elevating legs, floating in water, and compression wear.
SUN Time: 1:30 Time: 0:30	**Easy run/walk:** Zone 1–2 power run. Run 40 min as 5 min run at Zone 2, 1 min walk at Zone 1. Repeat for the duration of the run. **2nd run of the day:** Easy Zone 1–2 jog

Total time: 6:40

WEEK 2 Sub-3:30 Marathon Plan, 14 Weeks Specific Phase	
MON Time: 1:10	**Cruise intervals:** Warm up 15 min, building intensity through the warm-up, starting at Zone 1, then the last min at Zone 4–5. Then do 4 × 8 min, build to Zone 3–4 (2-min recoveries). Monitor pace, trying to be faster for the same power output. Cool down 15 min, at Zone 1–2.
TUES Time: 1:00	**Goal-pace tempo run:** Warm up well for about 15 min, building to Zone 4 for the last min. As you build, do a few surges at Zone 5, lasting about 10–15 sec each. Rest for a few min. Then do a 30-min tempo run at your marathon goal pace on a course similar to the race. Cool down for 15 min, easy Zone 1–2 jogging and walking.
Time: 0:40	**Easy run/walk:** Zone 1–2 power run. Run 40 min as 4 min run at Zone 2, 1 min walk at Zone 1. Repeat for the duration of the run.
WED Time: 1:00	**Envelope run:** Start easy in Zone 1–2 for the first 10–15 min, then work to a moderate pace on the edge of comfort/discomfort. Look at the power zone you are in, likely Zone 3–4. Stay in that zone, but find a way to go faster. Push that envelope, trying to be quicker without raising your watts. It's a balance of trying to hold or increase speed with technique. Focus on your rhythm, cadence, forward lean, soft foot strike, relaxation, eyes and head position. Last 10 min should be easy Zone 1–2 running.
Time: 0:30	**2nd run of the day:** Easy Zone 1–2 jog
THURS Time: 0:40	**Easy run/walk:** Zone 1–2 power run. Run 40 min as 4 min run at Zone 2, 1 min walk at Zone 1. Repeat for the duration of the run.
FRI Time: 1:00	**Envelope run:** Start easy in Zone 1–2 for the first 10–15 min, then work to a moderate pace on the edge of comfort/discomfort. Look at the power zone you are in, likely Zone 3–4. Stay in that zone, but find a way to go faster. Push that envelope, trying to be quicker without raising your watts. It's a balance of trying to hold or increase speed with technique. Focus on your rhythm, cadence, forward lean, soft foot strike, relaxation, eyes and head position. Last 10 min should be easy Zone 1–2 running.
Time: 0:30	**2nd run of the day:** Easy Zone 1–2 jog
SAT Time: 1:20	**Goal-pace tempo run:** Warm up well for about 15 min, building to Zone 4 for the last min. As you build, do a few surges in Zone 5, lasting about 10–15 sec each. Rest for a few min. Then do a 4 × 10-min tempo run at your marathon goal pace on a course similar to the race, with 2-min recoveries between. Cool down for 15 min, easy Zone 1–2 jogging and walking.
Time: 0:30	**2nd run of the day:** Easy Zone 1–2 jog
SUN Time: 1:30	**Envelope run:** Start easy in Zone 1–2 for the first 10–15 min, then work to a moderate pace on the edge of comfort/discomfort. Look at the power zone you are in, likely Zone 3–4. Stay in that zone, but find a way to go faster. Push that envelope, trying to be quicker without raising your watts. It's a balance of trying to hold or increase speed with technique. Focus on your rhythm, cadence, forward lean, soft foot strike, relaxation, eyes and head position. Last 10 min should be easy Zone 1–2 running.
Time: 0:30	**2nd run of the day:** Easy Zone 1–2 jog

Total time: 10:20

WEEK 3 Sub-3:30 Marathon Plan, 14 Weeks Specific Phase

MON Time: 0:40	**Easy run/walk:** Zone 1–2 power run. Run 40 min as 4 min run at Zone 2, 1 min walk at Zone 1. Repeat for the duration of the run.
TUES Time: 1:15	**Goal-pace tempo run:** Warm up well for about 15 min, building to Zone 4 for the last min. As you build, do a few surges at Zone 5, lasting about 10–15 sec each. Rest for a few min. Then do a 45-min tempo run at your marathon goal pace on a course similar to the race. Cool down for 15 min, easy Zone 1–2 jogging and walking.
Time: 0:30	**2nd run of the day:** Easy Zone 1–2 jog
WED Time: 0:40	**Easy run/walk:** Zone 1–2 power run. Run 40 min as 4 min run at Zone 2, 1 min walk at Zone 1. Repeat for the duration of the run.
Time: 0:30	**2nd run of the day:** Easy Zone 1–2 jog
THURS Time: 1:20	**Goal-pace tempo run:** Warm up well for about 15 min, building to Zone 4 for the last min. As you build, do a few surges at Zone 5, lasting about 10–15 sec each. Rest for a few min. Then do a 4 × 10-min tempo run at your marathon goal pace on a course similar to the race, with 2-min recoveries between. Cool down for 15 min, easy Zone 1–2 jogging and walking.
FRI Time: 1:00	**Envelope run:** Start easy in Zone 1–2 for the first 10–15 min, then work to a moderate pace on the edge of comfort/discomfort. Look at the power zone you are in, likely Zone 3–4. Stay in that zone, but find a way to go faster. Push that envelope, trying to be quicker without raising your watts. It's a balance of trying to hold or increase speed with technique. Focus on your rhythm, cadence, forward lean, soft foot strike, relaxation, eyes and head position. Last 10 min should be easy Zone 1–2 running.
Time: 0:30	**2nd run of the day:** Easy Zone 1–2 jog
SAT Time: 1:45	**Easy run/walk:** Zone 1–2 power run. Do this as 5 min run at Zone 2, 1 min walk at Zone 1. Repeat for the duration of the run. *The run/walk portion won't divide perfectly, so you will finish with a run. Walk a few minutes after.*
Time: 0:30	**2nd run of the day:** Easy Zone 1–2 jog
SUN Time: 0	**Day off:** Actively focus on recovery today: (1) stay off legs all you can; (2) watch nutrition closely (healthy carbs, lean protein, good fats); (3) stretch; (4) drink when thirsty. Other common recovery aids include massage, napping, elevating legs, and compression wear.

Total time: 8:40

WEEK 4 Sub-3:30 Marathon Plan, 14 Weeks Specific Phase	
MON Time: 0:40	**Easy run/walk:** Zone 1–2 power run. Run 40 min. as 4 min run at Zone 2, 1 min walk at Zone 1. Repeat for the duration of the run.
TUES Time: 1:10	**3/9-min Stryd test:** Warm up 15 min, preparing for hard effort at the end; conduct a 3-min interval at maximal effort; recover with 5-min walk, 10 min easy jog, 5 min walk, 5 min easy jog, 5 min walk (30 min total); conduct a 9-min interval at maximal effort; cool down 10–15 min easy. *Follow the protocol for this test and estimating rFTPw and rFTPa per Chapter 4.*
WED Time: 0:40	**Easy run/walk:** Zone 1–2 power run. Run 40 min as 4 min run at Zone 2, 1 min walk at Zone 1. Repeat for the duration of the run.
THURS Time: 0:40	**Easy run/walk:** Zone 1–2 power run. Run 40 min as 4 min run at Zone 2, 1 min walk at Zone 1. Repeat for the duration of the run.
FRI Time: 1:00	**30-min test:** Warm up 15 min, preparing for a hard effort at the end. Start a 30-min time trial (best effort) on a flat road or track, collecting power data (pace and HR data as well if possible). Cool down 10–15 min easy. *Follow the protocol for this test and estimating rFTPw and rFTPa in Chapter 4.*
Time: 0:30	**2nd run of the day:** Easy Zone 1–2 jog
SAT Time: 0	**Day off:** Actively focus on recovery today: (1) stay off legs all you can; (2) watch nutrition closely (healthy carbs, lean protein, good fats); (3) stretch; (4) drink when thirsty. Other common recovery aids include massage, napping, elevating legs, floating in water, and listening to music.
SUN Time: 2:00	**Easy run/walk:** Zone 1–2 power run. Do this as 9 min run at Zone 2, 1 min walk at Zone 1. Repeat for the duration of the run.
Time: 0:30	**2nd run of the day:** Easy Zone 1–2 jog

Total time: 7:10

WEEK 5 Sub-3:30 Marathon Plan, 14 Weeks Specific Phase	
MON Time: 0:40	**Easy run/walk:** Zone 1–2 power run. Run 40 min as 6 min run at Zone 2, 1 min walk at Zone 1. Repeat for the duration of the run. *This 7-min sequence won't divide evenly into 40, so you will finish on a run. Walk a few minutes after.*
TUES Time: 0:40	**Easy run/walk:** Zone 1–2 power run. Run 40 min as 6 min run at Zone 2, 1 min walk at Zone 1. Repeat for the duration of the run. *This 7-min sequence won't divide evenly into 40, so you will finish on a run. Walk a few minutes after.*
Time: 0:30	**2nd run of the day:** Easy Zone 1–2 jog
WED Time: 1:30	**8 × 1 mile:** Warm up well for about 15 min, building from Zone 1–2 to Zone 3–5. Find a flat stretch and run 8 × 1 mile (or 1.6 km) at your marathon goal pace, Zone 3. Do *not* go above Zone 3. Recover with 2-min jog/walk at Zone 1–2 between each mile. Cool down for 15 min with easy Zone 2 jogging and Zone 1 walking.
Time: 0:30	**2nd run of the day:** Easy Zone 1–2 jog
THURS Time: 1:30	**Envelope run:** Start easy in Zone 1–2 for the first 10–15 min, then work to a moderate pace on the edge of comfort/discomfort. Look at the power zone you are in, likely Zone 3–4. Stay in that zone, but find a way to go faster. Push that envelope, trying to be quicker without raising your watts. It's a balance of trying to hold or increase speed with technique. Focus on your rhythm, cadence, forward lean, soft foot strike, relaxation, eyes and head position. Last 10 min should be easy Zone 1–2 running.
Time: 0:30	**2nd run of the day:** Easy Zone 1–2 jog
FRI Time: 0:40	**Easy run/walk:** Zone 1–2 power run. Run 40 min as 6 min run at Zone 2, 1 min walk at Zone 1. Repeat for the duration of the run. *This 7-min sequence won't divide evenly into 40, so you will finish on a run. Walk a few minutes after.*
SAT Time: 1:45	**Goal-pace tempo run:** Warm up well for about 15 min, building to Zone 4 for the last min. As you build, do a few surges in Zone 5, lasting about 10–15 sec each. Rest for a few min. Then do a 4 × 15-min tempo run at your marathon goal pace on a course similar to the race, with 3-min recoveries between. Cool down for 15 min, easy Zone 1–2 jogging and walking.
Time: 0:30	**2nd run of the day:** Easy Zone 1–2 jog
SUN Time: 2:30	**Easy run/walk:** Zone 1–2 power run. Do this as 9 min run at Zone 2, 1 min walk at Zone 1. Repeat for the duration of the run.
Time: 0:30	**2nd run of the day:** Easy Zone 1–2 jog

Total time: 11:45

WEEK 6 Sub-3:30 Marathon Plan, 14 Weeks Specific Phase	
MON Time: 0:40	**Easy run/walk:** Zone 1–2 power run. Run 40 min as 6 min run at Zone 2, 1 min walk at Zone 1. Repeat for the duration of the run. *This 7-min sequence won't divide evenly into 40, so you will finish on a run. Walk a few minutes after.*
TUES Time: 0:40	**Easy run/walk:** Zone 1–2 power run. Do this as 7 min run at Zone 2, 1 min walk at Zone 1. Repeat for the duration of the run. *This 8-min sequence won't divide evenly into 40, so you will finish on a run. Walk a few minutes after.*
Time: 0:30	**2nd run of the day:** Easy Zone 1–2 jog
WED Time: 1:30	**5 × 2 mile:** Warm up well for about 15 min, building from Zone 1–2 to Zone 3–5. Find a flat stretch and run 5 × 2 mile (or 1.6 km) at Zone 3. Do *not* go above Zone 3. Recover with 3-min jog/walk at Zone 1–2 between each mile. Cool down for 15 min with easy Zone 2 jogging and Zone 1 walking.
Time: 0:30	**2nd run of the day:** Easy Zone 1–2 jog
THURS Time: 1:00	**Envelope run:** Start easy in Zone 1–2 for the first 10–15 min, then work to a moderate pace on the edge of comfort/discomfort. Look at the power zone you are in, likely Zone 3–4. Stay in that zone, but find a way to go faster. Push that envelope, trying to be quicker without raising your watts. It's a balance of trying to hold or increase speed with technique. Focus on your rhythm, cadence, forward lean, soft foot strike, relaxation, eyes and head position. Last 10 min should be easy Zone 1–2 running.
Time: 0:30	**2nd run of the day:** Easy Zone 1–2 jog
FRI Time: 0	**Day off:** Actively focus on recovery today: (1) stay off legs all you can; (2) watch nutrition closely (healthy carbs, lean protein, good fats); (3) stretch; (4) drink when thirsty. Other common recovery aids include massage, napping, elevating legs, and compression wear.
SAT Time: 2:00	**Goal-pace tempo run:** Warm up well for about 15 min, building to Zone 4 for the last min. As you build, do a few surges at Zone 5, lasting about 10–15 sec each. Rest for a few min. Then do a 4 × 20-min tempo run at your marathon goal pace on a course similar to the race, with 3-min recoveries between. Cool down for 15 min, easy Zone 1–2 jogging and walking.
Time: 0:30	**2nd run of the day:** Easy Zone 1–2 jog
SUN Time: 2:45	**Easy run/walk:** Zone 1–2 power run. Do this as 9 min run at Zone 2, 1 min walk at Zone 1. Repeat for the duration of the run. *The run/walk portion won't divide perfectly, so you will finish with a run. Walk a few minutes after.*
Time: 0:30	**2nd run of the day:** Easy Zone 1–2 jog

Total time: 11:05

WEEK 7 Sub-3:30 Marathon Plan, 14 Weeks Specific Phase	
MON Time: 0:40	**Easy run/walk:** Zone 1–2 power run. Run 40 min as 4 min run at Zone 2, 1 min walk at Zone 1. Repeat for the duration of the run.
TUES Time: 1:15	**5 × 1 mile:** Warm up well for about 15 min, building from Zone 1–2 to Zone 3–5. Find a flat stretch and run 5 × 1 mile (or 1.6 km) at Zone 3. Do *not* go above Zone 3. Recover with 3-min jog/walk at Zone 1–2 between each mile. Cool down for 15 min with easy Zone 2 jogging and Zone 1 walking.
Time: 0:30	**2nd run of the day:** Easy Zone 1–2 jog
WED Time: 0:40	**Easy run/walk:** Zone 1–2 power run. Run 40 min as 4 min run at Zone 2, 1 min walk at Zone 1. Repeat for the duration of the run.
Time: 0:30	**2nd run of the day:** Easy Zone 1–2 jog
THURS Time: 1:30	**5 × 2 mile:** Warm up well for about 15 min, building from Zone 1–2 to Zone 3–5. Find a flat stretch and run 5 × 2 mile (or 1.6 km) at Zone 3. Do *not* go above Zone 3. Recover with 3-min jog/walk at Zone 1–2 between each mile. Cool down for 15 min with easy Zone 2 jogging and Zone 1 walking.
Time: 0:30	**2nd run of the day:** Easy Zone 1–2 jog
FRI Time: 0:40	**Easy run/walk:** Zone 1–2 power run. Run 40 min as 4 min run at Zone 2, 1 min walk at Zone 1. Repeat for the duration of the run.
SAT Time: 2:30	**Goal-pace tempo run:** Warm up well for about 15 min, building to Zone 4 for the last min. As you build, do a few surges at Zone 5, lasting about 10–15 sec each. Rest for a few min. Then do a 3 × 30-min tempo run at your marathon goal pace, at Zone 3, on a course similar to the race, with 3-min recoveries between. Cool down for 15 min, easy Zone 1–2 jogging and walking.
Time: 0:30	**2nd run of the day:** Easy Zone 1–2 jog
SUN Time: 2:45	**Easy run/walk:** Zone 1–2 power run. Do this as 9 min run at Zone 2, 1 min walk at Zone 1. Repeat for the duration of the run. *The run/walk portion won't divide perfectly, so you will finish with a run. Walk a few minutes after.*
Time: 0:30	**2nd run of the day:** Easy Zone 1–2 jog

Total time: 12:30

WEEK 8 Sub-3:30 Marathon Plan, 14 Weeks Specific Phase	
MON Time: 0	**Day off:** Actively focus on recovery today: (1) stay off legs all you can; (2) watch nutrition closely (healthy carbs, lean protein, good fats); (3) stretch; (4) drink when thirsty. Other common recovery aids include massage, napping, elevating legs, and compression wear.
TUES Time: 0:40	**Easy run/walk:** Zone 1–2 power run. Run 40 min as 4 min run at Zone 2, 1 min walk at Zone 1. Repeat for the duration of the run.
WED Time: 1:10	**3/9-min Stryd test:** Warm up 15 min, preparing for hard effort at the end; conduct a 3-min interval at maximal effort; recover with 5-min walk, 10 min easy jog, 5 min walk, 5 min easy jog, 5 min walk (30 min total); conduct a 9-min interval at maximal effort; cool down 10–15 min easy. *Follow the protocol for this test and estimating rFTPw and rFTPa per Chapter 4.*
Time: 0:30	**2nd run of the day:** Easy Zone 1–2 jog
THURS Time: 0:40	**Easy run/walk:** Zone 1–2 power run. Run 40 min as 4 min run at Zone 2, 1 min walk at Zone 1. Repeat for the duration of the run.
FRI Time: 1:00	**Envelope run:** Start easy in Zone 1–2 for the first 10–15 min, then work to a moderate pace on the edge of comfort/discomfort. Look at the power zone you are in, likely Zone 3–4. Stay in that zone, but find a way to go faster. Push that envelope, trying to be quicker without raising your watts. It's a balance of trying to hold or increase speed with technique. Focus on your rhythm, cadence, forward lean, soft foot strike, relaxation, eyes and head position. Last 10 min should be easy Zone 1–2 running.
Time: 0:30	**2nd run of the day:** Easy Zone 1–2 jog
SAT Time: 2:30	**Goal-pace tempo run:** Warm up well for about 15 min, building to Zone 4 for the last min. As you build, do a few surges at Zone 5, lasting about 10–15 sec each. Rest for a few min. Then do a 3 × 30-min tempo run at your marathon goal pace, at Zone 3, on a course similar to the race, with 3-min recoveries between. Cool down for 15 min, easy Zone 1–2 jogging and walking.
Time: 0:30	**2nd run of the day:** Easy Zone 1–2 jog
SUN Time: 3:00	**Easy run/walk:** Zone 1–2 power run. Do this as 9 min run at Zone 2, 1 min walk at Zone 1. Repeat for the duration of the run.
Time: 0:30	**2nd run of the day:** Easy Zone 1–2 jog

Total time: 11:00

WEEK 9 Sub-3:30 Marathon Plan, 14 Weeks Specific Phase	
MON Time: 0	**Day off:** Actively focus on recovery today: (1) stay off legs all you can; (2) watch nutrition closely (healthy carbs, lean protein, good fats); (3) stretch; (4) drink when thirsty. Other common recovery aids include massage, napping, elevating legs, and compression wear.
TUES Time: 1:45	**Goal-pace tempo run:** Warm up well for about 15 min, building to Zone 4 for the last min. As you build, do a few surges at Zone 5, lasting about 10–15 sec each. Rest for a few min. Then do a 4 × 15-min tempo run at your marathon goal pace, at Zone 3, on a course similar to the race, with 3-min recoveries between. Cool down for 15 min, easy Zone 1–2 jogging and walking.
Time: 0:30	**2nd run of the day:** Easy Zone 1–2 jog
WED Time: 0:40	**Easy run/walk:** Zone 1–2 power run. Run 40 min as 4 min run at Zone 2, 1 min walk at Zone 1. Repeat for the duration of the run.
Time: 0:30	**2nd run of the day:** Easy Zone 1–2 jog
THURS Time: 1:10	**4 × 1 mile:** Warm up well for about 15 min, building from Zone 1–2 to Zone 3–5. Find a flat stretch and run 4 × 1 mile (or 1.6 km) at Zone 4. Do *not* go above Zone 4. Recover with 3-min jog/walk at Zone 1–2 between each mile. Cool down for 15 min with easy Zone 2 jogging and Zone 1 walking.
Time: 0:30	**2nd run of the day:** Easy Zone 1–2 jog
FRI Time: 0:40	**Easy run/walk:** Zone 1–2 power run. Run 40 min as 4 min run at Zone 2, 1 min walk at Zone 1. Repeat for the duration of the run.
SAT Time: 2:30	**Goal-pace tempo run:** Warm up well for about 15 min, building to Zone 4 for the last min. As you build, do a few surges at Zone 5, lasting about 10–15 sec each. Rest for a few min. Then do a 3 × 30-min tempo run at your marathon goal pace on a course similar to the race, with 5-min recoveries between. Cool down for 15 min, easy Zone 1–2 jogging and walking.
Time: 0:30	**2nd run of the day:** Easy Zone 1–2 jog
SUN Time: 3:00	**Easy run/walk:** Zone 1–2 power run. Do this as 9 min run at Zone 2, 1 min walk at Zone 1. Repeat for the duration of the run.
Time: 0:30	**2nd run of the day:** Easy Zone 1–2 jog

Total time: 12:15

WEEK 10 Sub-3:30 Marathon Plan, 14 Weeks Specific Phase	
MON Time: 0	**Day off:** Actively focus on recovery today: (1) stay off legs all you can; (2) watch nutrition closely (healthy carbs, lean protein, good fats); (3) stretch; (4) drink when thirsty. Other common recovery aids include massage, napping, elevating legs, floating in water, and listening to music.
TUES Time: 1:30	**5 × 2 mile:** Warm up well for about 15 min, building from Zone 1–2 to Zone 3–5. Find a flat stretch and run 5 × 2 mile (or 1.6 km) at Zone 3. Do *not* go above Zone 3. Recover with 3-min jog/walk at Zone 1–2 between each mile. Cool down for 15 min with easy Zone 2 jogging and Zone 1 walking.
Time: 0:30	**2nd run of the day:** Easy Zone 1–2 jog
WED Time: 0:40	**Easy run/walk:** Zone 1–2 power run. Run 40 min as 4 min run at Zone 2, 1 min walk at Zone 1. Repeat for the duration of the run.
Time: 0:30	**2nd run of the day:** Easy Zone 1–2 jog
THURS Time: 1:00	**Goal-pace tempo run:** Warm up well for about 15 min, building to Zone 4 for the last min. As you build, do a few surges at Zone 5, lasting about 10–15 sec each. Rest for a few min. Then do a 30-min tempo run at your marathon goal pace, at Zone 3, on a course similar to the race. Cool down for 15 min, easy Zone 1–2 jogging and walking.
Time: 0:30	**2nd run of the day:** Easy Zone 1–2 jog
FRI Time: 0:40	**Easy run/walk:** Zone 1–2 power run. Run 40 min as 4 min run at Zone 2, 1 min walk at Zone 1. Repeat for the duration of the run.
SAT Time: 2:00	**Goal-pace tempo run:** Warm up well for about 15 min, building to Zone 4 for the last min. As you build, do a few surges at Zone 5, lasting about 10–15 sec each. Rest for a few min. Then do a 4 × 20-min tempo run at your marathon goal pace, at Zone 3, on a course similar to the race, with 3-min recoveries between. Cool down for 15 min, easy Zone 1–2 jogging and walking.
Time: 0:30	**2nd run of the day:** Easy Zone 1–2 jog
SUN Time: 3:00	**Easy run/walk:** Zone 1–2 power run. Do this as 9 min run at Zone 2, 1 min walk at Zone 1. Repeat for the duration of the run.
Time: 0:30	**2nd run of the day:** Easy Zone 1–2 jog

Total time: 11:20

WEEK 11 Sub-3:30 Marathon Plan, 14 Weeks Specific Phase	
MON Time: 0	**Day off:** Actively focus on recovery today: (1) stay off legs all you can; (2) watch nutrition closely (healthy carbs, lean protein, good fats); (3) stretch; (4) drink when thirsty. Other common recovery aids include massage, napping, elevating legs, and compression wear.
TUES Time: 1:30	**Goal-pace tempo run:** Warm up well for about 15 min, building to Zone 4 for the last min. As you build, do a few surges at Zone 5, lasting about 10–15 sec each. Rest for a few min. Then do a 60-min tempo run at your marathon goal pace, at Zone 3, on a course similar to the race. Cool down for 15 min, easy Zone 1–2 jogging and walking.
Time: 0:30	**2nd run of the day:** Easy Zone 1–2 jog
WED Time: 0:40	**Easy run/walk:** Zone 1–2 power run. Run 40 min as 4 min run at Zone 2, 1 min walk at Zone 1. Repeat for the duration of the run.
Time: 0:30	**2nd run of the day:** Easy Zone 1–2 jog
THURS Time: 1:10	**4 × 1 mile:** Warm up well for about 15 min, building from Zone 1–2 to Zone 3–5. Find a flat stretch and run 4 × 1 mile (or 1.6 km) at Zone 3. Do *not* go above Zone 3. Recover with 3-min jog/walk at Zone 1–2 between each mile. Cool down for 15 min with easy Zone 2 jogging and Zone 1 walking.
Time: 0:30	**2nd run of the day:** Easy Zone 1–2 jog
FRI Time: 0:40	**Easy run/walk:** Zone 1–2 power run. Run 40 min as 4 min run at Zone 2, 1 min walk at Zone 1. Repeat for the duration of the run.
SAT Time: 2:00	**Goal-pace tempo run:** Warm up well for about 15 min, building to Zone 4 for the last min. As you build, do a few surges at Zone 5, lasting about 10–15 sec each. Rest for a few min. Then do a 4 × 20-min tempo run at your marathon goal pace, at Zone 3, on a course similar to the race, with 3-min recoveries between. Cool down for 15 min, easy Zone 1–2 jogging and walking.
Time: 0:30	**2nd run of the day:** Easy Zone 1–2 jog
SUN Time: 3:00	**Easy run/walk:** Zone 1–2 power run. Do this as 9 min run at Zone 2, 1 min walk at Zone 1. Repeat for the duration of the run.
Time: 0:30	**2nd run of the day:** Easy Zone 1–2 jog

Total time: 11:30

MON Time: 0	**Day off:** Actively focus on recovery today: (1) stay off legs all you can; (2) watch nutrition closely (healthy carbs, lean protein, good fats); (3) stretch; (4) drink when thirsty. Other common recovery aids include massage, napping, elevating legs, and compression wear.
TUES Time: 0:40	**Easy run/walk:** Zone 1–2 power run. Run 40 min as 4 min run at Zone 2, 1 min walk at Zone 1. Repeat for the duration of the run.
WED Time: 1:10	**3/9-min Stryd test:** Warm up 15 min, preparing for hard effort at the end; conduct a 3-min interval at maximal effort; recover with 5-min walk, 10 min easy jog, 5 min walk, 5 min easy jog, 5 min walk (30 min total); conduct a 9-min interval at maximal effort; cool down 10–15 min easy. *Follow the protocol for this test and estimating rFTPw and rFTPa per Chapter 4.*
Time: 0:30	**2nd run of the day:** Easy Zone 1–2 jog
THURS Time: 1:00	**Envelope run:** Start easy in Zone 1–2 for the first 10–15 min, then work to a moderate pace on the edge of comfort/discomfort. Look at the power zone you are in, likely Zone 3–4. Stay in that zone, but find a way to go faster. Push that envelope, trying to be quicker without raising your watts. It's a balance of trying to hold or increase speed with technique. Focus on your rhythm, cadence, forward lean, soft foot strike, relaxation, eyes and head position. Last 10 min should be easy Zone 1–2 running.
Time: 0:30	**2nd run of the day:** Easy Zone 1–2 jog
FRI Time: 0:40	**Easy run/walk:** Zone 1–2 power run. Run 40 min as 4 min run at Zone 2, 1 min walk at Zone 1. Repeat for the duration of the run.
SAT Time: 2:00	**Goal-pace tempo run:** Warm up well for about 15 min, building to Zone 4 for the last min. As you build, do a few surges at Zone 5, lasting about 10–15 sec each. Rest for a few min. Then do a 5 × 15-min tempo run at your marathon goal pace, at Zone 3, on a course similar to the race, with 3-min recoveries between. Cool down for 15 min, easy Zone 1–2 jogging and walking.
Time: 0:30	**2nd run of the day:** Easy Zone 1–2 jog
SUN Time: 0	**Day off:** Actively focus on recovery today: (1) stay off legs all you can; (2) watch nutrition closely (healthy carbs, lean protein, good fats); (3) stretch; (4) drink when thirsty. Other common recovery aids include massage, napping, elevating legs, floating in water, and listening to music.

Total time: 7:00

WEEK 13 Sub-3:30 Marathon Plan, 14 Weeks Specific Phase	
MON Time: 0:40	**Easy run/walk:** Zone 1–2 power run. Run 40 min as 4 min run at Zone 2, 1 min walk at Zone 1. Repeat for the duration of the run.
TUES Time: 1:10	**5 × 1 mile:** Warm up well for about 15 min, building from Zone 1–2 to Zone 3–5. Find a flat stretch and run 5 × 1 mile (or 1.6 km) at Zone 3–4. Do *not* go above Zone 4. Recover with 3-min jog/walk at Zone 1–2 between each mile. Cool down for 15 min with easy Zone 2 jogging and Zone 1 walking.
Time: 0:30	**2nd run of the day:** Easy Zone 1–2 jog
WED Time: 0:40	**Easy run/walk:** Zone 1–2 power run. Run 40 min as 4 min run at Zone 2, 1 min walk at Zone 1. Repeat for the duration of the run.
Time: 0:30	**2nd run of the day:** Easy Zone 1–2 jog
THURS Time: 0:40	**Fartlek:** Run of surges. Warm up well for about 15 min, building from Zone 1–2 to Zone 3–5. On rolling course, run 1–2-min pickups at faster than 5K pace (Zone 6–7), with recoveries at Zone 1–2 as long as you feel you need between the surges. Form! Cadence! Use the last 10 min to cool down with easy Zone 1 running/walking.
FRI Time: 0	**Day off:** Actively focus on recovery today: (1) stay off legs all you can; (2) watch nutrition closely (healthy carbs, lean protein, good fats); (3) stretch; (4) drink when thirsty. Other common recovery aids include massage, napping, elevating legs, and compression wear.
SAT Time: 1:20	**Goal-pace tempo run:** Warm up well for about 15 min, building to Zone 4 for the last min. As you build, do a few surges at Zone 5, lasting about 10–15 sec each. Rest for a few min. Then do a 3 × 15-min tempo run at your marathon goal pace on a course similar to the race, with 2-min recoveries between. Cool down for 15 min, easy Zone 1–2 jogging and walking.
Time: 0:30	**2nd run of the day:** Easy Zone 1–2 jog
SUN Time: 0:40	**Easy run/walk:** Zone 1–2 power run. Run 40 min as 4 min run at Zone 2, 1 min walk at Zone 1. Repeat for the duration of the run.

Total time: 6:40

WEEK 14 Sub-3:30 Marathon Plan, 14 Weeks Specific Phase

MON Time: 0	**Day off:** Actively focus on recovery today: (1) stay off legs all you can; (2) watch nutrition closely (healthy carbs, lean protein, good fats); (3) stretch; (4) drink when thirsty. Other common recovery aids include massage, napping, elevating legs, and compression wear.
TUES Time: 0:40	**5 × 2 min at Zone 3–4:** 15 min warm-up run, followed by 5 × 2 min, starting at Zone 3 for the first min, then building to Zone 4 in the last min, with 2 min easy recovery jog. Easy cool down in Zone 1–2 to make 40 min
WED Time: 0:40 Time: 0:30	**Easy run/walk:** Zone 1–2 power run. Run 40 min as 4 min run at Zone 2, 1 min walk at Zone 1. Repeat for the duration of the run. **2nd run of the day:** Easy Zone 1–2 jog
THURS Time: 0:30	**Run with surges:** First part of the run is easy, then do 5–7 × 7 sec surges at Zone 6–7 with long recoveries, getting faster over the course of the run. Really focus on forefoot strike, quick cadence, slight forward lean, and fluid motion, not forcing it.
FRI Time: 0:20	**Preview course:** Run start and finish of course. Note landmarks. Include several accelerations to race pace. Otherwise, keep power in Zone 1.
SAT	**MARATHON RACE**

Total time: 2:40

POWER METERS AND ANALYSIS SOFTWARE

To date, the number of programs designed to give you a deeper look into the training data from your power meter is fairly modest, but the programs below can already provide a robust analysis of your data. Updates to these programs, even in the short time between when this book was conceived to its publication, made them much more user friendly and comprehensive. We can expect that trend to accelerate as the popularity of these devices increases and they are adopted by more runners and coaches worldwide. I recommend that you check regularly for software updates from the manufacturer of your power meter and from the other software vendors you choose for your own analysis suite.

TRAININGPEAKS (TRAININGPEAKS.COM)

An online platform for collection of power data and analysis of files. User friendly. Works with a range of products. Allows athletes to share workouts through social media. Premium software analytics available for a monthly fee, but many valuable basic features are available for free.

WKO (TRAININGPEAKS.COM/WKO)

This TrainingPeaks product is an off-line suite that includes the ability to high-light and isolate different types of power meter data. Different versions can do different levels of in-depth analysis, but all are capable of delivering the type of analysis described in this book. All accumulated data can be uploaded to TrainingPeaks user account for backup storage.

THE PACING PROJECT (THEPACINGPROJECT.COM)

An advanced pace calculator based on course-specific terrain that can be used to create an optimal pacing strategy. At the time of this writing, this free online program does not offer power analysis or planning, but can help athletes better understand the demands of a course, and how pacing might be affected by the elevation profile. This is helpful for planning race-specific workouts, and simulating the racecourse. This is also a TrainingPeaks product.

GOLDEN CHEETAH (GOLDENCHEETAH.ORG)

This free, off-line open-source analysis software is continuously updated by its devoted user base, who donate their time. Very robust and always growing. This program can process all the analyses described in this book, and allows the athlete or coach to explore performance more deeply.

STRAVA (STRAVA.COM)

Originally a software program aimed at sharing different running and riding activities with others near you, this program now allows workout analysis. Requires a GPS unit (watch, phone, dedicated unit).

STRYD POWERCENTER (STRYD.COM/POWERCENTER)

Online-based program that works only with the Stryd Pioneer power meter. It helps users set rFTPw, review training sessions, and more. Also allows athletes to directly connect to Garmin Connect, TrainingPeaks, Strava, and other programs.

RPM2 (AVAILABLE IN SMARTPHONE APP)

Currently only available on smartphone or similar devices, such as tablets. The data analysis is extensive, allowing communication with a coach, graphical display of metrics, and ability to send the data to other analysis programs. This app is only compatible with the RPM2 power meter.

GARMIN CONNECT (CONNECT.GARMIN.COM)

For runners who use a Garmin device to connect with their power meter, this free online-based software program collects and displays many of the basic and key metrics from a run, and allows sharing through social media. It also connects directly with Stryd Power Center, TrainingPeaks, and more. The Connect IQ store allows users to create metrics to monitor on their wrist unit while running.

GLOSSARY

Acute Training Load (ATL). The recent workload of training, usually the previous seven days, expressed as TSS-per-day average.

Aerobic threshold. Point where the anaerobic energy pathways begin to be used more significantly in energy production than aerobic pathways.

Average power (AP). Total amount of power data collected from a session, divided by the number of time units, such as minutes.

Cadence. The rate at which steps are taken during a run.

Chronic Training Load (CTL). The long-term workload of training, usually the previous 42 days, expressed as TSS-per-day average.

Efficiency Index (EI). The metric to express the speed per watt of the runner. This is meters per minute divided by the average power for the duration.

EI@FT. The metric expressing the Efficiency Index of an athlete at functional threshold, for power and pace.

Force. Energy used to overcome resistance, pushing into the ground with the foot, while running.

Functional Threshold (FT). The best output one can perform for one hour.

Functional Threshold Pace (rFTPa). The best pace one can hold for one hour, on a flat course, with relatively low fatigue and in good conditions.

Functional Threshold Power (rFTPw). The best power one can hold for one hour, on a flat course, with relatively low fatigue.

Head unit. The hardware that collects and displays the data from the power meter to the runner, during or after a session. Can be a watch, tablet, smartphone, or a computer.

Horizontal power. Work rate being accomplished in the forward and back planes of movement.

Intensity Factor (IF). The ratio of a runner's Normalized Power to Functional Threshold Power. This is an indicator of how challenging or intense a workout or segment of a workout was.

Kilocalorie (kcal). The unit of measurement for biological energy expended while running, usually referred to as "calories."

Kilojoule (kJ). The unit of measurement for mechanical energy, or work, expressed as kJ.

Kilojoule per km (kJ/km). The metric to express how much work is required to run the distance of one km.

Lactate threshold. The intensity at which blood lactate levels accumulate faster than they can be reduced.

Lateral power. Work rate accomplished in the side planes of movement.

Normalized Power (NP). The average power of a run, adjusted for the variability of power within the session. A much better indicator of the intensity and metabolic cost of the effort, compared with average power.

Peak power (P). The highest average power a runner can achieve for a given unit of time, such as 2 seconds, 1 minute, 5 minutes, or 60 minutes. This is usually expressed as P followed by time in minutes. Five minutes would be P5, and 30 seconds would be P.5.

Performance Management Chart (PMC). An analysis tool available in many analysis software programs that allows the athlete or coach to monitor and manage CTL, ATL, and TSB.

Power meter. A device that measures or estimates the work rate of a runner, from either two planes of movement (2D) or three (3D).

Revolutions per minute (RPM). Cadence of the runner, isolating the average number of steps for a single foot in a minute.

Steps per minute (SPM). Cadence of the runner, as the average total number of steps for both feet in a minute.

Taper. A training model in which workload is reduced over a period of several days or more in order to eliminate fatigue for a peak event.

Tempo. A workout or effort done in Power Zone 3.

Training Stress Balance (TSB). A value that represents how well rested an athlete is, and the potential to perform well. Calculated by subtracting the ATL value from the CTL.

Training Stress Score (TSS). The workload of a run workout based on its intensity and duration.

Variability Index (VI). A value which helps show how well paced a session was. It is the ratio of Normalized Power to Average Power for that session.

Vertical power. Work rate being accomplished in the up and down planes of movement.

Watt (w). The unit of measure for power.

Watts per kilogram (w/kg). A ratio of a runner's power output and mass.

Work. Movement of a runner through a distance.

REFERENCES

CHAPTER 4: RUNNING INTENSITY

Tucker, Ross, Michael I. Lambert, and Timothy D. Noakes. "An Analysis of Pacing Strategies During Men's World-Record Performances in Track Athletics." *International Journal of Sports Physiology and Performance*, 2006; 1:233–245, http://www.humankinetics.com/acucustom/sitename/Documents/DocumentItem/6067.pdf.

CHAPTER 5: POWER FOR EFFICIENCY

Schepens, B., P. A. Willems, G. A. Cavagna, and N. C. Heglund. "Mechanical Power and Efficiency in Running Children." *Pflügers Archiv* 442, no. 1 (April 2001): 107–116.

CHAPTER 6: POWER ZONES

Coggan, Andy R. "Power Training Zones for Cycling." TrainingPeaks, October 10, 2008, http://home.trainingpeaks.com/blog/article/power-training-levels.

ACKNOWLEDGMENTS

Writing the first book on something so new and with so many unknowns can be a scary venture. Luckily, I had a great support group of friends, family, professionals, and peers who helped guide me. I would like to thank:

My high school cross-country and track coach, Mike Holman, who helped inspire my love for running and endurance sports, and showed me the value of a great coach at a young age.

My college coach at the University of Nebraska, Jay Dirksen, who taught me so much. I am proud to say I am a Husker cross-country and track and field alum, and I hope my contributions to the running community with this book are a testament to the quality of the program I was part of there.

Dr. Lydia Kualapai, at the University of Nebraska, who taught me the power of writing, and made me realize that I have ability as a writer. Without her guidance, I'm not sure I ever would have pursued writing anything of significance.

My coaches in the sport of triathlon who helped me learn so much about the highest levels of training and performance: Peter Reid, Greg Welch, Joe Friel, and Bob Seebohar.

My beautiful wife, Orlanda, and our two adorable boys, Alistair and Alden (a newborn when I started this book). Without their understanding and support, I could never have devoted time to this project. Being a dad and taking time away from my family to write a book sometimes seemed like a selfish endeavor, which made it even more challenging. But now that I'm seeing it come to fruition, the project feels even more rewarding.

My mom, Rhonda, and my dad, Bob, who pushed me to be better all the time, and provided opportunities that led me to this point in my life.

Ted Costantino of VeloPress was extremely patient with me as I pushed deadlines in order to find more time to research this new technology. This book was his idea, and his guidance and vision helped me immensely in forming it. His editing also made me look better than I really am.

Joe Friel, for his years of guidance as my coach, my mentor, my colleague, and my friend. I knew I had accomplished a lot when he helped critique this book and told me he was impressed.

Bobby McGee, with whom I have spent many hours, from my days as an athlete to countless hours on the phone in my days as a coach. I'll never be able to convey the true value of his guidance and respect. He always gives me the honest truth, and I certainly needed it with this project.

Gus Pernetz of Stryd, and the whole Stryd team, for their insight and info on the product and how it works. Their knowledge helped me establish the vision for the book much more clearly. Stryd's forums were also a great tool for hearing the questions athletes had and what they were experiencing.

Johnny Ross and his whole staff at RPM2, who enthusiastically supported me from the outset, gave me full access to the company, and presented a clear picture of the technology and what it can do.

Dr. Andrew Coggan, whose book on training with power for cyclists laid the foundation of my knowledge and experience in training with power as a triathlete. I have a new appreciation for his work after writing this. He answered many questions and gave me invaluable guidance based on his experience as an author and pioneer in training with technology.

The folks at TrainingPeaks who created the analysis tools that I relied on throughout this book. The TrainingPeaks metrics and software helped me learn a great deal about power for running. Without them, and my years of experience using TrainingPeaks, mastering these new power tools would have been much harder.

Alan Couzens, who I respect greatly, helped steer me to provide the directions that coaches want to use to help their athletes. He was excited to learn about this new technology, and it's an honor to help teach someone you respect.

The athletes who were devoted to using their power meters regularly so we could learn a lot in a short window of time: Frank Pipp, Brad Wenzel, Jason Bunch, Benedikt Imbach, Ron Richards, Patrick Flynn, and Gus Pernetz.

And finally, my friends Sally Meyerhoff, JT Tumilson, Dennis Clark, and Alex Lamme, all of whom left us too soon, in a short two-year span from 2011 to 2013. Sally was just 27 years old, and the others were only in their 30s. They were incredible people, and their deaths taught me that life is short—and I better do something worthwhile while I still have the chance. They were also runners, so I am hopeful this book is something they would have found worthwhile.

INDEX

ABOUT THE AUTHOR

Jim Vance is a former professional triathlete who trained under the guidance of the national team coaching staff at the US Olympic Training Center. He recorded two world championship titles as an amateur in XTERRA and International Triathlon Union. His range of performances also stretches to Ironman; he finished third overall at the 2006 Ironman Florida in a time of 8:37:09, running a 2:54 marathon in that race.

As the founder, team director, and head swim coach of Formula Endurance, a USA Triathlon High Performance Team in San Diego, Jim focused on developing youth and junior elite triathletes. He is also a Level 2 and Youth & Junior Certified Coach for USA Triathlon as well as an elite coach for Training-Bible Coaching. He has coached national champions and world championship podium finishers, both amateurs and elites. Jim has twice been named the USA elite head coach at the duathlon world championships.

Jim is the author of *Triathlon 2.0: Data Driven Performance Training*, which teaches athletes how to use technological training tools such as power meters, GPS, and heart rate monitors for Ironman triathlon racing based on their age, gender, and goals. In 2013, Jim coedited the book *Triathlon Science* with best-selling endurance training author Joe Friel.

Jim holds a BS in physical and health education, K–12, from the University of Nebraska, where he ran track and cross country and won two academic scholarships. He was a schoolteacher for six years before committing to triathlon full time in 2005. He retired from triathlon competition in 2010.

Jim currently resides in San Diego with his wife, Orlanda, and two young sons, Alistair JT and Alden James. He coaches high school swimming at Coronado High School and coaches a number of beginner and aspiring elite triathletes, runners, and cyclists. His website is CoachVance.com.